the BIG PICTURE *of* BUSINESS

"Hank Moore is a thought leader. Cognizant of the past, he weaves the accomplishments of others into dynamic strategies. I've worked with him and admire his writings."

—**George P. Mitchell**, Chairman of Mitchell Energy & Development. Developer of The Woodlands and downtown renovation in Galveston.

"Hank Moore truly embodies the concept of the Renaissance Man, from his worldly connections and involvement to his almost eerie sense of business acumen, in forecasting trends and patterns of commerce. To those of us who deal in the often delicate balance of customer and company, it is blessing to have, in Hank Moore, a resource we can depend on for fair, statesmanlike and balanced observation. I count him as a valued business friend."

—**Dan Parsons**, President, Better Business Bureau

"Every book that Hank Moore writes is a keeper. That's because of his thought leadership and ability to target what is paramount. Houston Legends is not only required reading, it is blessed reading for those of us who are Houstonians and those around the world who wish they were. Hank Moore brings out the grits and guts of these pioneers like nobody else could. You will be recommending this book to your friends."

—**Anthony Pizzitola,** MBA, CFM, CBCP, MBCI, Quality Assurance Manager, Jones Lang LaSalle.

"Hank Moore knows more people than a person who just got elected as President of the United States, and more importantly he knows how to bring out their traits. I don't know how he does it."

—**George W. Strake Jr.,** Chairman-President of Strake Energy, Inc.

"Hank Moore works miracles in changing stuck mindsets. He empowers knowledge from without by enthusing executives to reach within."

—**Dino Nicandros**, Chairman of the Board, Conoco.

"Mr. Moore is one of the true authority figures for business and organization life. He is the only one with an Ethics Statement, which CEOs understand and appreciate."

—**Ben Love**, Vice Chairman, Chase Bank.

"Hank Moore's Business Tree™ is the most original business model of the last 50 years."

—**Peter Drucker**, business visionary.

"Always ahead of the trends, Hank Moore's insights are deep, applicable beyond the obvious."

—**Lady Bird Johnson**, former First Lady of the United States.

"Hank Moore provides fresh approaches to heavily complex issues. His step-by-step study of the business layers makes sense. It shows how much success one could miss by trying to take shortcuts. There cannot be a price put on that kind of expertise."

—**Roy Disney**.

"How can one person with so much insight into cultural history and nostalgia be such a visionary of business and organizations? Hank Moore is one of the few who understands the connection."

—**Dick Clark**, TV icon.

"Hank Moore is a million dollar idea person. He is one of the few business experts whose work directly impacts a company's book value."

—**Peter Bijur**, Chairman of the Board, Texaco.

"30 minutes with Hank Moore is like 30 months with almost any other brilliant business guru. He's exceptional, unlike any other, and with a testimonial list to prove it. As a speaker, he's utterly content rich, no fluff, no 'feely-touchy' nonsense, right to the point and unashamed to tell the truth. There is nobody better. Every CEO needs him."

—**Michael Hick**, Director, Global Business Initiatives.

"I could not have wished for a better boss and mentor in my first professional job than Hank Moore. He leads by example, and taught me valuable lessons not only about business, but also professionalism and ethics that have stood me well throughout my career. Indeed, when I was in a position to mentor others, I've often repeated "Hank Moore stories" to my staff, and they've all heard of my first boss. Over time, I grew to understand more and more that Hank Moore treats others with respect, and thereby commands respect. I was privileged to be trained by this creative and brilliant thinker who gets more accomplished in a day than most do in a week."

—**Heather Covault**, Media Relations Manager,
Writer, Web Editor at Kolo, Koloist.com.

"Hank Moore is an outstanding professional, mentor, teacher, colleague and leader. He has given back to the community throughout the years to organizations and non-profits where his passion for their work is his focus. I have appreciate about him is his humbleness which counters his remarkable career and professional skills. He takes the time to talk or show up when you need him. Hank's achievements are plentiful but more importantly it is about who he is as a human being that endears him to the community. All the volunteer work he has contributed is making the world a better place in which to live."

—**Linda Toyota**, Houston Community College System

"Hank Moore brings alive the tales of these important individuals in a rich and detailed way that affords us all the opportunity to appreciate their contributions to our world and way of life. Well researched and experienced, Legends reflects Hank's personal relationships with those legends shaping the past, present, and future. Legends is a must read."

—**Nathan Ives**, Strategy Driven.com.

"Hank Moore has a wealth of knowledge. Not only is he fascinating to talk with, he's a fabulous writer as well. I'm so glad that he put all of his extensive knowledge of pop culture and business history down in a book for generations to come. Now we can all have access to the amazing stories behind many of the histories, corporations and who's who. Thanks Hank for sharing these wonderful stories. You Rock."

—**Kathryn C. Wheat**, author of the book *Networking: Naked and Unafraid.*

"Important Ideas Efficiently Presented. Hank Moore is a real king of business strategy in a time when there are all too many pretenders to that throne—and he knows how to write. The Business Tree is not for those who like their information presented slowly and interlaced with fluff. Moore's ideas are clearly and concisely presented. The book is all meat; and therefore needs to be read and pondered, then read again. Hank's books contain an enormous amount of useful information that will help any executive to function more effectively. Highly recommended."

—**Daniel Krohn**, attorney at law

"Hank Moore writes this book from a fascinating and unusual point-of-view. He is both an advisor to top-level managements of business and non-profit organizations, and an avid student of popular culture, especially of pop music. Combining these two perspectives, he offers valuable and entertaining insights about motivating excellence in organizational behavior. Hank's book is full of warmth and good humor, as well as keen insight. It is also stuffed with facts—my favorites are: a description of a sizeable list of young inventors and entrepreneurs (many under ten years of age, all under twenty), and a list of cities describing the origins of their names. This book is an enjoyable and thought-provoking read."

—**Thomas J. Perrone**

"Hank Moore is one of the legends of business, as well as pop culture. He connects the genres for ultimate wisdom. This is an adventurous book, his 10th. The next one, "Pop Music Legends," will go out of the stratosphere. This book series is a major undertaking. Hank Moore has crafted it masterfully."

—**Nancy Lauterbach**, *5.0 out of 5 stars* Must Read

"Hank Moore is a prolific writer with an amazing knowledge of his subject. Everyone will love this book."

—**Douglas B. Gehrman**

the BIG PICTURE *of*
BUSINESS

BIG IDEAS *and* STRATEGIES
7 Steps Toward Business Success

HANK MOORE

NEW YORK

LONDON • NASHVILLE • MELBOURNE • VANCOUVER

the BIG PICTURE *of* BUSINESS
BIG IDEAS *and* STRATEGIES
7 Steps Toward Business Success

Published in New York, New York, by Morgan James Publishing. Morgan James is a trademark of Morgan James, LLC. www.MorganJamesPublishing.com

The Morgan James Speakers Group can bring authors to your live event. For more information or to book an event visit The Morgan James Speakers Group at www.TheMorganJamesSpeakersGroup.com.

ISBN 978-1-68350-840-3 paperback
ISBN 978-1-68350-841-0 eBook
Library of Congress Control Number: 2017917355

Cover Design by:
Rachel Lopez
www.r2cdesign.com

Interior Design by:
Bonnie Bushman
The Whole Caboodle Graphic Design

In an effort to support local communities, raise awareness and funds, Morgan James Publishing donates a percentage of all book sales for the life of each book to Habitat for Humanity Peninsula and Greater Williamsburg.

Get involved today! Visit
www.MorganJamesBuilds.com

Dedicated to Joan Moore.

TABLE OF CONTENTS

ACKNOWLEDGEMENTS

Remembrances to some of the business legends whom I knew and worked with: Malcolm C. Baldridge, George R. Brown, George & Barbara Bush, Winston Churchill, Dick Clark, John & Nellie Connally, Stephen Covey, Philip B. Crosby, Michael Dell, W. Edwards Deming, Roy Disney, Peter Drucker, Michael Eisner, Bill & Melinda Gates, Max Gotchman, Dr. Norman Hackerman, Gerald Hines, Ima Hogg, Lee Iacocca, Lady Bird Johnson, Lyndon B. Johnson, Ben Love, Clare Boothe Luce, J. Willard Marriott, Glenn McCarthy, Marshall McLuhan, Harris & Carroll Masterson, George & Cynthia Mitchell, Bill Moyers, Dino Nicandros, Earl Nightingale, Cactus Pryor, Anthony Robbins, Eleanor Roosevelt, Colonel Harland Sanders, Vidal Sassoon, Peter Senge, Allan Shivers, Roger Staubach, Jack Valenti, Dottie Walters, Jack Welch, Gus & Lyndall Wortham.

Also, acknowledgements to Imad Abdullah, Sharon Connally Ammann, Tom Arbuckle, H.E. Madame Sabine Balve, Jim Bardwell, Robert Battle, Jennifer Bayer, Ann Dunphy Becker, Betty Bezemer, Judy Blake, Tom Britton, Robert Brooks, Dr. Lee P. Brown, Margie Nash Buentello, Sarah Buffington, Neil Bush, Crissy Butts, Tony Castiglie, Glenn Chisman, Johanna Chryssikos, Sandra Collins, George Connelly, Mike Contello, Rob Cook, John Cruise, Hector & Arleigh De Leon, Jenna & Michael Devers, R.J. Diamond, Kallen Diggs, Sue Ditsch, Deborah

Duncan, Tom & Anna Dutta, Alan Erwin, Kimberly N. Evans, Dr. Ron Evans, Margarita Farmer, Mike Flory, Felix Fraga, Dr. Yomi Garnett, Martin Gaston, Douglas Gehrman, Nick George, Andrea Gold, Diane Payton Gomez, Glen Gondo, Sonia Guimbellot, John Harris, Brett Hatfield, Phillip Hatfield, Bubba & Glenna Hawkins, Royce Heslep, Michael Hick, Mary Higginbotham, Bruce Hillegeist, Ann Hodge, Derrill Holly, Richard Huebner, Susan & Robert Hutsko, Hiett Ives, Chris Kelso, Dana Kervin, Soulat Khan, Jon King, Dan Krohn, Kirby Lammers, Nancy Lauterbach, Torre Lee, Wea Lee, Steve & Barbara Levine, Mike Linares, Craig & Vicki Loper, Stuart & Laura Lyda, Jackie Lyles, Carol & Michael Marcantel, Hon. Tammy Collins Markee RCC, Aymeric Martinoia, Wayne Mausbach, Cynthia Mazzaferro, Don McCoy, Bertrand McHenry, Kathleen McKeague, Bruce Merrin, Eugene Mikle, Mark Montgomery, Julie Moore, Larry Moore, Phil Morabito, Bill Nash, Keith Okano, Howard Partridge, Dan Parsons, Vaughn & Alisa Pederson, Monte & Linda Pendleton, Leila Perrin, Tom Perrone, Joe & Courtney Peterka, Sue Pistone, Anthony Pizzitola, Travis Posey, Dino Price, Michelle Puckett, Karen Griffard Putz, Doug Quinn, Sally Mathis Ramsay, Roy & Gail Randolph, Connie Rankin, David Regenbaum, Ronney Reynolds, Jimmy & Lindsey Rogers, Tamra Battle Rogers, Donna & Dennis Rooney, Mike Rosen, Rob Rowland, Tony Rubleski, Monica Ryan, Jordan Rzad, Rita Santamaria, Rick Schissler, Jack Shabot, Lisa Trapani Shumate, John Solis, Previn Sonthalia, Al Spinks, Bill Spitz, Maggie Steber, Rod Steinbrook, Kalen Steinhauser, Gail Stolzenburg, George Strake, Bill & Cindy Taylor, Deborah Taylor, Jon & Paige Taylor, Jane Moore Taylor, Charlie & Laura Thorp, Rich Tiller, James & Carolyn Todd, Linda Toyota, Candy Twyman, Carla Costa Upchurch, Kathryn van der Pol, David Wadler, Cameron Waldner, Jack Warkenthien, Louie Werderich, Kathryn C. Wheat, Sara Wilhelm, Robert Willeby, Chanel Williams, Melissa Williams, Ronald Earl Wilsher, Kyle Wilson, Beth Wolff, Dr. Martha Wong, R.D. Yoder, Tom Ziglar.

Special dedication to the Silver Fox Advisors.

Chapter 1

THE SIGNIFICANCES OF 7

S even is a very magical number and has an uncanny way of appearing in many situations.

I use the number 7 in business to symbolize both the parts of a successful company and the progressions that organizations must master to achieve optimum success. Under this model, each business must be viewed as a whole. Then, we examine the parts. Then, we comprehend the relationship of each part of each company to its other parts and to the whole.

Looking only at the parts of an organization out of context is counter-productive. Such practice by niche consultants and employees causes the organization to miss its marks and ultimately fail.

Concurrently, Branch 1 is the starting point. Each succeeding branch is a progression to #7, which constitutes long-term maximum success of the business. One must go through the progressive branches and cannot take short cuts.

The Significances of 7:

There are 7 days in the week.

One's telephone or fax number (excluding area code) has 7 digits.

You have to hear a concept 7 times before it fully sinks in.

A child begins formal school education in one's 7th year of life.

A child stops being a child in the 7th grade (entering adolescence).

The 7 Deadly Sins (Pride. Anger. Lust. Envy. Sloth. Covetousness. Gluttony.)

The 7 Heavenly Virtues (Faith. Hope. Charity. Fortitude. Justice. Temperance. Prudence.).

A full dinner consists of 7 courses.

Snow White knows 7 dwarves: Doc, Bashful, Dopey, Grumpy, Happy, Sleepy and Sneezy.

Seven is thought by many to be the ultimate symbol of perfection. In reality, there is no such thing as perfection. One continues to grow, achieve and amass successes. A process of Continuous Quality Improvement is recommended and more attainable. On the way to achieving goals (foundation #7), one travels through six progressions of improvement.

Researcher Howard Gardner studied what constitutes human intelligence. At the least, it constitutes a combination of varied abilities and skills. He believes there are seven intelligences: musical, logical-mathematical, spatial, bodily-kinesthetic, linguistic, interpersonal and intrapersonal.

A 45 RPM record is 7 inches in diameter. A VHS cassette videotape is 7 inches long.

There are 7 hills of Rome: Palatine (on which the original Romulus was built), Capitoline, Quirinal, Viminal, Esquiline, Caelin and Aventine.

There are 7 seas: the North Atlantic, South Atlantic, Indian Ocean, North Pacific, South Pacific, Arctic Ocean and Antarctic Ocean.

The 7 Habits of Highly Successful People.

There are 7 Wonders of the Ancient World: The Great Pyramid of Giza, The Hanging Gardens of Babylon, The Statue of Zeus at Olympia, The Temple of Artemis at Ephesus, The Mausoleum at Halicamassus, The Colossus of Rhodes and The Lighthouse of Alexandria.

"Hept" or "Sept" means seven. A heptagon is a figure with 7 sides.

A heptachord is a 7-stringed musical instrument.

A septennium is a period of 7 years and September used to be the seventh month in the year, but not any longer.

Among many things that come in sevens are the Seven Sisters, Shakespeare's Seven Ages of Man and the Seven Levels of Hell.

Netball and water polo are both played with teams of 7 players.

In Britain, the 20p and 50p coins both have 7 sides.

Under British law, when you reach the age of 7, you can open and draw money from a National Savings Bank account or a Trustee Savings Bank account.

7-Up is a soft drink. It was invented in the 1920s by C.L. Griggs of Missouri, who originally called it "Bib-label Lithiate Lemon-Lime Soda." Sales were poor, even though the drink tasted good, and so Mr. Griggs set about changing the name. After 6 attempts, he came up with 7-Up.

7-Up is also the name of a card game.

Seven is the number of perfection in the Bible. It appears 424 times from Genesis to Revelation.

John Sturges' 1960 western "The Magnificent Seven" is about a Mexican village that hires 7 gunmen for protection from bandits. The story is based on an earlier Japanese film made in 1954, Akira Kurosawa's "The Seven Samurai."

Roy Sullivan, a park ranger from Virginia, is the only person to have been struck by lightning 7 times. Between 1942 and 1977, he was struck on top of his head (twice), his eyebrows, his shoulder, his chest, his ankle and his big toe. Although he received hospital treatment for his injuries, he was extraordinarily lucky to escape death from so many strikes.

Ask a number of different people to give you any number between 1 and 10, and most will choose 7. Ask people to name their favorite number between 1 and 10, and again most will say 7.

In 1956, George Miller wrote an article "The Magical Number Seven Plus or Minus Two: Some Limits on Our Capacity for Processing Information." This showed that the amount of information which people can process and remember is often limited to about 7 items. One example of this is called the digit span.

Ask someone to repeat back to you exactly what you say. Begin with 4 digits chosen at random, e.g. 6625. Then give them 5 digits, e.g. 5 8450, then 6, and so on. Carryon increasing the number of digits until they make a mistake. The longest number of digits they get completely right is called their digit span, and for most people this is 7 digits.

Suppose someone is shown a pattern of dots for a very short time - just one fifth of a second - and they are asked to count the number of dots they saw. If the number is less than 7, they will be right almost every time, but with more than 7, they will make lots of mistakes.

Words Containing 7 Letters

Words are creative combinations of letters. Their meanings are determined by their completeness, rather than upon individual letters.

Words are used in conjunction with others to form sentences, paragraphs and complete ideas. To misspell words causes the communication to be distorted. Similarly, an organization cannot be successful if only focused upon selected parts.

Key English words comprised of 7 letters:

English	Spanish	Popular	Courage
Failure	Loyalty	Planning	Measure
Success	Compass	America	Tuesday
Setback	Roadmap	October	Seafood
Private	Mistake	Cover-up	Inquiry
Impeach	United	Serious	Reading
Actress	Florist	Citizen	Bedroom
Charity	Cooling	Science	Justice
Kitchen	Heating	Morning	Haircut
Calorie	Shampoo	Evening	Require

Key Spanish words comprised of 7 letters:

Estados	Espafiol
Nuestra	Cerveza
Estamos	Gracias
Palabra	Caramba
Pequeno	Poquito

Key Business 7-Letter Words
(per categories on "The Business Tree")

1. The business you're in

Actions	Execute	Oversee	Quality
Ascribe	Machine	Process	Skilled

Calibre	Monitor	Product	Utilize
Compile	Operate	Program	Workers

2. Running the business
Builder	Letters	Problem	Solving
Cabinet	Manager	Project	Systems
Conduct	Measure	Provide	Toolbox
Convert	Meeting	Quarter	Willing
Lawsuit	Passing	Section	Written

3. Financial
Account	Cashier	Economy	Receipt
Approve	Compute	Finance	Records
Actuary	Counters	Funding	Savings
Banking	Deficit	Million	Updates

4. People
Believe	Enlight	Nurture	Student
College	Involve	Perform	Support
Credits	Leaders	Respect	Synergy
Diverse	Linkage	Rewards	Teacher
Educate	Loyalty	Society	Trainer
Empower	Manners	Speaker	Wishing

5. Business development
Bargain	Connect	Markets	Preview
Booklet	Deliver	Network	Publish
Catalog	Listing	Opinion	Recover
Cluster	Mailing	Premium	Service

6. Body of Knowledge
Analyze	Leading	Promise	Stylize
Concept	Learned	Rebound	Success
Examine	Notable	Results	Thinker
History	Prepare	Reviews	Thought
Knowing	Profile	Setback	Worldly

7. The Big Picture
Advisor	Inspire	Planned	Reflect
Changes	Mastery	Predict	Supreme

| Company | Maximum | Present | Visions |
| Fortune | Picture | Prevent | Winners |

7 Levels of Visioning Programs, Determining How Far Organizations Evolve

1. Was Someone's Pet Idea. A program was initiated to fit a personal or political agenda. It was sold and accepted as such. Therefore, it will be pursued partially because its motivation is transparent or limited. Visioning is more than a "program." It is a process, encompassing change, behavioral modification, focus on growth and positive reinforcement.

2. Done Because It Was Forced or Mandated. A crisis, litigation, merger, loss of market share, government edict, competition with others or a combination of outside factors caused this to begin. Visioning here is a response, not a choice. The amounts of support and participation depends upon the circumstances and the spirit with which the mandate is carried out.

3. Done for Show or Image. Some organizations think that Visioning will make organizations look good. Actually, it makes them good. Visioning is not a substitute for public relations or marketing. It guides the organization which those other functions support. Visioning must focus upon substance, not just flash-and-sizzle.

4. With Partial Support and Resources. It is accorded just enough to begin the process but not quite enough to do it right. It is either the domain of top management or is delegated to the middle of the organization. Visioning must be a team effort and well-communicated in order to hit its stride, gather additional support and sustain.

5. Well Planned. The Visioning process begins with forethought, continues with research and culminates in a Strategic Plan, including the mission, core values, goals, objectives (per each key results area), tactics to address and accomplish, timeline and benchmarking criteria.

6. Well Executed. Visioning goes beyond the Strategic Plan. It sculpts how the organization will progress, its character and spirit, participation of its people and steps that will carry the organization to the next tiers of desired achievement, involvement and quality.

7. Well Followed and Benchmarked. Both the Strategic Plan and the Visioning process must be followed through. This investment is one-sixth that of later performing band-aid surgery on an ailing organization.

7 Steps Toward Wisdom

1. Information ... What We Know, Technologies—Tasks to Gather.
2. Education Teaching, Processing Information, Modeling.
3. Learning Mission, Absorbing Information, Techniques.
4. Insights Synthesizing Information, Values, Applicable Skills.
5. S. Knowledge ... Direction, Experience Bank, Inspired Thoughts.
6. Strategy ... Actions, Goals & Objectives, Viabilities, Creativity.
7. Vision ... Qualities, Strengths, Realizations, Big Picture Scope.

7 Layers of Wisdom

1. Glimmer of An Idea.
2. Learning Curve.
3. Applications for Lessons Learned.
4. Trial and Error, Success and Failure.
5. Teaching, Mentoring, Confluence of Ideas.
6. Deep Insights, Beliefs, Systems of Thought.
7. Profound Wisdom, Life Perspectives.

Chapter 2

MACROSCOPE: BIG PICTURE PERSPECTIVES OF BUSINESS

A Primer on Something Not Often Addressed in Business:
Big Picture Perspectives.

It seems so basic and so simple: Look at the whole of the organization, then at the parts as components of the whole and back to the bigger picture.

I advocate planning ahead and taking the widest possible view, embracing common sense and utilizing a series of bite-sized chunks of business growth activity. This is the approach to clients that I have taken as a senior business advisor for 40+ years. Even in times of crisis or when working on small projects, I use every opportunity to inspire clients look at their Big Pictures. The typical reaction is that my approach makes sense, and why haven't others taken it before.

The Big Picture exists, but companies have not found it for their own applications very often. Organizations know that such a context is out there, but most search in vein for partial answers to a puzzling mosaic of business activity.

The result, most often, is that organizations spin their wheels on inactivity, without crystallizing the right balance that might inspire success.

This chapter discusses the mission of business in society, the entrepreneurial environment, long-term investments in research and development, mergers and acquisitions, leadership and management in the new order. This is a primer on something not often addressed in business: Big Picture Perspectives. Suggestions are offered for the basics for Big Picture growth strategies and the criteria for looking wider-scope that should exist. This details priorities and strategies for growth companies.

The Big Picture can and should be painted. Obsession with certain pieces, comfort levels with other pieces and lack of artistic flair (business savvy) keep the work in progress but not resulting in a finished masterpiece.

Most of our energies are spent in reacting to the latest crisis, putting out fires. Organizations place too much focus upon the smallest pieces of the puzzle. That's why human beings and companies spend six times more on "band aid surgery" each year than if they planned ahead on the front end. That's why one-third of our Gross National Product is spent each year on cleaning up mistakes.

Municipal infrastructures have planning departments to focus upon traffic, sewers and real estate. They should be looking at all aspects of city life, services and the community's "book value."

Lawyers encourage clients to get advice earlier, in order to prevent lawsuits. Money managers are trying to maximize their clients' cash accounts. Engineers build structures to have lasting functionality. Many professionals have wider-scope textures to their service.

The hoopla over Y2K compliance put too much focus upon technological issues, thus diverting attention from the other 99.9% of business emphasis. Yet, it succeeded in getting the business culture to do "what if" situational analysis and commit resources to a form of planning.

The health care system is focused upon treating sicknesses, diseases and conditions. Many health care professionals advocate wellness, preventive and public awareness programs. It is tough to get insurance companies to cover wellness programs. The system just reacts to and supports after-the-fact treatments.

My job is to widen the frame of reference as much as possible. Under a health care model, I am the internist, a diagnostician who knows about the parts and makes informed judgments about the whole. This enables the specialists to then be more successful in their treatments, knowing that they stem from an accurate diagnosis and prescription.

In business, I explain to senior management in Big Picture perspectives the concepts behind the activities which the employees and consultants are conducting. For diversity, team building, sales, quality, customer service, training, technology, marketing and all the rest to be optimally successful, they must fit within a context, a plan and a corporate culture.

Businesses do not start the day with every intention of focusing upon the Big Picture. They don't get that far. It is too easy to get bogged down with minutia. This book and my advising activities are predicated upon educating the pitfalls of narrow focus and enlightening organizations on the rewards of widening the view.

Will every business ever become MacroScope focused? No, because vested interests and human nature want to keep attention on the small pieces. Those organizations with the wider horizons and the most creative mosaic of the small pieces will stand out as the biggest successes.

Alas, the Big Picture of business is a continuing realignment of current conditions, diced with opportunities. The result will be creative new variations. Masterpieces are not stagnant paintings … they can be continually evolving works in progress.

Basics of Big Picture Growth Strategies

There are three kinds of people in business: those who make things happen, those who watch and those who don't know what hit them. It is important to understand the differences in professional commitments among your team, customer base, competition and referral sources.

Know the business you're really in (core business, discussed in the next chapter). Prioritize the actual reasons why you provide services, what customers want and external influences. Where all three intersect constitutes the Growth Strategy.

Focus more upon service. Dispel the widely-held expectations of poor customer service. Building relationships is paramount to adding, holding and getting referrals for further business.

Plans do not work unless they consider input and practicalities from those who will carry them out. Know the people involved, and develop their leadership abilities. Plans must have commitment and ownership.

Markets will always seek new and more profitable customer bases. Planning must prepare for crises, profit from change and benchmark the progress. "More of the same" is not a Growth Strategy. A company cannot solely focus inward. Understand forces outside your company that can drastically alter plans and adapt strategies accordingly.

Evaluate the things that your company really can accomplish. Overcome the "nothing works" cynicism via partnerships and long-range problem solving. It requires more than traditional or short-term measures. He who upsets something should know how to rearrange it. Anyone can poke holes at organizations. The valuable ones know the processes of pro-active change, implementation and benchmarking the achievements.

Take a holistic approach toward individual and corporate development. Band aid surgery only perpetuates problems. Focus upon substance, rather than "flash and sizzle." Success is incrementally attained, and then the yardstick is pushed progressively higher.

Criteria for a Big Picture

Each year, thousands of companies seek to mount unrestrained growth for their own financial reasons. Yet, a very small percentage of firms will reach successful targets. An even smaller amount will sustain growth in the long-term.

I have worked with many companies in assessing potentialities and taking them public. Collaborating with niche advisors (attorneys and accountants), I've seen the relativity of a successful offering to a Strategic Plan that addresses the Big Picture … not just the financials. Once going through the process, the niche consultants see the wider scope too.

When companies go public, they must change mindsets and management styles. Evolving from entrepreneur to NYSE listed company means taking objective stock and re-engineering toward the future. Those who fail to take this process seriously will not be accorded proper attention on Wall Street.

In okaying stock underwriting, the investment community looks far beyond the desire for entrepreneurs to grow via expansion capital. Major brokers look at the organizational vision, planning potential, management structure, marketplace savvy and many more variables as indicators of each company's potential to go the distance.

The public company that sustains high book value must demonstrate its ability to focus on depth-and-substance, not just on flash-and-sizzle. Those who proclaim that hot ideas make great stock tips are dreamers selling flavors of the month, not public companies with staying power.

Taking a company public must be a process of guiding the organization through the levels of accomplishment. Sustaining book value is a thorough progression.

Management must develop critical thinking skills, through organizational processes, problem solving, challenges to take risks and daring to innovate.

You've got to have a unique product worthy of the marketplace. You've got to have something to trade in exchange for others supporting you.

The enlightened company must be structured, conduct planning and measure the accomplishments according to all seven categories on my trademarked Business Tree™: core business, running the business, financial, people, business development, Body of Knowledge (interaction of each part to the other and to the whole) and The Big Picture (who the organization really is, where it is going and how it will successfully get there).

Priorities, Strategies for Growth Companies

Evolve from entrepreneurial mindset to corporate culture. This necessitates evolving to a different kind of company … on a higher plateau. The investment community requires that valuable traded companies have Strategic Plans, cohesive training programs, management development and more.

Establish shareholder value. A company's book value is based upon perceptions, realities, transactions, image and other sophisticated factors. Such value is not established by accident and continually needs nourishing.

Evaluate and consider all non-financial aspects of the company. The profit motive is not the only measure of a successful company. Get beyond the bean counter mentality and think more globally. Consultants from outside the financial realm must advise public companies.

Management and leadership activities must be fine-tuned to the company's Big Picture. Most executives are not fully groomed to be top management and to develop corporate vision. From core business competencies, they are simply thrown into the pool and expected to swim. They tend to micro-manage and retain limited focus. Resources must be put toward developing the company's most valuable asset: its people.

Corporate communications (investor relations, public relations, community relations, government relations, stakeholder relations and more) must be weaved into a cohesive program, with qualified outside-the-company advisors. The Annual Report is symbolic of the company's growth and must be produced in tandem with the Strategic Plan.

Create and sustain corporate vision. It's not the whims of a few people. It's not an image campaign. It's something that is developed, fine-tuned, communicated and supported throughout the organization. It never stands still and reflects pro-active changes.

Achieve shareholder longevity, continuing value. Construct, provide and continue offering value. That is measured by addressing each of the previous six major areas on an ongoing, systematic basis.

Class is a person's way. Vision is an organization's way. Corporate culture is the methodology by which they successfully accomplish Vision.

For companies to succeed long-term, the Visioning process begins with forethought, continues with research and culminates in a Strategic Plan. A complete plan includes mission, vision, core values, goals, objectives (per each key results area), tactics to address and accomplish, timeline and benchmarking criteria.

Corporate Visioning goes beyond the Strategic Plan. It sculpts how the organization will progress, its character and spirit, participation of its people and steps that will carry the organization to the next tiers of desired achievement, involvement and quality.

Both the Strategic Plan and the Visioning process must be followed through. This investment is one-sixth that of later performing band aid surgery on an ailing organization.

Key Messages to Recall and Apply Toward Your Business
- Understand the Big Picture.
- Benefit from change.
- Avoid false idols and facades.

- Remediate the high costs of band aid surgery.
- Learning organizations are more successful.
- Plan and benchmark.
- Craft and sustain the vision.

Great Business and Life Lessons To Be Learned

- Acquire visionary perception.
- Never stop learning, growing and doing. In short, never stop!
- Offer value-added service. Keep the focus on the customer.
- Lessons from one facet of life are applicable to others.
- Learn from failures, reframing them as opportunities.
- Learn to expect, predict, understand and relish success.
- Contribute to the Big Picture of the company and the bottom line, directly and indirectly.
- Prepare for unexpected turns. Benefit from them, rather than becoming victim of them.
- Realize that there are no quick fixes for real problems.
- It is not when you learn, but that you learn.
- The path of one's career has dynamic twists and turns, if a person is open to explore them.
- Learn to pace and be in the chosen career for the long-run.
- Behave as a gracious winner.
- Find a truthful blend of perception and reality, with sturdy emphasis upon substance, rather than style.
- Realize that, as the years go by, one's dues-paying accelerates, rather than decreases.
- Understand what you're good at. Be realistic about what you're best at doing. Concentrate on those areas where good and best intersect.
- Continue growing as a person and as a professional, and quest for more enlightenment.
- Be mentored by others. Act as a mentor to still others.
- One learns to become his/her own best role model.
- There is always a next plateau, when we seek it.

Chapter 3

MASTERY OF THE BIG PICTURE: TRENDS AND ISSUES AFFECTING THE FUTURE OF BUSINESS

The business climate ahead is tough and filled with uncertainty, which translates into opportunities. Those who believe the old ways still work shall fall by the wayside. Innovation and the ability to fill new niches will signal the successful businesses of the future.

Take this quick test, as part of your strategic planning for the next two years:

- Does your company have a cohesive business plan, with results-oriented positioning and marketing objectives, updated every year?
- What is the nature of your business now, as compared to when you entered it?
- What has changed, and who are the new entrants?
- Which marketplace factors are out of your control?
- Which do your competitors control?
- Which are within your company's grasp?

- How well does the marketplace understand your organization and its value to the business bottom line?
- Are there misperceptions that need changing?
- Are you active in professional associations or chambers of commerce? Are they meeting your business needs?
- How much has your company given back to the communities that support you? Is there an organized plan of reciprocation, with a business development design?
- How well trained are your employees? Do they have the company vision? With some fine-tuning, how much could you multiply the effectiveness of your workforce?

The successful manager identifies and meets emerging issues before they take tolls. With informed outside counsel charts the company's course in a judicious manner. In an era of downsizing, cutbacks and a reluctance to expand, the same four principles of market dominance are still applicable:

1. Sell new customers. Without adding to the base, the business goes flat.
2. Cross-sell existing customers. They are easier to convince and see great credibility in your company. Most customers do not know all the product-service lines that you offer. It's your obligation to enlighten them, to facilitate their making wise buying choices.
3. Create and market new products-services. Having that mousetrap does not mean that the public will automatically beat a path to your door.
4. Joint-venture to create additional marketplace opportunities. By combining disciplines, you can attract new business and pursue new, creative solutions for clients. We can no longer do business as Lone Rangers.

Trends and Factors Shaping the Future Categorized

(per categories on "The Business Tree")

Based upon our studies of the business climate, counseling with top corporations and insight into business problems and challenges, I have identified the major emerging issues of the next two years. These factors will radically open new doors for those companies that are prepared.

1. The business you're in

Results-driven business.

Competition and changing marketplaces.

Deregulations.

Industry segments.

2. Running the business

Downsizing.

Technologies.

Business conducted at home.

Creating new efficiencies.

Rules, responsibilities and ethics.

3. Financial

Fluctuating economies.

Global economic development.

Incomes of companies vs. earnings.

4. People

Workplace illiteracy.

Societal changes.

Consequences to changing cultural panorama.

Workforce diversity.

Generational differences.

Drug testing (deemed legal in court challenges).

Age discrimination.

Back-handed ethnic discrimination, detriments to diversity.

Perceptions of a homogenous workforce.

Education of the workforce.

5. Business development

Branding and niche marketing.

Cause related marketing.

6. Body of Knowledge

Intellectual property issues.

Fear, failure and success ratios.

External influencers.

Regulators and government relations.

7. The Big Picture

Growing necessity for long-term strategy.

Strategic repositioning.

Corporate cultures.

7 Biggest Misconceptions About Business

1. Winning is paramount, no matter what the prize. Prove that you're right by making others wrong. It's not enough to win, but the competitors should suffer. "Might makes right" mentality blurs reasonable decisions by business leaders.

2. Executives know what they are doing. They are properly trained and have all resources necessary to manage. Many believe that executives have all talents, especially people skills. This puts company destiny in the hands of people who themselves need to be groomed-mentored.

3. Employees are sufficiently trained to do their jobs. Policies and procedures will take care of everything else. Employees know what they should do. This mindset leads to mis-use, mis-casting and costly make-goods by the company's most valuable resource, its people.

4. Technology and gadgets make the extra difference. Technology will solve all company problems. Besides, putting money into gadgets means that you don't have to address other shortcomings. People tend to focus more upon gadgetry than deeper organizational issues.

5. Flaws can be excused, patched or scapegoated elsewhere. If sales are up, then the company must be "doing something right." Temporary success

excuses company dysfunction. Artificial success is the downfall of every organization.

6.   Customers' opinions don't matter as much as that of the CEO. Don't ask for substantive input, nor evaluate what is uncovered. Efforts directed toward making the company policies right and, therefore, the customer wrong. This sabotages business development.

7.   There is a master plan. More often, the "plan" is a series of sales projections-quotas and says that problems will be handled via band aid surgery, only at such time as it is absolutely necessary. It's amazing how many companies rigidly refer to "plans" that don't really exist.

Fads, Panaceas and Quick Fixes Utilized by Businesses Rather than Focus Upon and Plan for the Big Picture

Activity-based costing

After-action review

Agile manufacturing

Benchmarking

Branding

Cognitive therapy

Commitment management

Continuous improvement and Total Quality Management processes

Core competencies

Customer focus

Cycle-time reduction

Dialog decision process

Downsizing and rightsizing

Economic value-added

Groupware

Information technology architecture and systems

Learning organizations

Outsourcing

Process engineering

Scenario planning

Self-directed teams

Sense and respond
Skill sets
Strategic alliances
System dynamics
Total quality management
Value chain analysis

These are valuable tactics and niche processes. Yet, people hear the terms and throw them out as rationales to their own version of the picture. It is not fair to business processes to let them become "flavors of the month" or talking points to a fully integrated and accepted business strategy.

Problems and Challenges Facing Growing Companies

Progress vs. Isolationism. For all we have achieved, our society is more polarized than ever. Like minds and appearances surround themselves with those like themselves. Diversity is not sought. Sameness is the mantra, by default.

Focus on Micro vs. Macro. It's easy and convenient to zero in on small details than to solve problems than to get at root causes of deeper issues. Very few managers have ever been taught to become skilled generalists. Big Picture thinking is not given much of a forum.

Band-Aid Surgery for All Business Problems. Society is predicated upon putting out the latest "fire," only when it arises. Most businesses deny the existence of a Big Picture and cannot plan for it. They don't utilize strategic planning and visioning processes because they were never taught any, nor know what they are. Thus, band aid surgery costs businesses six times more each year than the broader approach which this book advocates.

Workplace Illiteracy. Half of the corporate workforce is functionally illiterate, making costly decisions and failing to conserve company resources. They may have degrees and computer savvy, but thinking-reasoning skills, people experiences and professionalism have not been developed. The common denominator of today's workforce is lower than it was 25 years ago. Workplace illiteracy is at an all-time high. Educated people are making costly mistakes in business, and their supervisors do not comprehend the reasons why. Continuous quality improvement can and should be effected.

Poor and Nonexistent Customer Service. Customer service is presently at an all-time low … and getting worse. Business does not comprehend how it poorly treats, mistreats or neglects its means of support. We must always make the customer a priority. Customer service is something that we think and do, not an add-on sale. It must be inculcated into every dynamic of business, at every level in the organization and with accountability factors attached.

Technology Overload and Over-excuse. Technology is wonderful, yet it represents a fraction of a percent of organizational importance. In 1999, business spent $600 billion on Y2K compliance, thus diverting funds from planning, training, marketplace development and other priority issues. At least it was a form of planning, though proper front-end visioning would have precluded Y2K expenditures. Technology gets unfairly blamed and scapegoated for problems in other areas of the organization, becoming a barrier to customer service. More people have computer skills than people skills. We must utilize technology as the wonderful machinery that it is but not let it preclude holistic development of the business.

The High Cost of Hype. Some companies believe the statements that they are issuing. Some companies skillfully distort or lie to get what they think they want. Some may really believe themselves to be what they hype to publics who don't know any better. Many consumers are gullible, "name" crazy and susceptible to grandiose claims. They take what is said at face value because they have not or don't care to develop abilities to discern the comments and postures stated by others. They believe distortions faster than they believe facts, logic and reason. Consumers naively believe misrepresentations, to the exclusion of organizations that are more conservative, et substantive, in their informational offerings.

Further Spinning. People talk and perceive life in "spin doctor" bites, rather than true perceptions. This comes from teasers on TV newscasts, which lead to incorrect generalizations, which lead to patterns of thinking. Politicians and purposefully nebulous business leaders put more sophisticated "spins" on the same concepts. Thus, the average person emulates these patterns of talking, which become their methodologies for viewing life, which cloud objective thinking.

Button-Pushing Society. People want quick fixes, which usually lead to bills of goods that someone is selling. Our society continually seeks button-pushing answers for life's complex problems without paying enough dues toward a truly successful life. This book is the antithesis to that phenomenon … showing that business is an array of ideologies, processes and subtle nuances. Avoiding the temptation to short-circuit the necessary steps is really the road to gold.

Shoot, Ignore or Ostracize the Messenger. Most advice is obtained from the wrong consultants. Companies buy bills of goods from people who recommend what they're selling, rather than what is really needed. Thus, consultants are scapegoated and given a bad name. Blaming someone else is a way of avoiding the processes of improvement and quality.

Putting Tomorrow in Someone Else's Hands. Tomorrow is ours to craft, not that of vendors. Futurism is a process of thinking, reasoning, creative problem solving, interaction with others, thinking outside your frame of reference and personal commitment. Futurism is not esoteric, nor is it a quick fix. It is a process of change, which is 90% beneficial.

Management Challenges, Opportunities
(per categories on "The Business Tree")

1. The business you're in
Delivery of products and services.
Fewer safety nets, less reliance upon the old ways.

2. Running the business
Productivity through uncertainty.
Putting technology into perspective.
Quality.

3. Financial
Economies without borders.
Outsourcing and privatization.
Accountability, measurements and benchmarking.

4. People
Feminization and diversification of organizational culture.
Team building and team links.

Professional education, development and training.

Communications and trust.

Rights and respect.

Awards, incentives and recognition.

Performance reviews.

Personal visions and employee ownership of their productivity and, thus, the company.

Problem-solving skills.

5. Business development

Methods of communications.

Collaborating, Partnering and Joint-Venturing.

Customer relations.

Providing value-added.

E-business and debunking the e-business myths.

Research.

Human Intelligence.

The Court of public opinion.

6. Body of Knowledge

Front-burner business issues.

Institutionalization of rapid change.

New understanding of organizations.

Growth strategies programs.

Crisis management and preparedness.

Executive leadership.

Mentoring heir apparent and future executives.

Cooperation with government and the private sector.

Champions, inspirers and visionaries.

7. The Big Picture

Worldwide competition for new ideas.

Creative idea generation.

Strategies and stages in management implementation.

Strategic Planning and Corporate Visioning.

Steps in the Corporate Visioning Process

Synthesizing information, data.

Draw parallel analogies.

"What If" situational analysis.

Mapping strategies.

Create alternate visions.

Prioritizing visions.

Select the right vision.

Package the vision.

Communicate and articulate the vision.

Get buy-in.

Implement the vision.

Leadership development of executives.

Altering the organizational climate.

Organizational learning.

Organizational leadership.

Executive mentoring

Vision scope adjustments

Vision contexts (understanding, monitoring, updating).

Vision choices (contemplated, made, benchmarked).

Continuing Futurism.

Behavioral modification.

Commitments to do more, learn more, change more.

Reap realities of successes and failures.

Take vision to the next plateaus.

Short-Term Futurism

See how far the organization has come.

Continue to benchmark and recognize progress.

See what things that you could not do before this process began.

End goals are not the objective. Making definitive strides is highly important.

Recognize that no end goal may be reached.

Recognize that goals are constantly changing.

Create a "buddy system," a network of supporters for your pro-active process. See that change in realistic increments.

Factors of Futurism That Must Be Addressed

New kinds of products

A new company

The past as a teaching tool

Retreading old knowledge, technologies, marketing and products

Changing competition

Turning competitors into collaborators and sometime suppliers

Putting people above technology

Customer focus

The customer's customer

Information overhead, cutting through the clutter

Changing definitions of productivity

Where new ideas come from

Creating new business concepts, philosophies, processes

Levels of understanding

Developing insights-visions beyond information

Concurrent ee-engineering

Crisis management and preparedness

Taking Futurism out of the esoteric and into daily utilization

The past as a teaching tool

Top 21st Century Futures

1. E-Cybernation: Computers, TV, newspapers, and other media merge, along with their content, including entertainment, news, training, etc.

2. Bio-Age: Biotechnology transforms medicine, eliminating many human ills.

3. Personal Robot Slaves: Sentient but obedient robots will become affordable and commonplace.

4. Intelligent Things: Computer chips will be embedded in all of our stuff—and in ourselves.

5. Exploiting Outer Space: Exploration of our neighboring planets will lead to settling, mining, and manufacturing.

6. Quantum, Nanotech and Holodeck Computer Ages: Computers are destined to become a billion times more capable than today's systems.

7. Interactive TV Sitcoms: The entertainment industry will continue to be a key driver of technological advances.

8. Nonlethal Weapons: Public safety will increase thanks to advances in humane crime fighting and weapons technologies.

9. Redesigned Humans: Bioengineering will merge with computing to create healthier, wiser people.

10. Doubling of Human Life Spans: Reversing the physical and mental processes of aging may soon be within our reach.

7 Ingredients of Success

1. Finding knowledge in new and unique ways. Strive to learn something new everyday. Learn from examples (good and bad). Education leads to knowledge, which leads to wisdom. Develop continuing education, professional development and life philosophies.

2. Doing work that you're proud of. No matter what the job title, task or career orientation, work can be done professionally. If it doesn't mean something to you, it will not contribute to the marketplace or society at large. When you value it, they will begin to reciprocate.

3. Developing a philosophy of doing business, individually and organizationally. Analyze where you've been. Evaluate strengths and weaknesses. Analyze and strategize opportunities. Establish bigger goals this year than you had last year, with means and reasons for reaching them.

4. Handling mistakes and crises. Everyone makes mistakes. The mark of quality is how you handle them. Learn the art of diagnosing problems, taking input and effecting workable solutions. Planning for crises will divert them from occurring, 85% of the time. Waiting until the last moment to apply "band aid surgery" is self-defeating and costly.

5. Dealing with fear. Everyone has fear. Those who deny it the most are detrimental to your success and that of your organization. Understand

fears, and set plans to work with them. Remove barriers to success. Turn internal fears into motivating forces. Fears will never go away, but managing fears can facilitate the path toward success.

6.   Learning to read others' screens. Put yourself in other people's shoes, and communicate in their sphere, in order to achieve desired actions and results. Learn what motivates others and colors their take on life, in order to work well with diverse peoples and organizational cultures.

7.   Self fulfillment, purpose and commitment. Career-Life Vision, Body of Work. Develop a strategic plan, core values and action steps to accomplish your dreams. While others may roam aimlessly through life, you will achieve, sustain and share success. Commit to and thrive on change.

Charting the course of a company is a lofty responsibility, with so many factors riding on the outcome. It's lonely at the top, and most corporate executives are hard pressed to know where to turn for informed opinion. Effectively utilize outside advisors.

Having consulted and implemented programs in all of the above-listed areas for corporate, public sector and mid- sized business clients, we have quantified the efficiencies of front-end investment.

Planning facilitates a total and cohesive business approach. It signals the future and new, creative ways of doing things. Think to the future, and analyze where your company wishes to be. With strategic planning and implementation, success is attainable.

Chapter 4

THE BUSINESS TREE

Viewing Business as a Living, Growing Entity

Over many years as a business consultant, I kept getting called in to fix pieces of problems for companies. Most often, cutting expenses or having a new marketing program were the most common forms of band aid surgery that they thought would solve temporary problems.

Companies thought that selling more of something was all they needed, rather than what they were selling, to whom and the strains that increased volume and production capacity would have place upon other sectors of the organization. I remember one where the marketing people and the sales people would not communicate with each other, let alone coordinate activities. The results were increased sales with a multi-month time delay to produce products for a marketplace that was changing faster than was the equipment deliverability.

Through the years, I saw the wrong niche consultants being called in to fix the wrong problems, or what management incorrectly believed the problems to be. Most often, management was indeed the problem, or at least the logjam in the growth curve. The results were misspent funds, wasted efforts and the subsequent scapegoat of the consultants for what the companies could not or would not do.

Years of observations and follow-up advisory work for companies taught me that the root causes of problems in companies must be addressed, rather than to continue performing rounds of band aid surgeries. I also saw great nuggets of gold in those same companies, a bevy of talent, resources and a willingness to make the changes, all of which could be positively brought to bear for the benefit of their business.

Rather than go in and criticize management for short sightedness, bad policies and wrong actions, it occurred to me that getting their companies back to basics and planning for the next strata would offer the opportunities to right the wrongs in the least judgmental matter. Pro-active examinations followed by positively framed planning, to me, seemed to generate more results, foster more buy-in and create new strategies than would by playing the blame game.

Many times, I have been invited to present at board and management retreats. I always research the company, its products, its people and its competition. By talking with industry opinion leaders, key customers and other influencers, I always uncover gems that can be applied to new strategies.

The objective with companies is to reconnect present realities and opportunities with the visionary thinking that brought the company into existence. My "outside the box" material is presented as commensurate with enlightened thinking that had brought the company forward.

I like to go out of the way to credit each organization's internal innovations. I have always recognized the emerging leaders of each company, thus requiring infusions of visionary strategy, practical applications and the leadership quest necessary to climb the next plateaus.

The Business Tree™ is what evolved from doing many performance reviews, strategic plans and management retreats. It is predicated upon change, growth, and adapting to outside influences.

This model takes as its premise that every organization is a growing, living organism rather than something resembling a pie chart, with every department and function seen as a neat, separate, digestible slice. It is looks at business as a whole, then focuses upon each of the parts as they relate to the whole, and then back again on the whole. Look at the whole. Look at each part as it relates to the whole. Each part affects the behaviors of others and, thus, the whole.

The environment of a system affects the ability of its subset of parts to carry out successful functions. The parts of a system form a connected path, interacting directly and indirectly. The effect of any subset of parts depends upon the behavior of at least one other subset. A system is a whole that cannot be divided into independent parts without loss of essential functions.

This model has been used as the basis for company performance reviews, business plans, reorganizations and strategic plans that I have personally mentored. Through strategic planning, each part should see itself as it relates to the whole, not just to its own niche (as normally occurs in business).

With the tree symbolizing the organization as a whole, each major branch then represents a component of the company such as finance or business development. Limbs on each branch constitute departments. Twigs are analogous to individuals who keep the organization running, both staff employees and outside consultants and other operators.

No single branch—or business component—can constitute a healthy tree (organization). None of the limbs—or components—twigs (outside suppliers and consultants) and leaves on each branch (employees) provides all the nourishment required to maintain the health and growth of the tree. Each branch has its proper responsibility and needs to interact with each of the others.

In visualizing the organization as a Business Tree, we began at the roots, Category #7, which represents the direction where the organization is headed, how it will plan to get there and what factors, stakeholders and opportunities will affect it. Next, we focus upon the trunk, Category #6, representing the organization's body of knowledge, the relationship of the parts of the company tree to each other and the factors outside the company which affect its ability to do business.

Categories 6 and 7 support, water, feed and nourish branches 1 through 5. Naturally enough, The Business Tree will not stand without a trunk and roots. They keep the branches, limbs twigs, and leaves growing. Trees with thicker bases and deeper roots will sprout greener (last longer, be more successful), shed less often (fewer corporate flaws) and live longer (dominate its industry).

Branches 1 through 5 are the primary components of the business and represent its five primary functions. The numbers I've assigned them reflect the priority order in which most companies pay them attention, time and resources. Branch 1 (core business) is not the priority number, but merely a starting point. Companies then mature their tree by nurturing the other branches in descending numerical order.

Branch 2 (running the business) takes a widget from Branch 1 and turns it into a widget production company. Branch 3 represents financial. Branch 4 embodies people, the most valuable and most overlooked asset of any company. Branch 5 stands for business development, which is directly intertwined with Branch 3, the fiduciary ability to stay in business. A direct relationship between sales, marketing, research, advertising, public relations and customer service affects the financial strength of any organization.

Having conducted many performance reviews and company valuations, I've learned that most organizations address only three branches at any given time, some effectively and others not so well. Usually, they make Branches 1, 2 and 3—which should combine to 34% of the overall emphasis—into 100% of their focus, activities and what they believed to be planning.

Traditional management consultants only know how to focus upon Branches 1, 2 or 3. These include time-and-motion studies, just-in-time delivery, internal process controls, cost cutting procedures, re-engineering, quality controls and manufacturing. Traditional business models give short shrift to Branches 4 and 5, the largest and most enduring branches in a growth company (51% combined). Further, they neglect to address the wider scope emphasis of categories 6 and 7 (15% combined).

These are reasons why businesses experience recurring problems, often requiring consultant services to fix. They wrongly think that a branding program is a panacea to fix employee problems. Branding is a sub-set of marketing, which is a sub-set of corporate strategy, not the other way around. I find myself contextualizing for corporate management the strengths that reside within the company, while debunking the wrong advice they have gotten from the wrong consultants. Excellent consultants need to sell their services in the wider picture perspective, in order to hold maximum value.

The organization that does not address all five branches and their relationship to each other cannot remain profitable. Further, attention must be paid to the trunk and roots, in order to remain standing in the long term.

Developing Strategies, Realizing Business Opportunities

Over the years, I have been brought in to help clients assess their business dreams and strategize their proclivities to come to fruition. Most of the realistic ones came true.

What about the pipedreams that were more hype than substance? What did those who failed have in common? The emphasis was too much on having a copy of what someone else already had. The mousetrap they wanted to build was not fully delineated from others in the marketplace. Missteps are coupled with such factors as undercapitalization, insufficient business partners, few stakeholders, poor timing and inattentiveness to quality controls spelled missteps or disaster for those enterprises.

I met with the owner of a sandwich shop chain. He wanted to go public and establish a franchise organization. Turns out that putting a message on his napkins was the only way that he had to recruit franchisee inquiries. I very nicely held the "get real" meeting with him. I explained how a local restaurant chain goes national, citing case studies of the successful ones. I explained the process of going public, the funding that would be required and the shifts in management style that would be necessary to transform an entrepreneurial mindset company and take it public. I detailed how other chains in his state and industry had tried and failed.

I asked for a statement of his core business values. The answers were whimsical reminiscences of growing up in another part of the country and transforming those foods to a national sensation. Never mind that several other sub shops had already cornered the market. His "draw the line in the sand" comment was that he would not make compromises on what he considered an ideal menu. I explained that turning local restaurants into chains and local chains into corporations involved everything but the cut of meat and that compromise decisions were the rule of business life.

I observed that his casual hometown hangout ambience was great for a college town, but too many changes would need to be made in the company in order to become a chain to rival other established players. My recommendations were to stay local, enjoy the local fun, continue maintaining his defined levels of quality controls locally and be glad that he would not endure the headaches that would have been ahead in a publicly held company. He left the meeting feeling relieved. Who knows which roads those niche consultants would have taken his company down.

Business Tree lesson: Just because someone else has grown does not mean that all players in the same industry can expand rapidly. This company refined its core business to reflect a small company with standards that would have been changed in a rollout operation. They kept it back to basics.

How many times over the years have communities stated boldly that they would become the next Hollywood, that they would establish Third Coast film production facilities, only failing to raise the necessary funds. I have observed many and even advised some major cities against trying for the distinction.

Business Tree lesson: No community can re-vision itself by adding one niche industry alone. The community that expends resources into being a copycat of other communities or hoping in vein that resources will come to support a dream will find itself coming up short.

A group of doctor owned ambulatory surgical centers needed to devise strategies to reach its full potential. Applying the Business Tree, we examined Branch 1 (core business), we saw that the methods of healthcare delivery were changing and that such centers have proven to be a cost effective alternative to day surgeries at hospitals. Insurance companies and group health buyers were beginning to pick up on this and contract with ambulatory surgical centers as alternatives to more expensive hospitals for certain kinds of treatments. The insurers, rather than individual patients, were becoming the new customers that this client needed to target.

This set of circumstances resulted in changing Branch 2 (running the business). Doctor owned hospitals were popular investments in the 1980s, but they gave way to the corporate owned facilities. This ambulatory surgical center company was busy in packaging itself in order to sell to one of the for-profit chains. We researched other healthcare niches that the major companies did not own and decided that, rather than sell, this company would put together a rollup that included imaging centers, medical practice consulting arms and other service providers. They purchased other healthcare companies to make the new entity more full-service and thus more attractive to the insurance companies. The plan of reconfiguring the core business and the way in which service companies would run worked.

Business Tree lesson: The formation of corporate strategies is itself a "work in progress." Often, going through the process of rethinking and planning encourages some companies to change directions, retool its core business and broaden their business presences.

Communities as Living, Growing Business Enterprises

Entire communities can and must see themselves as business enterprises. When they make realistic, prudent efforts to diversify, grow or come back, this involves a combination of strategies, resources and people. Cities like Las Vegas, Nevada; Branson, Missouri; and Orlando, Florida, did not attain their designated glories purely by accident. All put formerly small towns on the international map by taking planned community status and marketing toward much wider audiences.

Following the 1999 shootings at Columbine High School, the City of Littleton, Colorado, made a concerted effort to come back as a strong community. That meant mounting an economic development effort, fostering quality of life and offering theirs as a beacon to communities set upon moving forward, putting themselves in a position to thrive at that next plateau.

When conducting leadership retreats for cities, I called attention to the overlapping and duplication of services by departments charged with planning functions. In each, there were three departments, one for real estate activities, one for roads and sewer infrastructure and another for traffic. I suggested that the term "infrastructure" relates more to quality of life and services to citizens, beyond the scope of just sewers, roads and bridges. Afterward, each city pursued a thoughtful process by staff that combined and expanded the planning functions to incorporate "quality of life" value to citizen services. The resulting cities achieved larger bond ratings, received positive marks for heightening citizen-friendly government and were better poised to face economic challenges.

Northern industrial cities have had to diversify their economies in the post-industrial age. The City of Syracuse, New York, mounted efforts to attract research, healthcare, technology and hospitality institutions into downtown hubs in order to re-energize its central city. I was invited to speak to citizen stakeholder audiences, giving case studies of how other cities came back from economic downturns, companies leaving town, loss of jobs and the business demands to diversify. I was impressed by the commitment of business visionaries who expended the capital necessary to foster local growth strategies and community visioning. I was inspired by the sincere desires of local businesses taking steps to strengthen the local economy.

Similar formal strategies to take communities to the next plateau have formed all over the United States. The private sector and public sector can both learn from concerted planning efforts, generated by crisis but rooted in thoughtful planning. While vertical cities have been losing population, mid-sized horizontal cities with high levels of educated workers have emerged as production centers in the technology age. These include Irvine, California; Austin, Texas; Chandler, Arizona; Boise, Idaho; Salt Lake City, Utah, and Raleigh-Durham, North Carolina. Austin, for example, mounted a concerted effort to create a technology corridor that subsequently drew more than 1,400 software production companies alone.

Other U.S. cities mounted visioning and planning efforts, thus attracting business, commerce, wealth and prominence. These communities include Boulder, Colorado; Santa Clara, California; Park City, Utah; Jackson Hole, Wyoming; Silicon Valley, California; and Fort Collins, Colorado.

Large cities represent grounds for rebirths because they have large immigration populations, many of whom are knowledge workers. These include Houston, Los Angeles, Dallas, San Jose, Miami, Phoenix, Philadelphia, Atlanta and San Diego. The economies of these regions display powerful opportunities to communicate, network, do business and enjoy community life. The energy and work ethics of immigrants tend to inject further vitality into these communities. These formerly unattached new urbanities constitute the critical new blood for the post-industrial urban economy.

Every major city and country of the world should undertake strategic planning and visioning programs, in order to move forward. Globalization is the biggest challenge of our time, accelerated by the infrastructures of communication, where the transfer of everything from ideas and data to goods and services has now become a staple of everyday business. Globalization impacts the safety of our nations, value of our currencies, condition of stock markets, products we buy, customers we serve and the competition that we face.

The globalization process considers different cultures, practices, and dilemmas faced within the realm of international business. The challenge of business planning is to understand and relate to the rest of the world. Human creativity and resilience are our primary economic resources.

Global business is more about exporting products and services, rather than the exporting of jobs. Understand the World's cultures and that world history repeats itself. Study how the global economy works. Visualize the possibilities, including trade blocs, geopolitics and strategic alliances. Interact with and help your customers develop their international activity.

I strongly recommend that every city and state governmental entity mount visioning programs, which incorporate strategic planning and much more. These are necessary for survival, usually create jobs, stimulate bond ratings and result in partnerships that benefit each participant.

Hold Up the Mirror, Conducting Performance Reviews

My Business Tree model has been utilized in visioning processes. One state saw it as the basis to expand the scope of Performance Reviews. I do not use the term "audit" when conducting organizational reviews and company valuations. That term portends to financial and "time and motion" measurements only. Some consulting firms conduct audits because those are the limited measurements they know how to make. In contrast, I see a performance review as more than just trimming the fat and criticizing incorrect activities in the organizational structure.

The term "audit" brings to mind an anticipated doom and gloom once the results are released. I recommend that it be replaced with a performance review, this being the precursor to the next strategic planning process. Such a formal review is a wider-scope look at all factors that contribute to an organization's well being. That means putting more emphasis upon factors that traditional audits do not. That also entails identifying factors that already contribute well to the organization, rather than simply looking for ways to cut, curtail or penalize.

This review is the basis for most elements that will appear in a strategic plan, including the organization's strengths, weaknesses, opportunities, threats, actions, challenges, teamwork, change management, commitment, future trends and external forces.

Among the components and professional specialties that could be represented in a performance review, per each branch on the Business Tree, include:

Branch 1: Core business, core industry.

Branch 2: Environmental, safety, IT systems design and computer software, training for computers and technology, architecture, engineering and legal

Branch 3: Accounting, banking, investments, financial planning, benefits programs, real estate, fund raising for non-profit organizations and investor relations services for public companies.

Branch 4: Training for diversity, team building, professional education and development, motivational and executive development-mentoring. Human resource administration, employee testing, behavioral research, executive search, talent pools, reorganizations, downsizing, executive outplacement, labor issues and negotiating.

Branch 5: Sales strategy, sales training, marketing strategy, customer service, advertising, direct marketing, public relations, special events, video production, promotional specialties, graphic design-production and website design-production.

Category 6: Business performance reviews, research, quality management programs, government relations, public policy, community relations and re-engineering.

Category 7: Corporate strategy, visioning, strategic planning, futurism, thought leader program and emerging business issues.

Grounding Factors for the Business Tree

Being stable does not mean that an organization stands still. Upholding traditions does not necessarily mean that one vehemently resists change. Being a family run company does not mean that outside stakeholders do not exist.

Authority figures must be effective disciplinarians. They must also be recognizable role models in order to inspire commitment from their team members.

The best leaders are adept at the balancing acts of business priorities. Organizations are collections of individuals, team clusters, operating units, departments, management philosophies and ideologies.

To gauge the company's future direction and avoid roadblocks to success, independent performance reviews must be conducted. The objective is to benefit from changes, rather than become the victim of them. By spotting trends and recognizing inner strengths of your existing company, you can compete and excel more effectively than without any strategy having been crafted at all.

Chapter 5

THE SEVEN LISTS: 7 STAGES— PROGRESSIONS TO BUSINESS SUCCESS

7 Tiers of Consultants and Business Advisers

1. Wanna-be consultants. They are vendors selling services. They often work as subcontractors. Out-of-work people often hang out "consulting" shingles in between jobs. These include freelancers and moonlighters, whose consultancy may or may not relate to their day jobs. (26%)

2. Entry-level consultants. Those who were downsized, out-placed, retired or changed careers, launching a consulting practice. Prior experience in company environment. (19.5%)

3. Grinders. Those who do the bulk of project work. They conduct programs designed by others. 1-10 years' consulting experience. (35.49%)

4. Minders. These are mid-level consultants, those with specific niche or industry expertise, starting to build a track record. 10-20 years' consulting experience. (13.5%)

5. Finders. These are firms which package and market consulting services. Most claim they have all expertise in-house. The more sophisticated ones

are skilled at building and utilizing collaborations of outside experts and joint ventures. (3.5%)

6.   Senior level. These are veteran consultants (25 years+) who were trained for and have a track record in consulting. That's what they have done for most of their careers. (2%)

7.   Beyond the strata of consultant. These are rare senior advisors, routinely producing original knowledge. They provide strategic overviews and are vision expeditors. These gurus have creativity and insights that are not available elsewhere.

7 Stages of Business Collaboration and Partnering

1.   Want to Get Business. Seeking rub-off effect, success by association. Sounds good to the marketplace. Nothing ventured, nothing gained. Why not try!

2.   Want to Garner Ideas. Learn how others work. Intend to package what the other does as your capabilities later. Each is scared of the other stealing business or scooping a client.

3.   First Attempts. Conduct programs that get results, praise, requests for more.

4.   Mistakes, Successes & Lessons. Crisis or urgent need led the consortium to be formed. Project required a cohesive team approach and multiple talents.

5.   Continued Collaborations. Consortium members are tops in their fields, truly understand teamwork and had prior successful experiences in joint-venturing. The sophisticated ones are skilled at building-utilizing collaborations of experts.

6.   Want and advocate teamwork. Members want to learn from each other. All are prepared to share risks equally. Early successes spurred future collaborations. Joint-venturing is considered an ongoing process, not a "once in awhile" action.

7.   Commitment to the concept and each other. Each team member realized something of value. The client recommended the consortium to others. Members freely refer business to team members, without jealousies or

the fear of not getting something in return. What benefits one partner benefits all.

7 Stages of Community Stewardship

1. Networkers. Pursue community involvement as a means of searching for contacts, resume credits, business referrals, make political friends, develop their careers.

2. Professional Networkers. Their job is to represent their company in charitable and civic activities. They have a budget to support programs, buy tables and build favor through the community. The goal is to optimally position their employers.

3. Non-Profit Leadership. Work for organizations that serve the community. They interface with the other six categories.

4. One-Issue Volunteers and Community Leaders. Deeply committed to and known for supporting one cause, issue, concern or primary subject area.

5. Community Molders-Stewards. Active volunteers. Serve on boards. Take visible leadership roles. Volunteerism becomes a lifelong passion-quest.

6. Agents of change. They teach the other five categories how to impact the community. They serve as inspirations for non-profit organizations, corporate stewardship and leadership programs. They amassed a long track record of credits.

7. Visionaries, Motivating Forces. Generate original thought. They provide influence and resource to the six other categories. They exhibit consistent and original creativity. They fund all time and resources out of their own pocket. They view life, work and community stewardship as a life-long scope body of accomplishments.

7 Stages of Business Growth Strategy

1. The business you're in. Clear understanding of what the business really is and why you've got what the target marketplace needs, expectations, challenges and deliverability.

2.   Running the business. Core industry people must learn how to be managers. Give administrative team enough rein-resources to do their jobs. Insist upon a holistic relationship to the rest of the tree-organization.

3.   Financial. Financial managers-personnel-consultants must focus beyond their own niche. Profit cannot be the only driving force. Show and measure full accountability.

4.   People. This is the largest, most overlooked branch of the tree-organization. Employees must be empowered. Management must develop people skills. Job descriptions, evaluations and advancements are documented-communicated. Train regularly.

5.   Business Development. Do all things necessary to capture and maintain market share. Maintain sales, marketing, advertising, public relations, research and product development programs, which must interact cohesively with each other.

6.   Body of Knowledge. Understand the relationship of each branch to the other. Research and know what's going on outside your doors. Develop the tools to change.

7.   The Big Picture. Business cannot grow without a holistic relationship to all parts of the tree-organization … what benefits one department benefits all. Keep existing roots living and sprout deeper, healthier ones (long-term planning). Master change. Shared Vision must be crafted, articulated and followed.

7 Phases in the Life Cycle of any Organization

1.   Conception.
2.   Birth.
3.   Childhood.
4.   Youth.
5.   Maturity.
6.   Avoiding the Traps-Downward Movement (stagnation, decline, death)
7.   Going the Distance Successfully.

Strategic planning fulfills a variety of practical and useful purposes. Business leadership should examine their organization's strategy and initiate—and periodically re-initiate—the strategic planning process when any of the following conditions exist:

1. There seems to be a need to change the direction of the organization.
2. There is a need to step up growth and improve profitability.
3. There is a need to develop better information to help management make better decisions.
4. Management is concerned that resources are not concentrated on important things.
5. Management expresses a need for better internal coordination of company activities.
6. The environment in which the organization competes is rapidly changing.
7. There is a sense that company operations are out of control.
8. Management of the organization seems tired or complacent.
9. Management is cautious and uncertain about the company's future.
10. Individual managers are more concerned about their own areas than for the overall well-being of the organization.

7 Benefits of Strategic Planning

1. Enhance problem prevention capabilities of the organization.
2. Group based strategic decisions reflect the best available alternatives.
3. Gaps and overlaps in activities should reduce.
4. Team motivation should be enhanced.
5. Resistance to change should be reduced.
6. Vehicle for monitoring organizational progress.
7. Disciplined thinking about the organization, its environment and future.

Each Strategic Plan should include these elements:

- Mission statement—Why we are in operation.
- Vision—What we want to become. It fulfills the mission.
- Goals—Broad statements of direction.
- Objectives—What we wish to accomplish.
- Tactics—Specific action steps to reach goals.

In order to be an effective Strategic Plan, it must be:

- Effective
- Measurable
- Motivating
- Realistic
- Consistent with the culture of the organization

7 Questions to Ask Your Company

1. Do you have goals for the next year in writing?
2. Are the long-range strategic planning and budgeting processes integrated?
3. Are planning activities consolidated into a written organizational plan?
4. Do you have a written analysis of organizational strengths and weaknesses?
5. Do you have a detailed, written analysis of your market area?
6. Do detailed action plans support each major strategy?
7. Is there a Big Picture?

After answering these questions, follow these guidelines for Strategic Planning:

- Utilize outside consultants. Do not conduct all planning internally. Keep objectivity.
- Budget enough time.
- Keep the procedure simple and disciplined.
- Develop the plan in stages. Set specific objectives.
- Set policies from this document.
- Tailor actions to the organization's culture.
- Ensure that the plan meets organizational needs.
- Find and keep a champion. Involve those who will implement the plan.
- Don't spread resources too thinly.
- Communicate results of the process to affected parties.
- Be willing to change as the process matures. Be open minded.
- Apply feedback to the continuing planning process.
- Keep the plan alive.

7 Values of an Annual Report

1. The Annual Report is the corporation's most important vehicle for communicating worth to current and potential shareholders. This is the best opportunity to share hopes and dreams for the company's future … and to muster support.
2. Corporate positioning has a direct relationship to stock price.
3. Check the certified public accounting statement first. It will be succinct and gives the numbers without embellishment.
4. Review footnotes, to interpret clarifying conditions. Footnotes will enable you to read the narrative with greater understanding.
5. The Chairman's Statement reflects the personality of the company, reasons for optimism and ability to empower employees toward future success. Watch for qualifying sentences. Which are clues to problems. If the narrative is straight forward and squarely places responsibility in the correct places, then the reader's confidence level increases.
6. Focus upon the future. The past is the past, with appropriate explanations offered. Company posturing for the coming fiscal year is crucial.
7. Visioning is a relatively new and highly sophisticated process. Every corporation should undertake Visioning. If this process is referenced in the Annual Report, then the organization is a superstar investment to watch.

7 Tiers on the Corporate Ladder, Contexts for Service Providers and Consultants

Within every corporate and organizational structure, there is a stair step ladder. One enters the ladder at some level and is considered valuable for the category of services for which they have expertise. This ladder holds true for managers and employees within the organization, as well as outside consultants brought in.

Each rung on the ladder is important. At whatever level one enters the ladder, he-she is trained, measured for performance and fits into the organization's overall Big Picture. One rarely advances more than one rung on the ladder during the course of service to the organization in question.

1. Resource. Equipment, tools, materials and schedules.
2. Skills and Tasks. Duties, activities, tasks, behaviors, attitudes, contracting and project fulfillment.
3. Role and Job. Assignments, responsibilities, functions, relationships and follow-through, accountability.
4. Systems and Processes. Structure, hiring, control, work design, supervision and decisions.
5. Strategy. Planning, tactics, organizational development.
6. Culture and Mission. Values, customs, beliefs, goals, objectives and benchmarking.
7. Philosophy. Organizational purpose, vision, quality of life, ethics and long-term growth.

7 Reasons to Embrace Change and the Benefits Provided

1. It beats the alternative. Organizations and professionals who become stuck in ruts and stubbornly cling to the past are dinosaurs, whom the marketplace will pass by.
2. Research shows that change is 90% beneficial. So why do people fight what's in their best interest? Change management is an art, not a death sentence.
3. Professionals, specialists and technicians owe their careers and livelihoods to change. Because they are educated and experienced at new techniques, they have market power.
4. Change is not as high-risk as some people fear. Failure to change costs the company six times more. Lost business, opportunity costs and product failures are signs of neglect, poor management, failure to plan, anticipate and grow the company.
5. Those who champion change advance their companies and careers. It accelerates the learning curve and success ratio. Those who do not get on the bandwagon will not last in the company. Those who excel will have developed leadership skills, empowered teams and efficiencies.
6. Change helps you do business in the present and helps plan for the future. Without mastering the challenges of a changing world, companies will not be optimally successful.

7. The company or organization that effectively manages change will remain successful, ahead of the competition and is a business-industry leader. Meanwhile, other companies will have become victims of change because they stood by and did nothing.

7 Ways to Measure the Success of Your Business

1. The business you're in. You're in the best business-industry, produce a good product or service and always lead the pack. Customers get what they cannot really get elsewhere.

2. Running the business. The size of your company is necessary to do the job demanded. Operations are sound, professional and productive. Demonstrated integrity and dependability assure customers and stakeholders that you will use your size and influence rightly. You employ state-of-the-art technology and are in the vanguard of your industry.

3. Financial. Keeping the cash register ringing is not the only reason for being in business. You always give customers their money's worth. Your charges are fair and reasonable. Business is run economically and efficiently, with excellent accounting procedures, payables-receivables practices and cash management.

4. People. Your company is people-friendly. Executives possess good people skills. Staff is empowered, likeable and competent. Employees demonstrate initiative and use their best judgment, with authority to make the decisions they should make. You provide a good place to work. You offer a promising career and future for people with ideas and talent. Your people do a good day's work for a day's pay.

5. Business Development. Always research and serve the marketplace. Customer service is efficient and excellent, by your standards and by the publics. You are sensitive to customers' needs and are flexible and human in meeting them.

6. Body of Knowledge. There is a sound understanding of the relationship of each business function to the other. You maintain a well-earned reputation and are awake to company obligations. You contribute much to the economy. You provide leadership for progress, rather than following along. You develop-champion the tools to change.

7.   The Big Picture. Approach business as a Body of Work, which is a lifetime track record of accomplishments. You have and regularly update-benchmark a strategy for the future, shared company Vision, ethics, Big Picture thinking and "walk the talk."

7 Truisms of a Healthy Business

1.   There is a difference between knowing a product-industry and growing a successful business. It is possible for a company and its managers to know much about certain arts and sciences without having the will to pursue them.

2.   Organizations do not set out to go bad. They just don't "set out" (little or no planning). Thus, they go off course.

3.   Much of the wisdom to succeed lies within. It must be recognized, fine-tuned and utilized. Much of the wisdom to succeed lies outside your company. It must be called upon, sooner rather than later.

4.   People under-perform because they are not given sufficient direction, nurturing, standards of accountability, recognition and encouragement to out-distance themselves. Organizations start to crumble when their people quit on each other.

5.   Unhealthy organizations will always "shoot the messenger" when change and improvements are introduced. Healthy organizations absorb all the knowledge and insight they can. They embrac change, continuous quality improvement and planned growth.

6.   Anybody can poke holes in an organization. The art and skill is to create programs and systems that inspire and accomplish something constructive.

7.   The level of achievement by a company is commensurate to the level and quality of its vision, goals and tactics. The higher its integrity and character, the higher its people must aspire.

7 Steps in the Corrective Action Process

The Corrective Action Process applies to all individuals operating in a business environment, divisions and entire companies. By employing these analytic tasks, problem solving may be turned into a marketplace advantage:

1. Identify customers for your goods or services, measuring their requirements and address problems incurred in delivering to the marketplace.
2. Understand, analyze and prioritize the problems.
3. Assign responsibilities for problem solving.
4. Apply appropriate problem-solving techniques, including checklists, process analysis, charts, diagrams and force field analysis.
5. Turn recommendations into implemented actions.
6. Review progress. Benchmark the accomplishments. Research serves as planning for the next project phase.
7. Analyze accomplishments in terms of overall organizational Vision and implications for successful achievement of long-term company objectives.

7 Factors Affecting Business Future

1. Workplace Literacy. Half of the workforce is functionally illiterate, making costly mistakes and failing to conserve company resources. Continuous quality improvement can and should be effected.
2. Workforce Diversity. We do not look the same anymore. Ethnic, cultural and societal differences should be studied, understood and fairly addressed by management. Issues of age and handicap status should be addressed in a pro-active manner.
3. Global Economic Development. For many years, we have successfully been a global economy. Hiding our heads in the sand will bury us. Open and cultivate new markets.
4. Team Building. People are your organization's most valuable commodity. Reduce wasted effort by empowering employees. Encourage training, professional development, service in professional organizations and community involvement. Employees work better when they think highly of their company and vice versa.
5. Customer Service Orientation. We must always make the customer the Number One priority. Companies who think otherwise will have a rude awakening.
6. Partnering-Collaborations-Joint Venturing. Put three parts together and come up with a five-edged arsenal. Matching disciplines

(complimentary or non-traditional) will create endless opportunities and give marketplace advantage.

7. Strategic Positioning. Companies must detect problems, create opportunities and assure that planned growth takes place. Champion and master change, rather than falling the victim of it.

7 Biggest Roadblocks to Business Growth

1. The business you're in. Not clear about the business you're really in, much less how-when-why to grow. Growth just for the sake of growth can ruin what you've built.
2. Running the business. Not properly trained or equipped to handle rapid influxes of business. Production, deliverability strained already. And it often gets worse.
3. Financial. Increased revenues, new sales and heightened profits are the only driving forces, without understanding how to protect the business you already have.
4. People. Employees are taught that corporate growth is the most important objective. Not empowered to make decisions or take risks. Management appears distant, with limited people skills. Employees don't really associate with company Vision because they're not sure what it is or what's in it for them.
5. Business Development. Customer service suffers the most. Company is likely to be killing the goose that laid the golden egg.
6. Body of Knowledge. Management doesn't take the time to understand how the company has grown or analyze the relationship of each branch to the other. Setting themselves up to avoid change, let alone grow without a Vision.
7. The Big Picture. Business will not grow because no Big Picture ever existed. They cannot truly grow without a crafted Vision for the future.

7 Stages of a Career

Version 1—Job—Worker, Bureaucrat.

1. Working Hierarchy—Workers versus managers. Each knows their place. Little communication. Mentoring and professional development will not likely occur.

2. Self Interests—Personal rewards, pay, benefits, time off are their only focus.

3. Using the System—Maintain the status quo. Resist change.

4. Dependency Upon the System—Don't wish to become management or advance beyond.

5. Don't Rock the Boat—Purge those who aspire. Surround with like minds.

6. Just a Job—Never will be anything more. No need to grow professionally.

7. Stagnated Career—Blocked at some point. Never will advance any further.

Version 2—Career—Professional, Leader, Executive

1. Education-Growth—Acquiring a profession, knowledge base and perspective.

2. Evolution—Paying substantial dues. Thinking as a manager, not as a shift worker.

3. Experience Gathering—Taking time in early career to steadily blossom. Being mentored by others. Measure output as a profit center to the company.

4. Grooming—Commitment to training and professional development. Sharpening people skills. Contribute to the bottom line, directly and indirectly.

5. Seasoning—Continues paying dues. Realizes there are no quick fixes. Has sets of standards. Emphasis upon substance, rather than style.

6. Meaningful Contributions—Learns to expect, predict, understand and relish success.

7. Body of Work—Acquiring visionary perception, career durability for the long-run.

7 Plateaus of Professionalism

1. Learning and Growing. Develop resources, skills and talents.

2. Early Accomplishments. Learn what works and why. Incorporate your own successes into the organization's portfolio of achievements.

3. Observe Lack of Professionalism in Others. Commit to sets of standards at role, job, responsibilities, relationships. Take stands against mediocrity,

sloppiness, poor work and low quality. Learn about the culture and mission of organizations.

4.   Commitment to Career. Learn what constitutes excellence, and pursue it for the long-term. Enjoy well earned successes, sharing techniques with others.

5.   Seasoning. Refining career with several levels of achievement, honors, recognition. Learn about planning, tactics, organizational development, systems improvement. Active decision maker, able to take risks.

6.   Mentor-Leader-Advocate-Motivator. Finely develop skills in every aspect of the organization, beyond the scope of professional training. Amplify upon philosophies of others. Mentoring, creating and leading have become the primary emphasis for your career.

7.   Beyond the Level of Professional. Never stop paying dues, learning and growing professionally. Develop and share own philosophies. Long-term track record, unlike anything accomplished by any other individual. All of these contribute toward organizational philosophy, purpose, vision, quality of life, ethics and long-term growth.

7 Levels of Mentorship

1.   Conveying Information. Initial exposure to the mentoring process. This may take the form of a one-time meeting or conference between mentors and mentees. The mentor is a resource for business trends, societal issues and opportunities. The mentor is an active listener, coaches on values and actions.

2.   Imparting Experiences. Mentor becomes role model. Insight offered about own life-career. Reflection strengthens the mentor and shows mentee levels of thinking and perception that was not previously available to the mentee.

3.   Encouraging Actions. The mentor is an advocate for progress and change. Empowers the mentee to hear, accept, believe and get results. Sharing of feelings, trust, ideas and philosophies.

4.   Paving the Way. Mentor endorses the mentee ... wants his-her success. Messages ways to approach issues, paths in life to take. Helps draw distinctions. Paints picture of success.

5. Wanting the Best. Continuing relationship between mentor and mentee. Progress is visioned, contextualized, seeded, benchmarked. Accountability-communication by both sides.

6. Advocating, Facilitating. Mentor opens doors for the mentee. Mentor requests pro-active changes of mentee, evaluates realism of goals, offers truths about path to success and shortcomings of mentee's approaches. Bonded collaboration toward each other's success.

7. Sharing Profound Wisdom. Mentor stands for mentees throughout careers, celebrates successes. Energy coaching and respect for each other continues throughout the relationship. Mentor actively recruits fellow business colleagues to become mentors. Lifelong dedication toward mentorship … in all aspects of one's life.

7 Degrees of Failure … Plateaus in the Learning Curve

1. Education-Growth—Didn't know any better. Made some dumb mistakes, based upon incorrect assumptions, insufficient information or lack of sophistication to "see beyond the obvious." Beginning to learn better approaches by analyzing the wrong ways of doing things.

2. Evolution—Tried some things that worked and some that didn't work. Beginning to understand that things do not fail without a reason or cause. Learns constructively from trial and error. Visualizing patterns of failure, as barriers to success.

3. Experience Gathering—Circumstances within and outside your control caused the projects to fail. Learns which external factors to trust and which cannot be controlled. The importance of research and marketplace understanding surface.

4. Grooming—The team let you down … understand why. Learns what you are capable of doing. Learns who to work with and in which capacities. Success-failure is a function of seizing-creating your own opportunities. No individual or organization can have success without experiencing and learning from failures.

5. Seasoning—Understand potential outcomes before they transpire and the myriad of failure-producing factors. Most people and organizations

fail due to never having control over certain ingredients, improper planning and the inability to change.

6.   Meaningful Contributions—Attitude is everything, affecting the approach to problems. People say they fear failure the most, when they, in fact, sabotage their own opportunities for success. Develops sophisticated understanding of attitudes, behaviors and interpersonal skills as the motivator to convert failures into bigger successes.

7.   Body of Knowledge—With time, seasoning, leadership development and a career track record, one experiences repeated successes and failures. Develops better understanding of cause-effect ratios. Develops profound insights and lifelong perspectives into the teachings of success and failure (learning three times more from failures than success).

7 Areas of Cutting Overhead Costs

1.   Core Operations. Trim inventory. Convert to a "just in time" concept. Discard idle equipment. Re-think your production processes. Prioritize core operations to see which costs and expenses are necessary and which may be reduced or curtailed.

2.   Administration. Exploit hidden assets. Rent idle space. Shrink shrinkage. Buy better. Get relief from the landlord. Cut insurance waste. Determine which assets to buy, lease or outsource.

3.   Financial. Practice "zero based budgeting" each year. Enjoy every allowable tax deduction. Collect receivables more quickly. Sell receivables that are troublesome or time-intensive. Tighten credit policies, and investigate customers' credit more closely before signing them.. Refinance bank notes. Utilize the company pension plan as an asset. Recoup pre-paid expenses. Save banking and finance charges. Reduce travel and entertainment costs.

4.   Personnel, Management. Ceremonially reduce the CEO's paycheck, to set a good example to the company. Reduce executive perks. Cut payroll costs by leasing personnel and outsourcing certain duties. Never skimp on training, since that enhances the productivity of employees. View all managers as profit centers, and make them accountable to the company.

5. Sales, Marketing. Raise prices to keep up with inflation. Practice bundle-selling. Sell an asset. Offer incentives to get advance cash from customers. Reduce advertising and marketing budgets, if they aren't producing desired results. Joint-venture when it makes sense.

6. Studying the Company. See that savings occur in all phases and that the company operates more holistically. Equate professional fees to an investment in company growth, not as a reward for loyal friends. Bring in consultants to recommend expense reduction and economy strategies. Realize that consultant fees are not the main problem, but budget for them wisely.

7. Company Long-term Growth. Visualize, adopt and benchmark a Strategic Plan. Without a rudder and the support by all, the organization will continue applying costly "band aid surgery." Progress must be expected, measured and celebrated. There must exist a Big Picture.

7 Means of Trimming Waste and Fat in Your Company

1. Core Operations. Reflect carefully upon what business you are really in. Sell obsolete inventory. Determine which equipment is worth keeping, repairing, updating or replacing. Seek to re-tool obsolete production processes.

2. Administration. Determine what can be automated, outsourced or dispensed with. Make judicious cuts at all levels. Determine who pulls their weight. Cut those who do not respond to retraining or perform according to the new organizational approach. Commit to an ongoing re-engineering program, in concert with and directed by a Visioning program.

3. Financial. Review and update accounting systems, cash flows, payables and receivables more regularly. Keep the "bean counter mentality" localized to financial areas and not let it spread to the "higher numbered branches."

4. Personnel, Management. Curb costs of rehiring by taking better care of existing employees … in ways beyond payroll. Investments in continuing education, empowerment, involvement and open communications

enable fewer people to do the work of more, with a better attitude. Commit to an ongoing Total Quality Management program.

5. Sales, Marketing. Research the marketplaces to determine which are viable and which are not. Participate in joint venture marketing promotions. Continually find new ways to improve customer service. Develop, package and advocate ways to deliver value-added to the marketplace.

6. Studying the Company. Cease conducting studies in-house. An investment in proper consultants makes better utilization of your staff. Find creative ways to integrate the sales staff with R&D and production, into a more cohesive organization. Commit to an ongoing program of Leadership Development.

7. Company Long-term Growth. Plan to reinvest profits. Plan strategically to grow. Plan to succeed. Commit to a Big Picture focus ... looking holistically at each branch of operation.

7 Major Areas Where a Business Fails

1. The business you're in. Not in the right business for well thought out reasons. Don't have a clearly unique product, rather an idea that isn't fully developed. Overdependence upon one product or service line. Diversifying beyond the scope of company expertise.

2. Running the business. They have poor controls, location, equipment, administrative support. Not properly trained or equipped to handle rapid influxes of business. Production, deliverability strained already, and it gets worse. Wrongful use of company resources, notably people.

3. Financial. Undercapitalized. Unprofitable pricing. They have poor payables-receivables policies., lack of accountability and excess overhead. Too much emphasis is placed upon getting rich, rather than steadily growing and improving. They rely only upon "bean counters" for company direction.

4. People. Insufficient investment in people on the front end, as the organization evolves and during rapid growth. Employees are not empowered to make decisions or take risks. Isolated or unrealistic management, possessing limited leadership development and people skills.

5. Business Development. They exhibit a marketplace naiveté. They maintain unrealistic sales policies, quotas and sales management. Unsuccessful marketing. Customer service is not good, doesn't improve and never is a major emphasis for the company. Marketing is more for ego reasons, rather than a careful strategy. Sales and marketing are not given enough support, especially management's personal participation. There is a lack of understanding about protecting existing business, entering new markets, new product development or collaborations.

6. Body of Knowledge. They have a failure to change and an inability to read the warning signs or understand external influences. They blame regulatory red tape. Management doesn't take the time to understand how the company has grown or analyze the relationship of each branch to the other. Setting themselves up to avoid change, failing to grow without a crafted and shared Vision.

7. The Big Picture. They fail to understand what business they're really in. They possess an inability to plan strategically. There appears a lack of an articulated, well-implemented vision. The business will not evolve because no Big Picture ever existed. They cannot truly grow without a crafted Vision for the future.

7 Stages in People's Willingness to Learn New Perspectives

1. Cluelessness-Apathy. Henry Ford said, "90% of the American people are satisfied." Will Rogers said, "Mr. Ford is wrong. 90% of the people don't give a damn." Content with the status quo. Taking a vacation from thinking. Not interested in learning more about life or seeing beyond one's realm of familiarization.

2. Basic Awareness. Latent readiness. Not moved to think differently, take risks or make decisions until circumstances force it. 90% don't care about specific issues until events that affect their lives force them to care about something. 5% affect decisions. 5% provide momentum.

3. Might Consider. The more one gathers information, they apply the outcomes of selected issues to their own circumstances. Begin learning through message repetitions.

4.   Taking in Information. Something becomes familiar after hearing it seven times. Gains importance to the individual through accelerated familiarity. The more one learns, the more one realizes what they don't know. At this plateau, they either slide back into the denial level of cluelessness or launch a quest to become mature via learning more about life.

5.   Beginning to Form Opinions. Triggering events or life changes cause one to consider new ideas, ways of thinking. Survival and the need-desire for self-fulfillment causes one to form strong desires to learn. Cluelessness and inertia are no longer options and are now seen as backward and self-defeating.

6.   Thinking and Analyzing. Changing paradigms. Behavioral modification ensues. There are ways we used to think and behave. We do these things differently now because we have learned preferable ways that cause better outcomes. Thus, we don't revert to the old paradigms.

7.   Behavioral Change and Commitment. Advocating positions. Creating own original ideas. Holding and further developing insights. Commitment to change and personal growth. Willing-able to teach and share intellect and wisdom with others.

7 Stages in the Evolution of Ideas, Concepts, Philosophies

1.   Information, Data. There is more information available now than ever before. Most of it is biased and slanted by vendors with something to sell. There exists much data, without interpretation. Technology purveys information but cannot do the analytical thinking.

2.   Perception. Appearance of data leads to initial perceptions ... usually influenced by the media in which the information exists. To many people and organizations, perception is reality because they do not delve any further. Thus, learning stops at this point.

3.   Opinion. Determined more by events-processes than words. Verbal statements are more important when people are suggestible and need interpretation from a credible source. Does not anticipate emergencies and only reacts to them. Many perceptions and opinions are self-focused

and affected by self-esteem. Once self-interest becomes involved, opinions do not change easily.

4.   Ideas and Beliefs. Formulated ideas emerge, as people-organizations learn to hold their own outside their shells. Two-way communication ensues. Opinion inputs and outputs craft ideas and beliefs. As people become more aware of their own learning, they tally their inventory of knowledge. Patterns of beliefs emerge, based upon education, experiences and environment.

5.   Systems of Thought and Ideologies. Insights start emerging at this plateau. Connect beliefs with available resources and personal expertise. Measure results and evaluate outcomes of activities, using existing opinion, ideas and beliefs. Actions are taken which benchmark success and accountability to stakeholders.

6.   Core value. Shaped by ideas, beliefs, systems of thought and ideologies. Becomes what the person or organization stands for. Has conviction, commitment and ownership. They are able to change and adapt. Behavioral modification from the old ways of thinking has transpired.

7.   Company, Career and Life Vision. They have an informed and enlightened plateau that few achieve. They are able to disseminate information, perceptions and opinions for what they really are. They are wisdom focused, an evolving flow of philosophies. There is a quest to employ ideologies and core values for benefit of all in the organization, committed to and thriving upon change.

7 Most Defeating Characteristics of Any Organization

1.   Thinking they've done enough homework. "Been there, done that" mentality. Feel they've learned all they need to know. Believe they have paid all the dues they needed to. Keep the troops in the dark about the bigger issues.

2.   Not grounded in realities of the business. Bureaucratic mentality, running a bureaucracy and keeping processes moving are paramount. Task orientation. People informed only on a "need to know" basis. They sustain closed, guarded and partial communications.

3. Bean counter mentality. Windfall profits at any cost. They advocate cost containment, without considering other consequences upon the business. Money and the bottom line are all that matter.

4. Wanting to always fix someone else. When morale is low, the tendency is to blame or discipline someone else, without studying organizational causes of recurring problems. Behaviors exhibited include back-pedaling, scapegoating, critiquing from the sidelines, passing the buck, avoiding risks and shooting the messengers of change-improvement.

5. Non-balanced approach. Band-aid surgery performed only at such time as it is glaringly necessary. Knee-jerk reactions to situations: (1) Flash and sizzle, without substance. (2) Hype, without customer service. (3) Public image, without quality improvement.

6. Corporate arrogance. Nobody can tell the CEO anything ... won't listen or cannot take advice. Management will not look at itself or pursue self-improvement.

7. Failure to dream, plan, execute, benchmark. They have an inability to move forward.

7 Ingredients of Success

1. Finding knowledge in new and unique ways. Strive to learn something new everyday. Learn from examples (good and bad). Education leads to knowledge, which leads to wisdom. Develop continuing education, professional development and life philosophies.

2. Doing work that you're proud of. No matter what the job title, task or career orientation, work can be done professionally. If it doesn't mean something to you, it will not contribute to the marketplace or society at large. When you value it, they will begin to reciprocate.

3. Developing a philosophy ... individually and organizationally. Analyze where you've been. Evaluate strengths and weaknesses. Analyze and strategize opportunities. Establish bigger goals this year than you had last year ... with means and reasons for reaching them.

4. Handling mistakes and crises. Everyone makes mistakes. The mark of Quality is how you handle them. Learn the art of diagnosing problems, taking input and effecting workable solutions. Planning for crises will

divert them from occurring, 85% of the time. Waiting until the last moment to apply "band-aid surgery" is self-defeating and costly.

5. Dealing with fear. Everyone has fear. Those who deny it the most are detrimental to your success and that of your organization. Understand fears, and set plans to work with them. Remove barriers to success. Turn internal fears into motivating forces. Fears will never go away ... but can facilitate the path toward success.

6. Learning to read others' screens. Put yourself in other people's shoes, and communicate in their sphere to achieve desired actions-results. Learn what motivates others and colors their take on life in order to work well with diverse peoples and organizational cultures.

7. Self fulfillment, purpose and commitment. Career-Life Vision, Body of Work. Develop a strategic plan, core values and action steps to accomplish your dreams. While others may roam aimlessly through life, you will achieve, sustain and share success. Commit to and thrive on change.

7 Biggest Misconceptions About Business

1. Winning is paramount, no matter what is the prize. Prove that you're right by making others wrong. It's not enough to win, but the competitors should suffer. "Might makes right" mentality blurs reasonable decisions by business leaders.

2. Executives know what they are doing. They are properly trained and have all resources necessary to manage. Belief that executives have all talents, especially people skills. This puts company destiny in the hands of people who themselves need to be groomed-mentored.

3. Employees are sufficiently trained to do their jobs. They are college educated ... so what more do they need? Policies and procedures will take care of everything else. Employees know what they should do. Professional development is a waste of money. This mindset leads to mis-use, mis-casting and costly make-goods by the company's most valuable resource, its people.

4. Technology and gadgets make the extra difference. Technology will solve all company problems. Besides, putting money into gadgets means that

you don't have to address other shortcomings. People tend to focus more upon gadgetry than deeper organizational issues.

5.   Flaws can be excused, patched or scapegoated elsewhere. If sales are up, then the company must be "doing something right." Temporary success excuses company dysfunction. Artificial success is the downfall of every organization.

6.   Customers' opinions don't matter as much as that of the CEO. Don't ask for substantive input, nor evaluate what is uncovered. Efforts directed toward making the company policies right and, therefore, the customer wrong. This sabotages business development.

7.   That there really is a master plan. More often, the "plan" is a series of sales projections-quotas and says that problems will be handled via "band aid surgery," only at such time as it is absolutely necessary. It's amazing how many companies rigidly refer to "plans" that don't really exist.

7 Levels of Authority Figure

1.   Self Appointed, Flash in the Pan. What they were doing five years ago has no relationship to what they're now marketing. They reap temporary rewards from momentary trends. They're here today, weren't an authority figure yesterday and likely won't be tomorrow. Yet, today, they're demanding your complete trust, respect and allegiance.

2.   Temporary Caretakers of an Office. Public officials. Appointed agency heads in a government bureaucracy. Respect is shown to the temporary trust which they hold. They're not going to be there for the distance, but they expect unparalleled deference now.

3.   Those Who We Think Control Our Destiny, for the Time Being. They are caretakers of corporate bureaucracies, departmental supervisors, short-term clients, referral sources for business development and those who dangle carrots under people's noses.

4.   Those Who Remain Through the Peter Principle. Supervisors and public servants who made fiefdoms by outlasting up-and-comers. Longevity is due to keeping their heads down and noses clean, rather than excelling via special talents-achievements. Still living on past laurels.

5.   Those Who Really Empower People. These are a rare breed … the backbone of well-run organizations. Some do what they do very well in poorly-run organizations. They may not be department heads, but they set exemplary standards and inspire others toward positive accomplishments. Category 2, 3 and 4 authority figures either resent them and try to claim credit for what they do … or are smart enough to place them in effective, visible roles. Some advance into management and encounter similar situations there too.

6.   Have Truly Earned Their Position-Respect. Also a rare breed. Those who excelled at every assignment given and each stage of their career. Never were too busy to set good examples, share ideas with others and help build the teams on which they played.

7.   Never Stop Paying Dues, Learning, Sharing Knowledge. The rarest breed of all. Distance runners who created knowledge, rather than conveyed that of other people. Though they could coast on past laurels, for them, the best is yet to come.

7 Levels of Values

1.   No Values. Either too young to know better or do not choose to develop further value systems. This is the crossroads … those who advance further will experience success in life.

2.   Values Held by Those with Whom We Interface. When we do business with them, we observe their values (which isn't entirely bad … one of the tenets of total quality management). Includes values of people temporarily in positions of authority, caretakers of our activities (such as public officials), and those with whom we must presently associate for business reasons. We may not agree with their values but understand how to work within them.

3.   Basic Teachings. Things we learned—or think we have assimilated—from parents, teachers, friends and community resources. Periodically, this needs to be re-examined, updated and reapplied to current life circumstances.

4.   Learning by Example, Trial and Error, Life Skills.

5.   Community Standards, Etiquette, Common Decency. When in Rome, we behave as the Romans do. Etiquette is sophisticated and must be mastered over time. If it's not the right thing to do, then a person has some real ethical considerations. By this stage, one is committed only to doing the right thing, doing it with class and inspiring others by example.

6.   Values Learned by Living, Learning, Earning. Take nothing for granted. Change is inevitable and brings opportunities for those who are adaptable, creative and innovative.

7.   Deeper Lessons from Mentorship, Risk Taking and a Balanced Life. Career and life Bodies of Work sprout from many roots. Must be viewed as a whole, the sum of the parts and the lessons learned to make each branch-limb-twig-leaf remain healthy.

7 Levels of Longevity ... How Companies Develop Staying Power

1.   Stuck around by default. Some companies are One Hit Wonders. They have limited utility and don't have what it takes to go the distance. They live short lives because that's all they've got in them. Some One Hit Wonders stay around a little longer than they should have, not because they are doing right things but because they have just stuck around.

2.   Needed for a Particular Niche. They don't try to be all things to all people. They have a specialized market.

3.   Show Promise to Develop into a Longevity Company. Made an effort to justify their niche, not just to fill it by default. Take pride in being the best in their area of expertise. Do business with other quality-oriented companies.

4.   Time Tested Products, Processes. They are good and plan to get better.

5.   Willing to Do Things Necessary for Growth. Products and processes only represent one-third of a company's picture. Growth companies take risks and address the other two-thirds (categories 4-7 on The Business Tree) on a regular, systematic basis.

6.   Earned Respect to Continue in Business. Dare to innovate. Commitment to Continuous Quality Improvement. Also look outward, rather than

focusing all resources internally. View their products, processes and people as a holistic organization.

7. Contributions Beyond the Bottom Line. Understand other reasons for being in business than just the dollars. Make healthy profits, while creating the best products, being a learning organization, setting-upholding standards and continuing to justify leadership position.

7 Stages of Change Management

1. Might. These are the 7 Stages in People's Willingness to Learn-Commit to New Perspectives: (1) Cluelessness-Apathy. (2) Basic Awareness. (3) Might Consider. (4) Taking in Information. (5) Beginning to Form Opinions. (6) Thinking and Analyzing. (7) Behavioral Change and Commitment.

2. Have To. Circumstances have forced change, including marketplace influences, litigation, mergers-acquisitions, regulations, new competition or other factors. These are the 7 Costs of Curing Corporate Problems: (1) Cleaning Up Mistakes. (2) Make-Good for Bad Work. (3) Make-Good for Bad Executive Decisions. (4) Reworked Processes-Systems. (5) Crisis Management. (6) Recovering Damaged Reputation. (7) Starting Over ... Changing Directions.

3. Ought To. Initial research and planning indicates forces and factors will necessitate changes in direction. Heed early warning signs to avoid costly damage control later.

4. Want To. Recognize The High Cost of Doing Nothing, It costs six times more to clean up damage than to take pro-active steps on the front end. Seek to remediate trouble sooner, rather than later. Process of crisis preparedness prevents trouble 85% of the time.

5. Will. Can be anticipated through Strategic Planning and Visioning. These are the 7 Levels of Change: (1) Natural Flow of Events. (2.) Changes Already Made and Realized. (3) Mandated by Others in Control. (4) Necessitated by Circumstances Outside Your Control. (5) Your Choices, Voluntary and Necessary. (6) Profound Commitment to Change. (7) Reaping the Benefits of a Continually Changing Life.

6.   Did. Successfully changed old paradigms. Behavioral modification ensued. Has effect upon overall company operations, with indicators for future growth.

7.   Continue To. Success becomes easier to replicate, and people find comfort levels with change. Organization develops, communicates and gets buy-in for an ongoing commitment to change and steady corporate growth. They are willing and eager to share insights and wisdom with others.

7 Stages of Education

1.   Teaching. Conveying information, insights and intelligence from various sources. Categorized by subject, grade level and methods of delivery. Expert teachers (fountains of learning material) are the building block in the educational process, and the student must be an active participant (rather than a non-involved or combative roadblock).

2.   Studying. One cannot learn just by listening to a teacher. Review of material, taking notes, seeking supplementary materials and questing to learn additionally must occur.

3.   Learning. The teacher instructs, informs and attempts to enlighten. The student accepts, interprets and catalogs the material taught. Periodically, the material is reviewed.

4.   Information. As one amasses years of learning, one builds a repository of information, augmented by experiences of putting this learning into practice.

5.   Analysis. One sorts through all that has been learned, matched with the realities of daily life. One determines what additional learning is necessary and desired. From this point forward, education is an ongoing process beyond that of formal schooling. If committed, the person turns the quest for knowledge into a life priority.

6.   Knowledge. A Body of Knowledge is derived from years of living, learning, working, caring, sharing, failing and succeeding. These are the 7 Plateaus of Knowledge: (1) Life. (2) Living Well. (3) Working Well. (4) Education. (5) Philosophy. (6) Self Fulfillment. (7) Purpose and Commitment.

7.   Wisdom. This requires many years of commitment to learning, compounded by the continuous development of knowledge. Few people attempt to get this far in the educational process. Those who do so have encompassed profound wisdom. These are the 7 Layers of Wisdom: (1) Glimmer of An Idea. (2) Learning Curve. (3) Applications for Lessons Learned. (4) Trial and Error, Success and Failure. (5) Teaching, Mentoring. (6) Insights, Beliefs, Systems of Thought. (7) Profound Wisdom, Life Perspectives.

7 Applications for Education

1.   Measurements. Test scores, grades, class rankings, GPA, SAT, professional certifications, licensing examinations, juried awards. Whether in school or business, we are all measured. Knowledge helps to make and predict society's measurements which are expected.

2.   Thinking-Reasoning Skills. What we learn is important. Further, what we do with lessons, how facts are interpreted, how we approach problems and the faculties of common sense are vital to economic, social and self-betterment success.

3.   Socialization-People Skills. Through trial-and-error, success-and-failure and the observation of other people's strengths-and-weaknesses, we learn how to live and work with others. Mastering people skills makes for win-win propositions.

4.   Professional Development. Education does not stop after the highest degree completed … it merely begins. Training, professional enrichment, membership in associations and constructive business interaction are vital for career longevity and economic independence.

5.   Mentorship. Learning from others takes a higher plateau when under the wings of experts. Mentorship (which has seven levels) is a stair-step process of bettering all participants. Meaningful lessons, paying dues and developing relationships empower those who make the effort "go the distance." Learning from different sources is the art of mentorship.

6.   Earning Power. Education (formal schooling, professional development and enhanced-relationship study) has a direct relationship to financial

rewards. It begins with school but bears fruit in the willingness to learn, change and grow professionally.

7. Future Life. A truly successful person commits to mentoring others, giving back, mastering change and never failing to learn. Education is more than confirming one's held beliefs. It plants knowledge roots, which sprout in ideas, applicable skills and lifelong insights.

7 Basics of Corporate Growth Strategies

1. There are Three Kinds of People in Business: (A) Those who make things happen. (B) Those who watch. (C) Those who don't know what hit them. Understand the differences, among your team, customer base, competition and referral sources.

2. Know the Business You're Really In. Prioritize the actual reasons why you provide services, what customers want and external influences. Where all three intersect constitutes the Growth Strategy.

3. Focus More upon Service and Less on Technology. Dispel the widely-held expectations of poor customer service. Building relationships is paramount to adding, holding and getting referrals for further business.

4. Must Have Commitment and Ownership. Plans do not work unless they consider input and practicalities from those who will carry them out. Know the people involved, and develop their leadership abilities.

5. Markets Will Always Seek New and More Profitable Customer Bases. Planning must prepare for crises, profit from change and benchmark the progress. "More of the same" is not a Growth Strategy. A company cannot solely focus inward. Understand forces outside your company that can drastically alter plans and adapt strategies accordingly.

6. Evaluate Things You Really Can Do. Overcome the "nothing works" cynicism via partnerships and long-range problem solving. It requires more than traditional or short-term measures. He who upsets something should know how to rearrange it. Anyone can poke holes at organizations. The valuable ones know the processes of pro-active change, implementation and benchmarking the achievements.

7. Take a holistic Approach to Individual and Corporate Development. Band-aid surgery only perpetuates problems. Focus upon substance,

rather than "flash and sizzle." Success is incrementally attained, and then the yardstick is pushed progressively higher.

7 Contributors to an Annual Report

1. Vendors—Printers, graphic designers, illustrators, typesetters, negative services, binders, shippers.
2. Process People Inside the Company—Those who chart, log and interpret specific pieces of data.
3. Financial Resources—Internal bookkeepers, accountants, payable and receivable staff. Outside auditing firm which prepares the financials.
4. Core Business Resources—Those who produce the product-service and assure its quality, consistency, deliverability throughout the year.
5. Outside Resources—Consultants to niche factors that will be addressed in the annual report: the core business, administration of the company, external communications, investor relations, organizational development, etc.
6. Company Management—Annual Report must reflect their Vision, strategies, corporate sensitivities, goals and beliefs.
7. Corporate Advisers—Advises senior management on all of the above. Sees that the Annual Report is a cornerstone of the corporation's worth, book value, sustaining growth and mirror of corporate strategy. Advises the company on ways to focus upon the future. Every corporation should undertake Visioning. If referenced in the Annual Report, then the organization is a superstar investment to watch.

7 Highest Costs of Neglect, Inactions and Wrong Actions

1. Product—Has somehow missed the mark. Does not have the marketplace demand that it once had. Others have streamlined your concepts, with greater success. Something newer has edged your company out of first place.
2. Processes—Operations have become static, predictable and inefficient. Too much band-aid surgery has been applied, but the bleeding has not been stopped. Other symptoms continue to appear ... often and without warning.

3. Financial Position—Dips in cash flow produce knee-jerk reactions to making changes. Cost cutting and downsizing are ready answers, though they take tolls on the rest of the company. Overt focus on profit and bean counter mentality cripples organizational effectiveness.

4. Employee Morale and Output—Those who produce the product-service and assure its quality, consistency and deliverability are not given sufficient training, empowerment and recognition. Team members fight the system and each other, rather than function as a team.

5. Customer Service—Customers come and go ... at great costs that are not tallied, noticed or heeded. After the percentages drop dramatically, management asks "What happened?" Each link in the chain hasn't yet committed toward the building of longterm customer relationships. Thus, marketplace standing wavers.

6. Company Management—There is no definable style, backed by Vision, strategies, corporate sensitivities, goals and beliefs. Whims, egos and momentary needs guide company direction. Young and mid-executives are not adequately groomed for lasting leadership.

7. Corporate Standing—Things have happened for inexplicable reasons. Company vision never existed or ceased to spread. The organization is on a downslide. Standing still and doing things as they always were done constitutes moving backward.

7 Costs of Flash and Sizzle ...
Paying High Costs for Smoke and Mirrors

1. Hype Doesn't Last. Gimmicks depend upon constantly changing audiences. They get your money and move on. Society unfortunately gravitates toward the "latest crazes," learns their lessons and moves on. The hype peddlers keep on selling false promises and unrealistic dreams until they are stopped cold.

2. Always Being Upstaged by Someone Else. The "number one at the box office" mentality is self-obsoleting. Week after next, someone else will be at their plateau. If the only value of a company or concept is this week's rating, then it does not merit your long-term trust, support and business.

3.   Public's Tastes are Fickle. The streets are strewn with the bodies of "one hit wonders." Flash-and-sizzle concepts dare the public to knock them off temporary pedestals. The public tires of their newness and, deep down inside, prefers organizations with consistency and solidarity.

4.   Artificial Measures Aren't Reliable. Sales statistics can be manipulated. Box office sensations do not always make projected profits … thus, their reason for creation failed. Creative accounting and spin-doctoring are justifications, not strategic business concepts.

5.   Deceptions Catch Up with Everybody. Truths are not always heard when first voiced. The public knows that much of what they're sold is "too good to be true." Only when it becomes their decision to seek and sustain the truth does it matter to them. Truths always emerge.

6.   At Some Point, We Become Accountable. Gimmicks run their course. Hard work and determination are the constant routes to success. As people see past the flash and sizzle, they move forward, and that's when they do their best work.

7.   High Costs Cause Changes in Business. Overcharges, waste, neglect, hucksterism and mis-representation ultimately cost you and me. The high costs are tallied and, much to our chagrin, are passed along to customers … only until such time as customers stand their ground and refute these costs back to the vendors with whom they do business.

7 Biggest Career Killers … the first 10 years.

1.   Insufficient Life Preparation. Home environment, parenting, school experiences, social interactions and life experiences influence the direction of a career. All of us are under-prepared … the way in which we overcome and grow is what spawns success.

2.   Not Wanting or Seeking a Niche. Waiting too long to establish a marketable niche causes the young person to ramble and search. Society tends to place labels, and the aimlessly searching young professional will get saddled with one that is not likely appropriate.

3.   Waiting to Make Professional Commitments. One must do work that is satisfying, but opting for fun and thrills over a professional commitment sets life patterns. Holding a job is not the same thing as building a career

foundation. Those who hold jobs are forever restless. Those who steadily build careers are more rewarded, in every sense of the word.

4. Underdeveloped People Skills. Saying irretrievable things, championing the wrong causes and holding grudges does the individual damage. One catches more flies with honey … oh, if only people had told us about this sooner! Continuing patterns of underdeveloped social skills hold one back, daily and for the long-term. Those who really succeed cultivate and nourish people first, work product secondarily and processes thirdly.

5. Reality Based Education. Early preparation and formal schooling are valuable first steps. One must fulfill a plan of professional and leadership enhancement to be successful in the long-term. Corporations value you in relation to their objectives, not yours.

6. The Corporate Culture. You're only as valuable as the marketplace judges that you are. Job performance and exhibited professionalism make the difference. The successful professional must communicate with others. Doing great work matters little unless it collaborates with corporate cultures in which it exists. Document your worth and activities.

7. The Long Distance. Life and business test us constantly. It's not personal against us … it's the system. Within the unfairness, inequities and confusion lie opportunities for the young professional to develop a niche, conceptualize a dream and pursue success professionally.

7 Levels of Sales on the Internet

1. Gimmick Marketing. They use terms like "100% free" to lure your credit card. These are baits … but not enough to be considered a "free sample" of actual product sold. Let the buyer beware … or otherwise encounter large charges. The best sales are out-front and obvious.

2. "Customer Service" Facade. Increasingly, companies direct customers to websites, in order to standardize messages and cut costs for live support. This is dangerous and disturbing, since it creates frustration for customers, reduces human contact and leaves more room for error. What many companies call "customer service" is really cross-marketing for other products to sell more, rather than emphasizing service beyond the sale.

3. Institutional Promotion. Companies want and need to project good images of themselves. These sites are both institutional and instructional. They enlighten customers of what they are and what they do. The sell is relatively soft … simply reinforcing corporate images.

4. Links to Discover Other Sources. The best thing that a company can do is to link up with colleagues. Business collaboration is one vital wave of the future. Websites can cross-promote each other, the goal to get each sites' share of an increasingly larger pie.

5. Catalog Sales. Catalog buying has been a fixture of society for 150 years. Internet technology creates kinds of catalogs that could not have afforded to print, mass-mail and distribute before. Specialty catalogs and clearinghouses now have homes on websites. The wise ones will still collaborate with each other … yielding value-added to customers and assuring repeat visits.

6. Materials Not Available Elsewhere. Enlightens audiences to resources not widely known before. This level goes far beyond sales. It nourishes credibility relationships with customers, suppliers and business collaborators. It stimulates further creation of quality materials.

7. Responsible Use of the Infant Medium. Those who excel at Categories 4, 5 and 6 on this list will develop a genuine pride that the hucksters and fast-buck artists will never explain. Internet sales resources that last will develop, advocate and increase standards of quality and value.

7 Limitations of the Internet, Opportunities to Grow

1. Newness. As with fax machines and telecommunications, the uniqueness commands current attention. As the novelty wears off, higher standards will be set. New generations of usage for this infant medium will spend efforts and knowledge toward upgrading it.

2. Limited Audiences. People now on the net have the equipment, time and interest. Vast audiences who truly need the net's capabilities still need to be recruited. A word of caution: make recruitment customer-friendly. Too much pseudo-technology snobbery exists toward non-users, many of whom resist because they feel spurned.

3.   Hucksterism. Presently, there are many people selling on the net. It's a haven for wanna-be hucksters, some with insignificant products. As time passes, fast-buck artists will move on. It is the responsibility of consumers to patronize reputable websites with solid products.

4.   Customer Assertiveness. Shuffling customers off to websites only aggravates the situation and causes more confusion. Poor customer service should not be blamed on the Internet. Poor customer service is jointly stoked by the companies and the customers themselves. Consumers must learn to demand their rights, stand their ground, insist upon personal service and utilize the Internet for informational support. Customers who do not assert their rights and continue to accept impersonal service deserve what they get or do not get.

5.   Collaborations and Alliances. This communications medium can foster consortiums of individuals and organizations … for purposes of doing business and much more. This technology is a tool of the trade, not an end in itself. How human beings interact with each other depends upon their abilities, willingness and attentiveness to do so.

6.   Educational Advantage. They say that the net is "the world's largest library." To date, it's more of a catalog. Educational institutions must open their contents … realizing their obligations to public education and community outreach.

7.   Responsibilities. Those who make money, court public favor and are chartered to inform must benchmark their progress in responsible use of this medium. Their right to stay in business is based upon how the public's only true "free speech medium" is upheld and upgraded.

7 Stages of Relationship Building: Customers and Partners

1.   Want to Get Business. Seeking rub-off effect, success by association. Sounds good to the marketplace. Nothing ventured, nothing gained. Why not try!

2.   Want to Garner Ideas. Learn more about the customer. Each team member must commit to professional development, taking the program to a higher level. Making sales calls (mandated or voluntarily) does not constitute relationship building.

3. First Attempts. Conduct programs that get results, praise, requests for more. To succeed, it needs to be more than an advertising and direct marketing campaign.

4. Mistakes, Successes & Lessons. Competition, marketplace changes or urgent need led the initiative to begin. Customer retention and enhancement program requires a cohesive team approach and multiple talents.

5. Continued Collaborations. Collaborators truly understand teamwork and had prior successful experiences at customer service. The sophisticated ones are skilled at building and utilizing colleagues and outside experts.

6. Want and advocate teamwork. Team members want to learn from each other. All share risks equally. Early successes inspire deeper activity. Business relationship building is considered an ongoing process, not a "once in awhile" action or marketing gimmick.

7. Commitment to the concept and each other. Each team member realizes something of value. Customers recommend and freely refer business to the institution. What benefits one partner benefits all.

7 Levels of Standards and Ethics

1. Base Level. Just needing and attempting to get by. Pursuing the basics of food, clothing and shelter. Knowing right from wrong. Trying to pursue a good life and aspire to something higher.

2. Society's Lowest Common Denominators. Although knowing better, subscribing to prevailing philosophies and behaviors of others. This leads some to take advantage of the system, want more than one's share and fail to be accountable. Sadly, the common denominators are below what they used to be, and society continues to lower them. The mission of a successful person or organization is not to succumb quite that low.

3. Lessons from the School of Hard Knocks. Learning by experiences, trial and error, successes, life skills. Becoming more familiar with one's strengths, weaknesses, opportunities and threats. Understanding what an organization can and cannot accomplish, represent and become. Maximizing one's resources to the most practical advantage.

4. Launching a Quest. Striving to learn more and go further. Includes intellectual pursuits, professional realities, nurturing of people skills and executive abilities. At this point, people change careers, and organizations revisit their goals and crystalize new visions.

5. Standards. Set and respect boundaries. Many times, people and organizations will attempt to violate those standards or fail to acknowledge their existence. The test is how consistently one sets, modifies and observes one's own standards.

6. Values and Vision. No person or organization stands still. It is not enough to accept change but more importantly to benefit from it. It is not enough to see yourself on a higher plateau and quest for more. Success comes from charting a course, encompassing value systems and methodically reaching goals.

7. Code of Ethics. Nurture a robust portfolio of fundamental canons, rules of practice, professional obligations, accountability-measurability, professional development, integrity, objectivity and independence. Maintain the commitment to uphold and enforce codes of ethics (yours and those of others) and the ethical responsibilities of members in business.

7 Priorities, Strategies for New Public Companies

1. Evolve from entrepreneurial mindset to corporate culture. Necessitates evolving to a different kind of company … on a higher plateau. The investment community requires that valuable traded companies have Strategic Plans, cohesive training programs, management development and more.

2. Establish share holder value. Stock value is based upon perceptions, realities, transactions, image and other sophisticated factors. Book value is not established by accident and continually needs nourishing.

3. Evaluate and fine-tune all non-financial aspects of the company. Profit motive is not the only measure of a successful company. Get beyond the bean counter mentality and think more globally. Consultants from outside the financial realm must advise public companies.

4. Management and leadership activities. Most executives are not fully groomed. From core business competencies, they are simply thrown into the pool and expected to swim. They tend to micro-manage and retain limited focus. Resources must be put toward developing the company's most valuable asset: its people.

5. Corporate communications. Investor relations, public relations, community relations, government relations, stakeholder relations and more must be weaved into a cohesive program, with qualified outside-the-company advisors. The Annual Report is symbolic of the company's growth and must be produced in tandem with the Strategic Plan.

6. Create and sustain corporate vision. It's not the whims of a few people. It's not an image campaign. It's something that is developed, fine-tuned, communicated and supported throughout the organization. It never stands still and reflects pro-active changes.

7. Achieve share holder longevity, continuing value. Construct, provide and continue offering value-added. That is measured by addressing each of the previous six major areas on an ongoing, systematic basis.

7 Levels of Thinking-Reasoning Skills

1. Don't Have Them … Don't Understand That They're Essential. Some people are too consumed with just getting by. Some are preoccupied with getting more than their share from the system. Some are busy doing things without thinking them through.

2. Thinking That They're Thinking … Abdicating to Someone Else. If they believe that external forces (such as technology) will "do it all" and create the future, then their thinking skills stop here on Branch 2. Abdicating to others and reacting to situations without applying other thought processes is just acting out, not thinking out.

3. Beginning to Develop … Learning from Experiences. Trial and error. Success through learning from failures. Learning from doing, experiencing and witnessing becomes a habit.

4. Continue Adding to Their Knowledge Base. Beginning to understand how and why things happened. Noticing paradigms and patterns of behavior … in ourselves, others and situations we get ourselves into.

5.   Develop Insights into Situations, Life. Maximizing the learning curve. Comprehending how to avoid pitfalls and make the most of circumstances. This leads to enlightened views of life and results in a more fulfilled usage of time and resources.

6.   Develop Insights into Reasons Why, Motivations, Implications, Consequences. Learn outside one's sphere, seeing and studying the paradigms of others. Developing the tools to function better through a Body of Knowledge.

7.   Generate and Continue to Seek Wisdom. Only through progressively navigating from Branches 3-6 can one arrive at plateaus of wisdom. The truly wise person inventories what he-she does not know and accelerates the learning tracks.

7 Levels of Answers Given to Questions

1.   Easy, Obvious Ones. Based upon the only information available, assumptions, conclusions, innuendo or heresy. Sometimes, answers are just enough to get rid of someone or to discourage certain people from asking deeper questions or conducting more substantial research.

2.   Knee-Jerk, Shoot from the Hip. Based upon surface conclusions or generalities. Quoting other people, mass media or popular sayings. Not based upon original thought or investigation of the facts or circumstances.

3.   Party Line, Politically Correct. Bureaucracies like to give out pat answers that cover their obligation to respond, but they are not saying much. Some answers echo company policies and wishes (either actual or perceived as just enough to avoid blame). Some are targeted at certain audiences.

4.   Tell People What They Want to Hear. These are phony and are usually justified in the mind of the person giving the answers. The sophisticated questioner will pursue further. After the stock answer, ask for what they really think or believe.

5.   Factual, Complete Explanations. Rich on content, backup descriptions and inviting further questions.

6.   Answers That Get Them Thinking Further. Offer what you do with the information and the longer implications.

7. Deep Wisdom. Having been there, considered the situation and offering insights into the deeper aspects of your question. These are the rare people worth listening to.

7 Levels of Decision Making

1. Quoting the Book. Avoid decisions, deferring to others or simply doing nothing. Nebulous sources quoted serve as barriers to making and standing by decisions.

2. Carrying Forward Prevailing Philosophies. It's amazing how many organizations do something the same way twice, and it is hence heralded as "the way it is." What's worse, if repeated often enough, it is labeled a "tradition." This level is based upon blocking change, which is 90% positive and can benefit any company.

3. Guesses. Offering things that we may believe to be true, rather than what we have researched. Many people and organizations claim and quote policies that never really existed. That's just their interpretation of certain rules. Guesses sometimes prove true, and the only way to know is to research hunches before offering them as opinion.

4. Niche Decisions. Related to the subject matter. What's best for that department, division or circumstances. The organization that supports empowered decisions at the niche level is willing to widen its scope when it comes to the Bigger Picture decisions. Great place for a truly successful organization to start.

5. Taking Risks, Blazing Horizons. Citing applicable precedents, yet exploring creative new ways of dealing with old problems. Looking at decisions as opportunities, rather than as obstacles.

6. Long-term Decisions. Look at the pieces of the company "pie" in terms of their inter-relationship to the other. Determine patterns of decisions that may serve multiple objectives ... setting precedents for a more enlightened level of decision making throughout the organization.

7. Profound Wisdom. Truly wise executives listen to others and seek informed counsel by advisors and qualified outside consultants. Truly wise executives have made their share of bad decisions ... the greatest

learning curves of all. They celebrate the guts and instincts of other trusted employees to make and stand by decisions.

7 Biggest Paradoxes-Challenges Facing Business

1. Progress vs. Isolationism. For all we have achieved, our society is more polarized than ever. Like minds and appearances surround themselves with those like themselves. Diversity is not sought. Sameness is the mantra, by default.

2. Focus on Micro vs. Macro. It's easy and convenient to zero in on small details than to solve problems, than to get at root causes of deeper issues. Very few managers have ever been taught to become skilled generalists. Big Picture thinking is not given much of a forum.

3. Worshipping Inanimate Objects. Computer groupies say that "technology" is all that matters. They banish those who are not quite as passionate. Organizations put disproportionate amounts of money, time and attention behind equipment ... while forsaking and slighting the most important priority: people (employees, customers, stakeholders).

4. Coveting Flash and Sizzle. People believe exaggerated claims faster than factual research. The public does not comprehend substance and wisdom because it is bombarded with half-baked ideas created by sellers and promoters.

5. Band-Aid Surgery Approach. By dealing with problems only at such time as they can no longer be avoided, the average organization pays six times more than if planning and strategy had been applied on the front end. This is The High Cost of Doing Nothing™.

6. Shoot, Ignore or Ostracize the Messenger. Most advice is obtained from the wrong consultants. Companies buy bills of goods from people who recommend what they're selling, rather than what is really needed. Thus, consultants are scapegoated and given a bad name. Blaming someone else is a way of avoiding the processes of improvement and quality.

7. Putting Tomorrow in Someone Else's Hands. Tomorrow is ours to craft, not that of vendors. Futurism is a process of thinking, reasoning, creative problem solving, interaction with others, thinking outside your frame of

reference and personal commitment. Futurism is not esoteric, nor is it a quick fix. It is a process of change, 90% beneficial.

7 Tenets of Diversity

1. Core Values. Diversity is not something that is mandated or unpleasant. It opens windows of opportunity for all who choose to learn, grow and prosper. Organizations that seek and foster diversity will be more successful than those who are mandated to change.

2. Business Realities. Good business is all-inclusive of ideas, methodologies and approaches to the work at hand. The "book value" of a company has a direct relationship to its biggest resource, its people.

3. Workforce Dynamics. Diversity is about more than race, age, physical abilities and lifestyle. It welcomes substance, commitment, creative ideas and constructive participation of employees in the operation of their organization.

4. Legal, Ethical Responsibilities. Certainly the letter of the law must be abided. Diversity reflects the manner in which crises are avoided upfront and the manner in which the spirit of the law is exceeded. Companies that do the right thing consistently will minimize costly band-aid surgery. It costs six times more to clean up problems than to address them on the front end. Resources spent on pro-active initiatives are wiser than after-the-fact damage control.

5. Opportunities to Grow. Diverse organizations attract the best people, with the best work ethics. Inclusiveness is an important ingredient in the quality process, re-engineering and organizational mission.

6. Benefits to All. Valued employees are more productive and loyal. The more that communications are open and continuous, the more efficient the operation.

7. Corporate Vision. Closed, rigid corporate philosophies are inevitably replaced with enlightened approaches. Futurism is the process of thinking through the opportunities, mustering the resources and creating the best possible organization. Visions do not magically appear, nor or they handed down from ivory towers. Diversity of thought, if properly harnessed and applied, constitutes the organization of the future.

7 Basics of E-Mail

1. Content. When you need to say things short and sweet, e-mail is a handy resource. It cannot take the place of face-to-face communications and formalized business communications, but it opens additional opportunities to convey information and solicit feedback.

2. Business Etiquette. Though some people exercise relaxed protocol and use jargon slang, don't follow suit … the same standards as formal business letters should apply to e-mail. It is said that first impressions are lasting ones, and the language with which one communicates is indicative of other ways in which he-she does business. Though the format is new, e-mail does not require a lesser level of etiquette.

3. Timeliness. Part of e-mail protocol is that one responds in as timely a manner as has the sender. Partially-returned and non-returned responses send messages in themselves.

4. Audience Customization. Think of e-mail as though you're having a private conversation or sharing a hand-written letter. It is possible and advisable to have boiler plate sections that you may drop in. However, some degree of customization is necessary and enhances your chances to get desired results … in ways that faxes, letters and mass mailings cannot.

5. Avoiding Junk E-Mail. Be selective about giving out your e-mail address. It is easier to get on e-mail solicitation lists than any others. Though messages can be deleted, junk e-mail still wastes your valuable time. Be selective about getting into chat rooms, newsgroups and other outlets where you will get mass e-mailings.

6. Confluence with Other Communications. E-mail communications must be compatible in content, substance, demeanor and professionalism with annual reports, newsletters and other official publications. It should be part of a cohesive written corporate communications program, not the antithesis of it.

7. Follow-up Opportunities. Make and take the chances to communicate further and more frequently with key stakeholders. Keep communications friendly, focused and succinct.

7 Steps Toward Strategic Vision

1. Analyze the company's future environment, resources and capabilities.
2. Clarify management values.
3. Develop a mission statement. It is a starting point, not an end in itself.
4. Identify strategic objectives and goals.
5. Generate select strategic options.
6. Develop the vision statement.
7. Measure and review the progress.

7 traits of a successful Visioning Program include:

1. Effective visions are inspiring.
2. Effective visions are clear and challenging … involving excellence.
3. Effective visions have marketplace purpose, savvy and flexibility.
4. Effective visions must be stable, yet prudently updated.
5. Effective visions are role models, when all else is in turmoil.
6. Effective visions empower the organization's people first and the customers secondly.
7. Effective visions honor the past and prepare for the future.

7 Pitfalls to avoid include:

1. Settle short-term problems. Otherwise, they will fester and grow.
2. Never let the vision lapse.
3. Effective visions are lived in details, not in broad strokes.
4. Be sure that all sectors of the organization participate.
5. Periodically, test and review the process.
6. Never stop planning for the next phase.
7. Don't forget that change is inevitable.

7 Levels of Visioning Programs

1. Was Someone's Pet Idea. A program was initiated to fit a personal or political agenda. It was sold and accepted as such. Therefore, it will

be pursued partially because its motivation is transparent or limited. Visioning is more than a "program." It is a process, encompassing change, behavioral modification, focus on growth and positive reinforcement.

2. Done Because It Was Forced or Mandated. A crisis, litigation, merger, loss of market share, government edict, competition with others or a combination of outside factors caused this to begin. Visioning here is a response, not a choice. The amounts of support and participation depends upon the circumstances and the spirit with which the mandate is carried out.

3. Done for Show or Image. Some organizations think that Visioning will make organizations look good. Actually, it makes them good. Visioning is not a substitute for public relations or marketing. It guides the organization which those other functions support. Visioning must focus upon substance, not just flash-and-sizzle.

4. With Partial Support and Resources. It is accorded just enough to begin the process but not quite enough to do it right. It is either the domain of top management or is delegated to the middle of the organization. Visioning must be a team effort and well-communicated in order to hit its stride, gather additional support and sustain.

5. Well Planned. The Visioning process begins with forethought, continues with research and culminates in a Strategic Plan. A comprehensive plan includes the mission, core values, goals, objectives (per each key results area), tactics to address and accomplish, timeline and benchmarking criteria.

6. Well Executed. Visioning goes beyond the Strategic Plan. It sculpts how the organization will progress, its character and spirit, participation of its people and steps that will carry the organization to the next tiers of desired achievement, involvement and quality.

7. Well Followed and Benchmarked. Both the Strategic Plan and the Visioning process must be followed through. This investment in careful and thoughtful planning is one-sixth that of later performing band aid surgery on an ailing organization.

7 Levels of Handling Problems

1. Do Nothing. Think that things will work themselves out or that causes of problems will go away. Research shows that doing nothing results in creating 3-6 more affiliated problems.

2. Deny, Actively Avoid. Don't see problems as such. Keep one's head in the sand and remain impervious to warning signs of trouble. Go to great lengths to put positive spins on anything that may point back to one's self, department or organization as being problematic.

3. Cover Up. Cover-ups cost 6-12 times that of addressing problems upfront. In addition to financial, cover-up costs can include the effects upon morale, activity levels, productivity, decision making, creativity, adaptation and innovation. Even after the cover-up has fully played out, there is an additional cost: the period of recovery and restoration of confidence.

4. Partially Address. Perform band aid surgery, at such time as action is demanded. Address signs and symptoms, without addressing root causes. This shows that something is being done, but it is often the wrong thing at the wrong time.

5. Handle in Politically Correct Terms. Some problems are addressed, partially or fully, because bosses, regulators or stakeholders expect it. Some are handled for fear of repercussion. This motive results in tentative actions, with lip service paid to deep solutions.

6. Address Head-On. Problems are, of course, opportunities to take action. Everyone makes mistakes, and success lies in the way that problems are recognized, solved and learned from. The mark of a true manager is to recognize problems sooner, rather than later. The mark of an effective leader is the ability and willingness to take swift and definitive actions. The mark of an empowered team is its participation in this process. The mark of a successful organization is its endorsement and insistence upon this method of action.

7. Address in Advance, Preparing for Situations. Pro-actively study for patterns. 85% of the time, crises that are predicted, pre-addressed, planned and strategized are averted. The skill in pre-managing problems is a fundamental tenet of a quality oriented organization.

7 Levels of Leader

1. Sets a Good Example. Individuals and organizations prove themselves by their characters, not just words, promises or personalities. Flash-and-sizzle wears thin and shows itself relatively soon.

2. Was a Good Team Player. The person who took instruction from others and served as a good organization member has the makings of an effective leader. Poor team players, however, will remain so.

3. Abilities to Lead. Some people want to lead. Some have limited opportunities to take charge. Of those, few are "natural leaders." It takes experience, finesse and an understanding of human dynamics to excel as a leader. Credit must be paid to second-line and third-line influencers. They inform, affect and steer the leaders.

4. Track Record. The leader's past accomplishments, especially abilities to encounter adversity and group discord, are indicative of his-her style. One leads by example.

5. Abilities to Inspire. The inspiring leader empowers followers to want and advocate good teamwork. It's more than an inspirational message, and the team cares to be involved, rather than just following along.

6. Still a Team Player. A true leader serves on other people's teams, supports their objectives and flexibly functions in a variety of settings. One does not always lead in front but proves his-her measure through mentoring and complimenting other leaders.

7. Further Advance the Concept of Leadership. The proof is in the body of causes, relationships, projects, people, collaborations, objectives and accomplishments. Leaders don't just lead the process. They develop expertise in subjects, group dynamics, community alliances and other outlets for guided teams to be effective.

7 Stages of Fear

1. The Unknown
2. Circumstances Beyond Your Own Control
3. Failure
4. Taking Risks

5. Being Creative
6. Making Meaningful Contributions
7. Success

7 Stages of FEAR, Find Excellence After Reflection
1. Whatever measure you give will be the measure that you get back.
2. There are no free lunches in life. The joy is in the journey, not in the destination.
3. The best destinations are not pre-determined in the beginning, but they evolve out of circumstances. Circumstances can be strategized for maximum effectiveness.
4. You have to give in order to get. Having and being given talent and results are not the same thing.
5. One cannot live entirely through work. One doesn't just work to live. As an integrated process of life skills, career has its place.
6. A Body of Work doesn't just happen. It's the culmination of a thoughtful, dedicated process, carefully strategized from some point forward.
7. The objective is to begin strategizing sooner rather than later and keep it going.

7 Stages of Fixing Problems
1. Band aid surgery for what we think is the problem.
2. Fixing what vendors who are selling their "consultative services" tell us need fixing.
3. Fixing what will make management look like problem solvers.
4. Patchwork to cover all bases and rear-ends.
5. Earnest initial efforts to solve actual problems with effective procedures.
6. Deep insight as to the real problems and causes.
7. Planning, actions and measurements for profound solutions to long-term problems.

What Happens at Each Stage
1. One problem looks solved. Look the other way, or else its stitches will come undone.

2. A patchwork of vendors … not a cohesive diagnosis of the organization's needs.
3. Look-good activities, which will unravel as band aid surgeries soon enough.
4. Reactions, rather than strategies.
5. Earnest initial results. But don't rest on early laurels.
6. It takes courage to focus clearly and then to take specific actions. Relish the journey.
7. It's not a one-meeting or management edict procedure. Plan and interact organizationally.

What You Get
1. A band-aid surgery mindset that perpetuates itself.
2. Shoot the messenger when you don't get the answers that you want or expect.
3. Steer clear of recommendations that will facilitate change in the organization.
4. The rear end that is exposed will embarrass the whole organization.
5. Sincere intents to try harder, activities that are pro-active and focuses upon quality.
6. Paradigm shifts, empowered employees and enlightened management.
7. A growth organization. Each challenge is met successfully.

7 Levels of Advice Given

1. Answers to Questions. There are 7 levels of answers which may be given, depending upon how extensive one wants: Easy and Obvious Ones, Knee-Jerk Reactions, Politically Correct, What People Want to Hear, Factual and Complete Explanations, Answers That Get Them Thinking Further and Deep Wisdom.
2. Observations on Situations. These take the forms of "When this happened to me, I did X," or "If this occurred with me, I would Y." It's often good to see things through someone else's perspective.
3. Subjective Viewpoint. Friends want what is best for you. This level of advice is usually pro-active and is influenced by the advisor's experiences with comparable situations.

4. Informed Opinion. Experts have core-business backgrounds upon which to draw. Advisors bring facts, analysis and methodologies of applying their solutions to your case. Niche consultants provide quality viewpoints, as it relates to their talents and skills. Carefully consider the sources of advice and expertise.

5. Researched Options. Investments in research (formal, informal, attitudinal, demographic, sociological) will avert unnecessary band aid surgery expenses later. Research leads to planning, which is the best way to accomplish tasks and benchmark success.

6. Discussion of Outcomes-Consequences. Most actions and decisions in an organization affect many others. At this level, advisors recommend that sufficient planning be conducted … please take their advice. The more strategic and Big Picture in scope, then planning reaps long-term rewards.

7. Inspiring Directions. This gets into Visioning. Planning and going to new heights are stimulating. The mannerisms and substance by which any organization achieves its Vision requires sophisticated advice, deep insights and creative ideas.

7 Levels of Seminar-Workshop

1. Niche player wants to put it on.
   - Seeking business.
   - Because someone else had a conference.
   - Think it is a requisite thing to do.
   - Glorified sales pitch.
   - Gimmick marketing.
   - Ego based. Done for show or image.
   - Niche webinars.
   - Was Someone's Pet Idea. A program was initiated to fit a personal or political agenda. It was sold and accepted as such. Therefore, it will be pursued partially because its motivation is transparent or limited.

2. Playing to the base.
   - Group think version of first category.
   - Conferences by niche business groups, chamber of commerce expos, etc.

- Conferences by networking groups.
- College showcase programs.
- Boot camps.

3. Conveying information.
    - Grew out of the second category.
    - Supplier and customer forums.
    - Institutional Promotion. Imparting experiences.
    - Done Because It Was Forced or Mandated. A crisis, litigation, merger, loss of market share, government edict, competition with others or a combination of outside factors caused this to begin.
    - Done With Partial Support and Resources. It is accorded just enough to begin the process but not quite enough to do it right. It is either the domain of top management or is delegated to the middle of the organization.

4. Programs with purpose.
    - Outlook conferences.
    - Links to discover other resources and colleagues.
    - Business collaboration is one vital wave of the future.
    - Answers to Questions.
    - Observations on Situations.
    - Subjective Viewpoint.

5. Events that reach out.
    - Widen the scope of material.
    - Pertinent, timely and applicable to business.
    - Encouraging actions.
    - Informed Opinion. Experts have core-business backgrounds upon which to draw. Advisors bring facts, analysis and methodologies of applying their solutions to your case. Niche consultants provide quality viewpoints … as it relates to their talents and skills. Carefully consider the sources.
    - Researched Options.
    - Discussion of Outcomes-Consequences.

6. Wishing to stimulate, encourage and share.
    - Paving the way.

- Messages ways to approach issues, paths. Helps draw distinctions.
- Paints pictures of success. Wanting the best.
- Continuing business relationship between mentor and mentee.
- Progress is planned, contextualized, seeded, benchmarked.
- Accountability-communication by participants.
- Material Not Available Elsewhere. Enlightens audiences to resources not widely known before. This level goes far beyond sales. Iit nourishes credibility relationships with customers, suppliers and business collaborators. It stimulates further creation of quality materials.

7. Sharing meaningful knowledge and wisdom.
    - Thought leader forums.
    - Advocating, Facilitating.
    - Bonded collaboration toward each other's success.
    - Sharing Profound Wisdom.
    - Respect for each other continues throughout the relationship.
    - Well Planned. Well Executed. Well Followed and Benchmarked.
    - Inspiring Directions. This requires sophisticated advice, deep insights and creative ideas.

Levels of Teaching Others:
1. Information … What We Know, Technologies-Tasks to Gather.
2. Education … Teaching, Processing Information, Modeling.
3. Learning … Mission, Absorbing Information, Techniques.
4. Insights … Synthesizing Information, Values, Applicable skills.
5. Knowledge … Direction, Experience Bank, Inspired Thoughts.
6. Strategy … Actions, Goals & Objectives, Viabilities, Creativity.
7. Vision … Qualities, Strengths, Realizations, Big Picture Scope.

7 Types of Crises

1. Those Resulting from Doing Nothing. The biggest problem with business, in a one-sentence capsule, is: People exhibit misplaced priorities and impatience, seeking profit and power, possessing unrealistic views of life, and not fully willing to do the things necessary to sustain orderly growth and long-term success.

2. Doing Things As We Always Have. This leads to inflexible work conditions, obsolete policies-procedures, procrastination, resistance to innovation and failure to change.

3. Those We Bring Upon Ourselves. Having insufficient management skills or resources to do something well. Ignoring small problems as they occur. Won't listen to advice.

4. Circumstances Beyond Our Control. Miscalculations, disasters, shifting resources, changing marketplaces, regulations and bureaucracies all serve to trigger crises.

5. Bad Work, Make-Good Actions. Damage control for what someone else did wrong, sub-standard, behind schedule, in poor taste, without regard for quality or poorly prepared.

6. Averted Crises. 85% of the time, planning and forethought will prevent trouble and crises from brewing. So, why don't organizations and individuals remediate potential problems sooner rather than later?

7. Intervention. Getting past the current crisis does no good unless one takes steps to prevent it from recurring. Planning is necessary to reduce current and future high crisis costs.

What Causes Crises:
1. Refusal to take action.
2. Letting problems fester until they become epidemic diseases.
3. Lack of accountability.
4. Waiting until it is too late to avert a crisis.
5. Taking correctional measures after too much damage has been done.
6. Waiting too late to make good for damage. Saying one is sorry is not enough.
7. Living life for the moment, without comprehending the implications and repercussions.

7 Levels of Planning Utilized by Organizations

1. Information Gathering Process. Snapshot of the realities of situations, as well as facts and figures. Understand the organization's truths.

2. Studying How the Organization Operates. Conduct performance reviews of successful activities, while also looking for efficiencies.
3. Enhance Efficiencies, Economies, Profitability. Shareholder value.
4. Process For and About Teams. Empowering and involving the organization's most valuable resource, its people.
5. Adapting to Changing Marketplaces, Relationships. Connect beliefs with expertise. Actions are taken with measurements of success and accountability to stakeholders.
6. Strategic Planning. Study the organization's core values. Has commitment and ownership. Able to change and adapt to changing situations and marketplaces.
7. Futurism, Vision and Change Focused. Everything is done based upon beliefs and systems of thought. Committed to and thriving upon change.

7 Levels of Addressing Public Opinion

1. Those Resulting from Doing Nothing. The biggest problem with business, in a one-sentence capsule, is: People exhibit misplaced priorities and impatience, seeking profit and power, possessing unrealistic views of life, and not fully willing to do the things necessary to sustain orderly growth and long-term success.
2. Doing Things As We Always Have. This leads to stifled Visioning attempts, stagnant company image, obsolete policies-procedures, procrastination about taking pro-active positions, inactions, resistance to innovation and failure to change.
3. Selling, Marketing, Promoting.
4. Spin Doctoring. Organizations and individuals try to put "spins" on situations in order to meet crises and benefit their immediate interests. Such situations are complicated through: (a) Refusal to take action, (b) Letting problems fester until they become diseases, (c) Lack of accountability, (d) Waiting until it is too late to avert a crisis, (e) Taking correctional measures after too much damage has been done, (f) Waiting too late to make good for damage.
5. Taking an Educational Stance.

6. Being an Informed, Enlightened Citizen. Being successful in business for the long haul goes beyond just communicating what the organization does. A well planned and executed public affairs program sculpts how the organization will progress, its character and spirit, participation of its people and steps that will carry the organization to the next tiers of desired achievement, involvement and quality.

7. Raising the Standards, Going the Distance. Communications practices begin with forethought, continues with research and culminates in a plan ... incorporating and enriching the mission, core values, goals and objectives of the organization.

7 Measures of Customer Focused Management

1. Being Your Best Self. It is not acceptable to be a clone of what you perceive someone else to be. Those organizations and managers who use terms like "world class" are usually wanna-be's who won't ever quite make the measuring stick.

2. Being Consistently Excellent ... and Upholding Standards to Remain So. There is no such thing as perfection. Yet, excellence is a definitive process of achievement, dedication and expeditious use of resources. Exponential improvement each year is the objective.

3. The Ability to Change, Adapt and Lead.

4. Learning from Experiences, Successes and the Shortcomings of All.

5. Thinking, Planning, Reflecting and Benchmarking.

6. Committing to the Next Great Challenge.. Do not fall into the trap of some false commitment to "tradition" (an excuse used by many to avoid change and accountability).

7. Ability to Communicate and Share with Others.

7 Levels of Motivation for Things that We Wish to Accomplish

1. Do by Direction. Do as a favor to someone or as an expedient way of accomplishing overall objectives. Sometimes, actions are because we were instructed, mandated or coerced to do.

2. Do by Default. Things done because it was the only choice.

3. Need to.

4. Want to.
5. In our best interest to do so.
6. Should, would and could do.
7. Committed, energized and eager to do or achieve.

7 Levels of Paying One's Dues in Business

1. Learn from Others' Mistakes.
2. Gain Experiences.
3. Lead Because You've Been There.
4. Timing is a Major Factor.
5. Can't Succeed Without Paying Dues. The process of failing and evaluating spawns success.
6. Chart the Changes.
7. Things Are Rarely Ours When We First Want Them.

Chapter 6

REVIEW OF RECENT RECESSIONS
AND THEIR AFFECTS ON BUSINESS

P erhaps because we had seen such a long period of prosperity, the current economic recession is causing inordinate panic. The media is helping this panic with headlines such as "Economy shrinks at fastest pace in 26 years," "Over One-Third of Americans Believe Nation in a Depression," and "Wall Street Tumbles to 1997 Levels on Bank, Recession Fears."

It's important to read beyond the headlines and remember that recessions are actually a normal part of the business cycle. Recessions do have a valuable purpose in that they clear away weak companies and force people to spend less and save more. While this recession appears to be lasting longer than a normal recession, history has shown we will eventually emerge to a new period of economic growth and the stock markets will eventually recover their losses and hit new highs.

It is easy to forget that we have had seven recessions since 1967. While the most recent recession (2008-2010) may seem "different" for various reasons, it is important to remember that recessions usually have "different" causes or related events new to our history. Here are some examples:

1973-1974 Stock Market Crash and 1973 Oil Crisis (1973-1975) lasting two years.

- Between January 11, 1973, and December 6, 1974, the Dow Jones Industrial Average benchmark lost over 45% of its value.
- The unemployment rate jumped from the 5% level to nearly the 9% in about a year and a half.
- The Arab members of OPEC declared they would no longer ship oil to the United States and other countries if they supported Israel.
- In 1972, the price of crude oil was about $3.00 per barrel and by the end of 1974 the price of oil had quadrupled to over $12.00.
- In the United States, the retail price of a gallon of leaded regular gasoline rose from a national average of 39 cents in 1973 to 53 cents in 1974.
- The New York Stock Exchange shares lost $97 billion in value in a six-week period.
- Inflation jumped from 3.4% in 1972 to 12.3% in 1974.

Early 1980s recession (1980-1982) lasting two years.

- The unemployment rate reached 10.8%.
- Bank failures reached a high of 42, and in the first half of 1983 an additional 27 banks failed.
- In 1984, the Continental Illinois National Bank and Trust Company, the nation's seventh-largest bank failed. Members of Congress felt Continental Illinois was "too big to fail." In May 1984, federal banking regulators were forced to offer a $4.5 billion rescue package to Continental Illinois.
- 415 savings and loan associations in the US failed.
- In 1979, inflation reached 13.3%7 and the Prime lending rate jumped to 21.5% by December 1980.

Early 1990s recession (1990-1991) lasting one year.

- By 1989, over half the Savings and Loan banks had failed, along with the FSLIC fund that was created to insure their deposits.

Early 2000s recession (2001-2003) lasting two years.

- By the end of 2001, the S&P 500 average price-to-earnings ratio was 46.50, well above the historical average of 15, and it was thought that "earnings didn't matter" in the valuation of stocks.

- The NASDAQ lost 78% of its value following the collapse of the Dot-com bubble.
- From March 2000 to October 2002, technology companies lost $5 trillion in market value.
- After the September 11, 2001 terrorist attacks, the Dow Jones Industrial Average suffered its worst one-day point loss and biggest one-week losses in history up to that point.
- Unprecedented accounting scandals at companies such as Enron and Worldcom.

Crisis Management, Learning From the Titanic

This is the first use of the Titanic as an analogy to business. The Titanic was a monument to human folly and arrogance. It started with pomp and potential. Yet, it turned into a lot of what-ifs and missed opportunities. So, too, is business, who should learn the lessons from the economic downturn and the corporate scandals.

One of the greatest tragedies in history, the sinking of the Titanic, can be attributed to carelessness, insufficient planning and stubborn pride.

People literally went down with the ship while still quoting the ship's marketing hype, "Everybody knows this ship cannot sink." They really believed the spin and rationalized it as a false hope to avert disaster. They were so sure, thought tragedy could not happen to them, believed themselves to be invincible, had false senses of security and exhibited unnecessarily stoical behavior when confronted with the harsh realities of death.

In 1912, the Titanic, a Trans-Atlantic ship on its maiden voyage, hit an iceberg and sank. Though some people escaped by life boats, there were still 1,502 people killed.

If any of these had occurred, chances are that every life would have been saved. The Titanic would not have sunk if any of these precautions-actions had occurred:

- Management ... had the ship's officers heeded one of the six iceberg warnings.
- Planning ... had the ship's design required better lighting to see a potential collision.

- Timing ... had the ship hit the iceberg 15 seconds sooner or 13 seconds later.
- Planning ... had the water tight bulkheads been one deck higher.
- Supplies ... if the ship had carried enough life boats.
- Regulations ... had the distress signal to a nearby ship been heeded and acted upon.

Not only did the people die, but it was the end of an era in travel. Credibility toward steamships was shaken. Safety became more important in the luxury travel industry. Other forms of travel could serve customers better, faster and cheaper. Concern for corporate savings at the expense of quality was raised.

Think of other disasters that brought similar concerns home and forced major changes in planning, policy, safety, implementation and accountability:

- Fires and collapses in commercial buildings, due to use of sub-standard materials or improper safety precautions.
- Citizen outcries over prejudice, hate and bigotry actions by people in charge.
- Unnecessary duplication of services by public sector and non-profit entities.
- Chemical plant explosions.
- Improper discharge of substances into the ozone.
- Maneuvers, where improper planning cost property and lives.
- Insensitivity of organizations to their customers.

Learning More from History

The basic cause of World War II was a failure to uphold the peace treaty following World War I. Countries let circumstances fester (notably the Hitler regime) that paying attention to and adhering to the peace treaty would have precluded.

"They can't hang you for saying nothing," quipped President Calvin Coolidge in the 1920s. He spent more time doing chores at his farm and taking long naps than taking care of the nation's business. Coolidge prided himself upon doing little and, thus, failed to see crises brewing during his presidency. A person once joked to President Coolidge that he could get him to say three or more words, to which

Coolidge quipped, "You lose." This "keep your head in the sand" mentality is prevalent of people who move slowly and let others clean up the damage.

Throughout the 1920s, the U.S. spent $50 million per year in trying vainly to enforce the highly unpopular Prohibition Act. Bootleggers, racketeers and mobsters made billions of dollars and established footholds in territories that were impossible to retract. An unpopular law spearheaded by a zealous few was never really enforced, and its criminal perpetrators became "folk heroes" to many.

People at Work

The current success rate for organizational hires is 14%. If further research is put into looking at the total person and truly fitting the person to the job, then the success rate soars to 75%. That involves testing and more sophisticated hiring practices.

Retaining good employees, involving training, motivation and incentives, is yet another matter. According to research conducted by the Ethics Resource Center:

- Employees of organizations steal 10 times more than do shoplifters.
- Employee theft and shoplifting accounting for 15% of the retail cost of merchandise.
- 35% of employees steal from the company.
- 28% of those who steal think that they deserve what they take.
- 21% of those who steal think that the boss can afford the losses.
- 56% of employees lie to supervisors.
- 41% of employees falsify records and reports.
- 31% of the workforce abuses substances.

One out of every 20 employees has substance or alcohol abuse problems, with resulting behaviors which in turn adversely effect another 20 people in their lives. Employees with substance abuse problems cost their companies $7,000 per year in downtime or lost days, $9,500 in make-good and work redo and another $15,000 in opportunity and credibility costs to the organization. Companies with good Employee Assistance Programs reduce these high costs and retain the services of valuable workers.

The old adage says: "An ounce of prevention is worth a pound of cure." One pound equals 16 ounces. In that scenario, one pound of cure is 16 times more mostly than an ounce of prevention.

Human beings as we are, none of us do everything perfectly on the front end. There always must exist a learning curve. Research shows that we learn three times more from failures than from successes. The mark of a quality organization is how it corrects mistakes and prevents them from recurring.

Running a profitable and efficient organization means effectively remediating damage before it accrues. Processes and methodologies for researching, planning, executing and benchmarking activities will reduce that pile of costly coins from stacking up.

Doing nothing becomes a way of life for many people and organizations. It is amazing how many individuals and companies live with their heads in the sand. Never mind planning for tomorrow, and we will just deal with problems as they occur. This mindset, of course, invites and tends to multiply trouble.

There are seven costly categories of doing nothing, doing far too little or doing the wrong things in business:

1. Cleaning Up Problems: Waste, Spoilage. Poor controls. Down-time. Lack of employee motivation and activity. Back orders because they were not properly stocked. Supervisory involvement in retracing problems and effecting solutions.

2. Rework: Product recalls. Make-good for shoddy or inferior work. Poor location. Regulatory red tape. Excess overhead.

3. Missed Marks: Poor controls on quality. Fallout damage from employees with problems (For example, a substance abuser negatively impacts 20 people before treatment is applied.) Under-capitalization. Unsuccessful marketing. Unprofitable pricing.

4. Damage Control: Crisis management. Lawsuits incurred because procedures were not upheld. Affirmative action violations. Violations of OSHA, ADA, EEOC, EPA and other codes. Disasters due to employee carelessness, safety violations, oversights, etc. Factors outside your company that still impede your ability to do business.

5.   Recovery and Restoration: Repairing ethically wrong actions. Empty activities. Mandated cleanups, corrections and adaptations. Employee turnover, rehiring and retraining. Isolated or unrealistic management. Bad advice from the wrong consultants. Repairing a damaged company reputation.

6.   Retooling and Restarting: Mis-use of company resources, notably its people. Converting to existing codes and standards. Chasing the wrong leads, prospects or markets. Damage caused by inertia or lack of progress. The anti-change "business as usual" philosophy. Long-term expenses incurred by adopting quick fixes.

7.   Opportunity Costs: Failure to understand what business they're really in. Inability to read the warning signs or understand external influences. Failure to change. Inability to plan. Over-dependence upon one product or service line. Diversifying beyond the scope of company expertise. Lack of an articulated, well-implemented vision.

Chapter 7

SITUATIONS CAUSING THE 2008-2010 ECONOMIC DOWNTURN AND 2000S CORPORATE SCANDALS

E very business, company or organization goes through cycles in its evolution. At any point, each program or business unit is in a different phase from the others. Every astute organization assesses the status of each branch on its Business Tree™ and orients its management and team members to meet constant changes and fluctuations.

It's not that some organizations "click" and others do not. Multiple factors cause momentum, or the lack thereof. As companies operate, all make honest and predictable mistakes. Those with a willingness to learn from the mistakes and pursue growth will be successful. Others will remain stuck in frames of mind that set themselves up for the next round of defeat or, at best, partial-success.

The saddest fact is that businesses do not always know that they're doing anything wrong. They do not realize that a Big Picture must exist or what it could look like. They have not been taught or challenged on how to craft a Big Picture.

Managers, by default, see band aid surgery as the only remedy for problems … but only when problems are so evident as to require action.

Is it any wonder that organizations stray off course? Perhaps no course was ever charted. Perhaps the order of business was to put out fires as they arose, rather than practicing preventive safety on the kindling organization. That's how Business Trees in the forest tend to wither and burn like wildfires.

This article studies obsolete management styles and corporate cultures that exist in the minds of out-of-touch management. Reliance upon many of these management tenets subsequently brought Enron and many others down.

This includes the characteristics of addictive organizations, their processes, promises and forms. It reviews the Addictive System, the company way and the organization as an addict. This chapter studies communications, thinking processes, management processes, self-inflicted crises and structural components of companies that go bad, or maybe never do what it takes to be good. Topics discussed include the society that produced business scandals, accountants and auditors, pedestals upon which CEOs are placed, spin doctoring, compensations and accountability issues with managers.

Companies are collections of individuals who possess fatal flaws of thinking. They come from different backgrounds and are products of a pop culture that puts its priorities and glories in the wrong places, a society that worships flash-and-sizzle over substance.

In my professional opinion, these were the factors that led to the great recession:

- Running business in "fantasy land."
- Failure to keep it real.
- Deregulation, going back to the deregulation of the banking industry in 1984.
- An ill-informed marketplace
- A culture that tolerated and worshipped hype.
- Speculation by the ego driven.
- Complicity by the media.
- Inaction by the public.

- Lack of safeguards.
- A society that does not support or reward accountability.
- Business education that is behind the times.

Characteristics of Corporate Arrogance

- Support others who are like-minded to themselves.
- Scapegoat people who are the messengers of change.
- Blame others who cannot or will not defend themselves.
- Find public and vocal ways of placing blame upon others.
- Shame those people who make them accountable.
- Neither attends to details nor to pursue a Big Picture.
- Perpetuate co-dependencies.
- Selectively forgets the good that occurs.
- Find three wrongs for every right.
- Do little or nothing.
- At all costs, fight change, in every shape, form or concept.
- Making the wrong choices.
- Inability to listen. Refusal to hear what is said.
- Stubbornness.
- Listening to the wrong people.
- Failure to change. Fear of change.
- Comfort level with institutional mediocrity.
- Setting one's self up for failure.
- Pride.
- Avoidance of responsibilities.
- Blaming and scapegoating others.
- People who filter out the truths.
- Non-risk-taking mode.
- Inaccessibility to independent thinkers.
- Calling something a tradition, when it really means refusal to change.
- Pretense.
- Worshipping false idols, employing artificial solutions.
- Preoccupation with deals, rather than running an ongoing business.

- Arrogant attitudes.
- Ignorance of modern management styles and societal concerns.
- Failure to benchmark results and accomplishments.

Incorrect Assumptions that People Make:
- That wealth and success cure all ills.
- That business runs on data. That data projects the future.
- That data infrastructure hardware will navigate the business destiny and success.
- That all athletes are role models. That all well-paid celebrities are national heroes.
- That the CEO can make or break the company single-handedly.
- That doctors do not have to be accountable to their customers.
- That education stops after the last college degree received.
- That TV newscasters are celebrities and community leaders.
- That having an E-mail address or a website makes one an expert on technology.
- That the Internet is primarily an educational resource.
- That technology is the most important driving force in business and society.
- That buying the latest software program will cure all social ills and create success.
- That community stewardship applies to other people and does not require our own investment of time.
- That white-collar crime pays and that highly paid executives will avoid jail time.
- That senior corporate managers have all the answers and do not need to seek counsel.
- That return on shareholder investment is the only true measure of a company's worth.
- That all people who grew up in the south are racist.
- That government bureaucrats are qualified to make decisions about taxpayer money.
- That activists for one cause are equally open-minded about other issues.

- That corporate mid-managers with expense accounts are community leaders.
- That deregulation is always desirable and in the public's best interest.
- That home-based businesses are more wealth-producing than holding a job.
- That professionals can get by without developing public speaking and writing skills.

Fatal Quotations Voiced to Justify Fatal Thinking
- "Might makes right. Take no prisoners. Wear the other side down."
- "Everyone knows who we are and what we do."
- "Our accountants will catch it and take care of it."
- "It's none of their business. The public be damned."
- "We're not paying people to think, just to do what they are told. Make them understand."
- "We don't need outsiders coming in and hogging the credit."
- "If you don't cooperate with me, I'll bring you down."
- "We cannot do that right now. Once this crisis is past, we can think about the future."
- "How does this contribute to our bottom line?"
- "If it does not contribute directly to the bottom line, we're not interested."
- "We have more business than we can handle."
- "Too much competition destroys free enterprise. We need to eliminate competition."

Addictive Organizations
Addictive organizations are predicated upon maintaining a closed system. Alternately, they are marked by such traits as confusion, dishonesty and perfectionism. They are scarcity models, based upon quantity and the illusion of control. Only the high performers get the gold because there are not enough bonuses to go around. Addictive organizations show frozen feelings and ethical deterioration.

Addictive organizations dangle "the promise" to employees, customers, stockholders and others affected. People are lured into doing things that enable the addictive management's pseudopodic ego.

All that is different is either absorbed or purged. The addictive organization fabricates personality conflicts in order to keep people on the edge all the time. There exists a dualism of identifying the rightness of the choice and a co-dependence upon the rewards of the promise.

In such companies, the key person is an addict. The CEO and his chosen lieutenants have taken addictions with them from other organizations. The organization itself is an addictive substance, as well as being an addict to others. They numb people down and addict them to work-aholism.

The addictive system views everything as "the company way." The entity is outwardly one big happy family. It is big and grandiose. The emphasis is upon the latest slogans of mission but does not look closely at how its systems operate. The term "mission" is a buffer, excuse, putdown and roadblock.

Rather than embrace the kinds of Big Picture strategies advocated in this book, the addictive system seeks artificial fixes to organizational problems, such as bonuses, benefits, slogans and promotions of like-minded executives.

Communications are always indirect, vague, written and confusing. People are purposefully left out of touch or are summarily put down for not co-depending. Secrets, gossip and triangulation persist, as a result. The addictive organization does communicate directly with the news media and often adopts a "no comment" policy. Company officers (who should be accessible to media) are cloistered and unavailable. The addictive organization does not recognize that professional corporate communications are among the best resources in their potential arsenal.

The addictive system does not encourage managers to develop thinking and reasoning processes. The system portrays forgetfulness, selective memory and distorted facts into sweeping generalizations. We are expected to take them at their word, without requesting or demanding facts to justify.

In the addictive organization, those who challenge, blow whistles or suggest that things might be better handled are neither wanted nor tolerated. Addictive managers project externally originated criticism back onto internal scapegoats. There is always a strategy of people to blame and sins to be attributed to them.

Management processes tend to exemplify denial, dishonesty, isolation, self-centeredness, judgmental nature and a false sense of perfectionism. Intelligent people know that perfectionism does not exist and the quest for quality and excellence is the real game of life and business. Addictive organizations do not use terms like "quality" and "excellence" because such terms must be measured, periodically reexamined and communicated ... the organization does not want any of that to occur.

There persists a crisis orientation, meaning that everything is down to the wire on deadlines (not to be confused with just-in-time delivery, which is a good concept). Things are kept perennially in turmoil, in order to keep people guessing or confused. Management seduces employees into setting up competing sides in bogus feuds and manipulating consumers.

Structural components include preserving the status quo, fostering political games, taking false measurements and pursuing activities that are incongruent with the organization's announced mission.

7 Layers of Organizational Addictiveness, Companies That Go Bad and Their Self-Inflicted Crises

1. Self Destructive Intelligence. There exists a logic override. Since the company does not believe itself to be smart enough to do the right things, then it creates a web of rationalism. Since the mind often plays tricks on itself, management capitalizes upon that phenomenon with people who may question or criticize.

2. Hubris. This quality destroys those who possess it. Such executives exhibit stubborn pride, believing their own spin doctoring and surrounding themselves with people who spin quite well on their behalf. They adopt a "nobody does it as well as we can" mentality. Such companies scorn connections, collaborations and partnering with other organizations.

3. Arrogance. Omnipotent fantasies cause management to go too far. The feeling is that nothing is beyond their capacity to succeed (defined in their minds as crushing all other competition).

4. Narcissism. Company executives possess excessive conceit. They are disconnected from outside forces, self-centered and show a cruel indifference to others. The view is that the world must gratify them.

5. Unconscious Need to Fail. These companies try too hard to keep on winning. With victory as the only possible end game, all others must be defeated along the way. In reality, these people and, thus, their

organizations, possess low self-esteem. Inevitably, they get beaten at their own games.

6. Feeling of Entitlement. Walls and filters have been established which insulate top management from criticism (which is viewed as harming the chain of armor, rather than as potentially constructive). Anger stimulates many of their decisions. The feeling is that they deserve it all. Power satisfies appetites. These executives have poor human relations skills. They believe that excesses are always justified.

7. Collective Dumbness. Such organizations have totally reshaped reality to their own viewpoints. The emperor really has no clothes, but everyone overlooks the obvious and avoids addressing it forthrightly. The organization dumbs down the overall intelligence level, so that people are in the dark and cannot readily make judgment calls. Cults of expertise function in vacuums within the company. Neurotic departmental units do not interface often with others. Employees are slaves of the system. There exists total justification for what is done and an ostrich effect toward calls for accountability.

Chapter 8

WHAT BUSINESS MUST LEARN

**Putting the Recessions, Economic Downtowns
and Recent Events into Perspective**

T he public does not react to any crisis until it is big enough and far-reaching to affect their daily lives. When business news gets on Page 1 of every day's newspaper and every evening TV newscast, then the public notices and cares.

Business and organizational stories do not hit the public consciousness until there is a crisis. People decry the scandals and rest assured that such doings are not happening in their companies. Often, it is assumed that some protector or regulator will adequately address the issues. When the outcomes are of high magnitude, the outcry becomes larger. As people see the events as having a direct effect on the economy and their livelihood, they take notice and follow the stories more thoroughly.

The recent years succeeded in exploding a great many myths and presumptions about business. Formerly sainted icons went down in disgrace. Tactics deemed as "standard operating procedure" for some companies were exposed and ridiculed by others. A few whistle blowers were lauded in the efforts, though others were attacked as the perpetrators of the chaos shuffled aside.

One must ask many simple and pertinent questions about a seemingly unsettling business future:

- How did business get this far?
- Why did the scandals and corporate disrepute occur?
- What are the implications of Enron and other corporate scandals upon business?
- Where are the next trends and opportunities?
- How do we cope in the new environment?
- What beacons of opportunity do we look for?
- What will it now take to succeed and fail?
- How do we react to and benefit from changes, rather than become victims of them?
- Do we still take band aid approaches (such as buying enterprise software)? Or, do we now see the need and importance to embrace longer-term approaches?
- How far will we go to excel?
- How creative must we become in the New Order of Business?
- How far-reaching are business practices?
- How much further should we extend ethics?
- Where will the pendulum swing next?

Business in the 21st Century is real and dangerous. People suddenly feel lost. They are no longer in a safe port. They don't know how to cope. Yesterday's strategies simply do not work anymore.

Many of the old assumptions which business previously held have proven untrue and unworkable. We really must examine what we assumed before and what we can assume now. Business is at a juncture and needs new focus.

The victims' fear and the public's apathy enabled the crises to occur. This is the perfect climate for unethical people to have gotten away with murder. Sadly, many of the perpetrators did not see lapses in ethics. To them, it was legal and just business to them.

It takes tragedies occurring in order for the system to stand back, take focus and fix what is wrong. It's a whole new world. By maintaining an awareness of further changing environments, there are further opportunities to be successful, ethical and move ahead of the competition..

The term CEO has recently been held in disfavor. We decry CEOs for the same reasons that we formerly sainted and canonized them. People are envious of the power, status and wealth of company heads. Yet, most CEOs were never trained on how to be CEOs, with all the responsibility, people skills, leadership and ethical management that must go along with the job.

The game of duping and fooling shareholders, customers and employees has ended, as well it should move forward. We cannot ignore or compartmentalize board members, stockholders, employees and stakeholders anymore. We cannot fool them. We must listen to them and respect them.

Every organization in the world must reexamine how we will keep score in the New Order of Business. Continuing to justify blind spots will blur accountability. Having maintained too much of a myopic focus is what got so many companies in trouble already.

Thinking that we dodged the bullet while others got caught is a mentality that will still bring many other companies down in value and defeat. The scandals are not all aired in public yet. Up to 25% of our businesses are in peril and must take corrective actions, lest they be brought down in disgrace too.

Most of the downfalls, stumbles, false starts and incorrect handling of situations stemmed from business' lack of focus on the macro and over-emphasis upon certain micros, to the exclusion of other dynamics.

This chapter puts business events of the last two years into perspective, covering a broader scope of subjects than has been reported and discussed. This book states the case for more of a macro-focused approach to management. An analysis of business encompasses much more than accounting fraud and stated values of stocks.

What we do with fear and uncertainty determines who we are. It is time for fresh thinking, heightened ethical behavior and a shift to a macro focus. Rules and responsibilities within each sector of companies are changing. Each of us must ask what we can contribute and our roles in adapting to the crises.

High Costs and Learning Curves

Corporate scandals of each of the years cost the U.S. economy more than $200 billion in lost investment savings, jobs, pension losses and tax revenue. The scandals resulted in one million job cuts. 401(k) plans dropped $13 billion as a result of these events alone. Recent corporate scandals have cost good businesses in reputation, credibility and support, by virtue of being lumped with some bad apples. Thus, consumer confidence dipped, and it will take years to fortify the trust in business.

Losses from 401(k) investment accounts alone totaled $175 billion, making them worth 30% less than they were two years ago. Public pension funds nationwide lost at least $6.4 billion as the stock market plummeted, amid a crisis of investor confidence. More than a million workers lost their jobs at the affected companies, while company executives cashed out billions of dollars of their stock.

This demonstrates the impact of accounting failures at high-profile companies. There has been $13 billion in lost federal tax revenue from companies with questionable accounting practices underreporting their profits to the IRS. 23 companies under investigation have laid off 162,000 workers.

We have been subjected to the second longest bear market in history, the longest being that of the Great Depression. The stock market went down 25%. There are 25 million small businesses in America, all affected in some way by corporate scandals. Steroid scandals periodically rock the sports world. The public decries the use of steroids but secretly supports the results that they yield (athletic records being set). The steroids usage norm in some team sports has the effect of institutionalizing breaking the rules, even though the health of some is seriously endangered. Temptations to break the rules for the hope of future financial gain are at the heart of corporate arrogance, greed, deceptions and double-dealings, as well as in the minds of some sports promoters.

Operational Statistics

One out of every 12 businesses fails.

90% of all e-businesses fail.

97% of all internet websites do not make a profit.

Retailers make 70% of their earnings in the fourth quarter of each year. That is why holiday sales are vital to their bottom line and, thus, the economy.

Airport screeners fail to detect fake bombs and guns 24% of the time.

52% of all high school students know someone who brought a weapon to school. 61% of those students did nothing about it.

52% of all high school students know someone who made a weapon-oriented threat. 56% of those students did nothing about it.

Shoplifting costs American business $10 billion per year.

Airlines say that delays caused by air traffic controllers cost them a combined $4 billion per year. For every 1-cent reduction in the cost of jet fuel, the airlines save $170 million.

Cargo theft costs the U.S. economy $6 billion per year. The victimized companies pass their recoveries from losses along to the customers. For example, $125 of the cost of each new personal computer goes to reimburse companies for previous thefts.

Consumers are cheated at gas pumps of self-serve marts each year in excess of $1 million because of faulty computer chips.

On any given day in the United States, over 100 convenience stores are robbed.

Every day in the U.S., people steal $20,000 from coin-operated machines.

The average bank teller loses about $250 every year.

One third of our nation's Gross National Product is spent in cleaning up mistakes. Yet, only 5.1% is spent on education, which is the key to avoiding mistakes on the front end.

Fires cost more than $150 billion per year in damage. Most fires are caused by carelessness: overloading electrical sockets, smoking in bed, failure to turn off kitchen burners, malfunctions with space heaters, allowing trash to accumulate, failure to repair electrical wiring and electrical breaker explosions. Electricity-related incidents account for half of all fires.

Learning the Lessons and Moving Forward

The U.S. Congress enacted the Sarbanes-Oxley Act, corporate reform legislation, in 2002. The bill delineated new regulations, in response to the accounting scandals at WorldCom, Enron, Tyco and other large companies that left thousands of employees without retirement savings and investors with worthless stock shares.

The bill was intended to prevent malfeasance, restore investor confidence and crack down on corporate cheaters. It set up new regulations for corporate auditing practices and creates strict penalties for executives who hide debt in accounting tricks. It was the largest reform since changes were made to halt the Depression-era slide into bankruptcy.

Sarbanes-Oxley instituted extensive corporate governance reforms, including standards for advisors representing public companies and their nonpublic subsidiaries. Under it, business leaders are expected to embrace both the letter and spirit of the bill and other existing laws, designed to protect investors, employees and other stakeholders.

Unfortunately, the material covered by Sarbanes-Oxley represents only two percent of Corporate Responsibility and Ethics. As one who has conducted ethics audits and put programs into practice, I know that the reform did not go far enough. This contributed to the economic downtown in 2008-2010. A more holistic approach to ethics would have averted many of the crises.

In moving forward, one must review those junctures where leaders and their companies recognize when a business is in trouble. These are the high costs of neglect, non-actions and wrong actions, per categories on The Business Tree™:

1. Product, Core Business. The product's former innovation and dominance has somehow missed the mark in today's business climate. The company does not have the marketplace demand that it once had. Others have streamlined their concepts, with greater success. Something newer has edged your company right out of first place.

2. Processes, Running the Company. Operations have become static, predictable and inefficient. Too much band aid surgery has been applied, but the bleeding has still not been stopped. Other symptoms of trouble have continued to appear … often and without warning.

3. Financial Position. Dips in the cash flow have produced knee-jerk reactions to making changes. Cost cutting and downsizing were seemingly ready answers, though they took tolls on the rest of the

company. The overt focus on profit and bean counter mentality has crippled the organizational effectiveness.

4. Employee Morale and Output. Those who produce the product-service and assure its quality, consistency and deliverability have not been given sufficient training, empowerment and recognition. They have not really been in the decision making and leadership processes, as they should have been. Team members still have to fight the system and each other to get their voices heard, rather than function as a team.

5. Customer Service. Customers come and go … at great costs that are not tallied, noticed or heeded. After the percentages drop dramatically, management asks "What happened?" Each link in the chain hasn't yet committed toward the building of long-term customer relationships. Thus, marketplace standing wavers.

6. Company Management. There was no definable style in place, backed by Vision, strategies, corporate sensitivities, goals and beliefs. Whims, egos and momentary needs most often guided company direction. Young and mid-executives never were adequately groomed for lasting leadership.

7. Corporate Standing. Things have happened for inexplicable reasons. Company vision never existed or ceased to spread. The organization is on a downslide … standing still and doing things as they always were done constitutes moving backward.

These situations are day-to-day realities for troubled companies. Yes, they brought many of the troubles upon themselves. Yes, they compounded problems by failing to take swift actions. And, yes, they further magnify the costs of "band aid surgery" by failing to address the root causes of problems.

Each year, one-third of the U.S. Gross National Product goes toward cleaning up problems, damages and otherwise high costs of failing to take proper action. On the average, it costs six times the investment of preventive strategies to correct business problems). This concept was addressed in another of my books, The High Cost of Doing Nothing™.

There are seven costly categories of doing nothing, doing far too little or doing the wrong things in business:

1. Waste, spoilage, poor controls, lack of employee motivation.
2. Rework, product recalls, make-good for inferior work, excess overhead.
3. Poor controls on quality, under-capitalization, under-utilization of resources.
4. Damage control, crisis management mode.
5. Recovery, restoration, repairing wrong actions, turnover, damaged company reputation.
6. Retooling, restarting, inertia, anti-change philosophy, expenses caused by quick fixes.
7. Opportunity costs, diversifying beyond company expertise, lack of an articulated vision.

Chapter 9

LESSONS ABOUT BUSINESS TO BE LEARNED FROM THE Y2K BUG

T he U.S. economy spent between $800 billion and one trillion dollars fixing and treating the Y2K Bug in 1999 and 2000. Certainly, aspects of the bug were treated successfully, and troubles were averted because of professional actions. No doubt, public hype contributed to a "sky is falling" situation that made computer consultants rich.

My concern was that money was diverted from other aspects of organizational wellness toward treating one symptom of one disease. I advocated a balanced approach toward planning, visioning and the Big Picture.

Rather than bash those who neglected other aspects of the organization in favor of Y2K Readiness, let's refocus what we did and learned.

Among the lessons which we learned from the Y2K Bug exercise were:

- When they want to do so, company leadership will provide sufficient resources to plan for the future, including crisis management and preparedness (of which computer glitches are one set of "what ifs.")

- When they want to do so, company leadership will provide leadership for change management and re-engineering ... two of the many worthwhile concepts that should be advocated every business day.

- People are the company's most valuable resource, representing 28% of the Big Picture. Today's work force will need three times the amount of training that it presently gets in order for the organization to be competitive in the millennium.

- Change is good. Like change ... don't fear it. Change is 90% positive. Without always noticing it, individuals and organizations change 71% per year. The secret is to benefit from change, rather than become a victim of it.

- Pro-active change involves the entire organization. When all departments are consulted and participate in the decisions, then the company is empowered.

- Fear and failure are beneficial too. One learns three times more from failure than from success. Failures propel us toward our greatest future successes.

- When we work with other companies and the public sector, we collaborate better. All benefit, learn from each other and prepare collectively for the future.

- In the future and in order to successfully take advantage of the future, make planning a priority, not just a knee-jerk reaction.

Calculating Each Organization's High Costs

People and organizations are wont to throw money at things that pop up at the moment or that look good at external publics. It is easier to tinker with machines than to admit that the organization has deep management and philosophical issues. After all, 92% of all organizational problems stem from poor management decisions.

Our society is infested with the band aid surgery way of treating things as they come up. This approach costs six times that of doing things correctly on the front end ... meaning planning, sequential execution and benchmarking progress.

Each year, one-third of the U.S. Gross National Product goes toward cleaning up problems, damages and otherwise high costs of doing either nothing or doing the wrong things.

On the average, it costs six times the investment of preventive strategies to correct business problems (compounded per annum and exponentially increasing each year). In some industries, the figure is as high as 30 times. Six is the mean average.

The old adage says: "An ounce of prevention is worth a pound of cure." One pound equals 16 ounces. In that scenario, one pound of cure is 16 times more mostly than an ounce of prevention.

Human beings as we are, none of us do everything perfectly on the front end. There always must exist a learning curve. Research shows that we learn three times more from failures than from successes. The mark of a quality organization is how it corrects mistakes and prevents them from recurring.

"They can't hang you for saying nothing," quipped President Calvin Coolidge in the 1920's. He spent more time doing chores at his farm and taking long naps than taking care of the nation's business. Coolidge prided himself upon doing little and, thus, failed to see crises brewing during his presidency. This "keep your head in the sand" mentality is prevalent of people who move on and let others clean up the damage.

Doing nothing becomes a way of life. It's amazing how many individuals and companies live with their heads in the sand. Never mind planning for tomorrow … we'll just deal with problems as they occur. This mindset, of course, invites and tends to multiply trouble.

7 Categories of High Costs

1. Cleaning Up Problems. Waste, Spoilage. Poor controls. Productivity down-time. Lack of employee motivation and activity. Back orders because they were not properly stocked. Supervisory involvement in retracing problems and effecting solutions.

2. Rework. Product recalls. Make-good for shoddy or inferior work. Poor location. Regulatory red tape. Excess overhead.

3. Missed Marks. Poor controls on quality. Fallout damage from employees with problems. Undercapitalization. Unsuccessful marketing. Unprofitable pricing.

4. Damage Control. Crisis management. Lawsuits incurred because procedures were not upheld. Affirmative action violations. Violations of

OSHA, ADA, EEOC, EPA and other codes. Disasters due to employee carelessness, safety violations, oversights, etc. Factors outside your company that still impede your ability to do business.

5.   Recovery and Restoration. Repairing ethically wrong actions. Empty activities. Mandated cleanups, corrections and adaptations. Employee turnover, rehiring and retraining. Isolated or unrealistic management. Bad advice from the wrong consultants. Repairing a damaged company reputation.

6.   Retooling and Restarting. Mis-use of company resources, notably its people. Converting to existing codes and standards. Chasing the wrong leads, prospects or markets. Damage caused by inertia or lack of progress. The anti-change "business as usual" philosophy. Long-term expenses incurred by adopting quick fixes.

7.   Opportunity Costs. Failure to understand what business they're really in. Inability to read the warning signs or understand external influences. Failure to change. Inability to plan. Over-dependence upon one product or service line. Diversifying beyond the scope of company expertise. Lack of an articulated, well-implemented vision.

Remediating the High Costs

7 Primary Factors of The High Cost of Doing Nothing™:
1.   Failure to value and optimize true company resources.
2.   Poor premises, policies, processes, procedures, precedents and planning.
3.   Opportunities not heeded or capitalized.
4.   The wrong people, in the wrong jobs. Under-trained employees.
5.   The wrong consultants (miscast, untrained, improperly used).
6.   Lack of articulated focus and vision. With no plan, no journey will be completed.
7.   Lack of movement really means falling behind the pack and eventually losing ground.

What Could Have Reduced These High Costs:
1.   Effective policies and procedures.
2.   Setting and respecting boundaries.

3.   Realistic expectations and measurements.
4.   Training and development of people.
5.   Commitments to quality at all links in the chain.
6.   Planning.
7.   Organizational vision.

7 Levels of Handling Problems, Determining Effectiveness

1.   Do Nothing. Think that things will work themselves out or that causes of problems will go away. Research shows that doing nothing results in creating 3-6 more affiliated problems.

2.   Deny, Actively Avoid. Don't see problems as such. Keep one's head in the sand and remain impervious to warning signs of trouble. Go to great lengths to put positive spins on anything that may point back to one's self, department or organization as being problematic.

3.   Cover Up. Cover-ups cost 6-12 times that of addressing problems upfront. In addition to financial, cover-up costs can include the effects upon morale, activity levels, productivity, decision making, creativity, adaptation and innovation. Even after the cover-up has fully played out, there is an additional cost: the period of recovery and restoration of confidence.

4.   Partially Address. Perform band aid surgery, at such time as action is demanded. Address signs and symptoms, without addressing root causes. This shows that something is being done, but it is often the wrong thing at the wrong time.

5.   Handle in Politically Correct Terms. Some problems are addressed, partially or fully, because bosses, regulators or stakeholders expect it. Some are handled for fear of repercussion. This motive results in tentative actions, with lip service paid to deep solutions.

6.   Address Head-On. Problems are, of course, opportunities to take action. Everyone makes mistakes, and success lies in the way that problems are recognized, solved and learned from. The mark of a true manager is to recognize problems sooner, rather than later. The mark of an effective leader is the ability and willingness to take swift and definitive actions. The mark of an empowered team is its participation in this process. The

mark of a successful organization is its endorsement and insistence upon this method of action.

7.   Address in Advance, Preparing for Situations. Pro-actively study for patterns. 85% of the time, crises which are predicted, pre-addressed and strategized are averted. The skill in pre-managing problems is a fundamental tenet of a quality-oriented organization.

If postured properly, the process of planning and visioning remediates opportunity costs before they occur. Running a profitable and efficient organization means effectively remediating damage before it accrues. Processes and methodologies for researching, planning, executing and benchmarking activities will reduce that pile of costly coins from stacking up.

Chapter 10

BUSINESS LESSONS TO BE LEARNED FROM THE ENRON SCANDAL

T his is my own Big Picture full-scope analysis of the Enron debacle. It far transcends financial analyses made by other people.

I have been carefully observing Enron with interest since 1984 and saw the trouble coming for most of those years. The company cried "case study" from the very beginning, when it segued from the former Houston Natural Gas moniker. I have been chagrined as to why people could not or would not see through the facade. But, human nature being what it is, people are more easily duped than they are taught to appreciate the attributes of quality and substance.

I once had a client who felt that he owed Ken Lay a favor. Thus, when Lay (CEO of Enron) was chairing a non-profit fund raising drive, Lay asked for 100% participation from the client's firm, and the client reciprocated by requiring donations from his 200+ employees. This client was a prime example of a leading CEO who served his community, profession and firm well. Lay was the outsider who wanted status with the downtown CEO clique.

I thought that demanding participation in one person's pet cause was too punitive to the company's employees and told the client so. I further made recommendations that future charitable requests would go through committee and that the client's partners and key executives were better suited by serving on community boards, thus polishing their own luster. The company's emphasis shifted from making ad hoc contributions to chunks of time, whereby the firm got recognition, the partners became better leaders, and the community benefited from their expertise.

In the ensuing years, I saw Lay get lots of community credit, but his other executives and friends in different companies who aided the causes rarely got billing. For a period of time, Enron had an excellent foundation that steered it toward important community activities. Yet, when the company shifted from being an energy supplier to the energy trader, the charitable activities were dispensed with. So were professional development programs, rewards for random acts of kindness and other empowerment initiatives.

Executives never stayed long. Enron routinely fired 10% of its top salaried people each year, fostering a lean-and-hungry spirit among producers of business.

The Enron scandals of 2001 and 2002 focused only upon cooked books audit committees and deal making. There was so much more to look at, from the perspective of learning from the trouble and inspiring other companies to more forward.

Enron's debacle can serve all of us with lessons learned. Within that spirit and out of respect to many fine professionals who tried to save that company, I offer this analysis. These are my considered opinions, having conducted Performance Reviews, Strategic Planning and Visioning for other companies over 35+ years. I never worked for Enron … they never would have related to my Big Picture of business scope. I would have asked too many tough questions, and that was not what they wanted consultants for.

These observations are intended to contextualize the Enron case studies in broader terms than were reported in the news media:

1. Conditions Allowing It to Occur. The pivotal event was the passage of the Securities Reform Act of 1995, also dubbed the "Securities Rip-off Act." Corporations lobbied for and got major loopholes and a relaxed posture

on the part of the Securities & Exchange Commission. As a result of that act, the SEC is no longer a watchdog but is a sideline to brokerage houses and major financial institutions. In my opinion, deregulation, as a whole, has worked negatively upon business and society (banking, airlines, trucking, and broadcasting), and the SEC is no exception.

2. Congressional Hearings. It was a public and media curiosity, though becoming a good opportunity for the public to understand business better. Many of those investigating Enron had received campaign contributions from the company, yet kept maximum objectivity. Several committees competed with each other for the spotlight. After the hearings, there was little follow-through. Granting immunity often sets dangerous precedents, making it hard to get the complete truth. While frying some fish, immunity lets other more culpable ones off the hook.

3. Corporate Culture. At Enron, it was dictatorial and repressive to new ideas. It was very "old school" (a management style that was 40 years obsolete), though it pretended to be "new school." It fostered a false sense of security for employees, paying higher salaries than the marketplace, thus keeping employees dependent upon the system via golden handcuffs. It demanded blind loyalty, hired ISTJ personality types for support and rewarded dogmatic sales types for trading deals. Employees were expected to live the same ways (even in the same neighborhoods) and have common outside interests, with little individuality.

4. Core Business. Enron (like many other companies) got into areas beyond their core competencies. They got into business ventures on whims or for flashy reasons, utilizing concepts that were untried.

5. The Deals. The company did more than 4,000 deals ... most risky and without research, planning and benchmarking. Stock was transferred to partnerships simply to lock in gains on balance sheets. Many deals were put on the books in order to inflate the price of Enron stock, which the insiders sold at peak price levels. The audit committee of the board would not sign off on behalf of the deals, which just kept happening and developing secret lives of their own.

6. Attitude with Suppliers and Vendors. They took posture that nobody could say "no" to Enron and that suppliers and vendors work with Enron

on their terms only. The attitude was non-collaborative, with business units acting as Lone Rangers and often in competition with each other. There were no checks and balances for members of the supply train. This archaic mindset flies in the face of progressive supply chain management, which successful companies now embrace.

7.   Communications. They were secretive and guarded from the beginning. The manner in which company and unit name changes were handled exemplified a non-communicative executive suite, with lack of media or public access to top management. Spokespersons were not media-trained, nor media-friendly. The company issued everything through written news releases. No on-camera interviews were sought or granted No pro-active corporate communications campaigns were ever waged. The Annual Reports carried and permeated this communications aloofness. The way the California energy crisis was handled speaks to Enron's disdain for media openness.

8.   The News Media. Though it took a field day with the Enron story, the media itself had played a part in crowning Enron as the king in previous years. In absence of substantive business reporting and asking the tough questions, the media tends to pander to the hype and flash that the companies themselves dish out. Financial media indeed bought and published Enron's version of the story without checking as far as journalists have recently.

9.   Concept of Examining the Company. Bean counters set the perimeters at Enron and ran the company. The term "audit" is too micro-niche and limited. Companies should be doing full-scope Performance Reviews. Without Strategic Planning, there is no benchmarking of specific tactics. When goals are only in financial terms, the company is disproportionately lopsided.

10.   Accounting. Enron paid too much for outside auditing services. ($1 million per week) Every company should re-examine its major professional services relationships every five years, take competitive bids (especially from talented mid-sized firms) and look at options available from service providers. Enron did not demand enough accountability, fairness, ethics and operational autonomy from its outside auditor.

11. Auditing. In their marketing, accounting and auditing firms claim to be full-service business advisors, in order to get business. In reality, audit, tax and management consulting services are competing business profit centers within large firms. Enron's auditor said that its scope was limited. The outside auditor took unfair advantage of not being watched. It charged too much money and got away with it (because mid-managers but brand names of firms). After the scandals hit, the auditor played the Blame Game, without admitting itself of wrong-doing. The CEO of auditing firm tacitly dismissed the whole issue as, "A company failed because the economics did not work."

12. Executives. No executive development program was held at Enron. Ken Lay's management style was that he sat in the tower and had people to filter the bad news out. Other executives were brash, exhibited poor management judgment and made windfall money by selling stock due to insider trading information, when employees could not cash-out. The roles of other executives were to keep quiet and look the other way.

13. Bonuses. Doing deals was the mantra … quickly and with great flash. Exorbitant bonuses and side "consulting fees" for executives were the goals … and what were most aggressively pursued.

14. Employees, Morale, The Workforce. Employees pledged blind loyalty to Ken Lay, though few ever had access to him. They worshipped the emperor from a distance. Individuals blindly accepted the company's 401k directives but could have managed their money alternately. Employees emulated the corporate culture. Egos and working mannerisms did not produce the most productive workforce. Too many bought into the hype and lost objectivity. Employees were better paid than the marketplace, thus forcing many to stay or not question policies. They'll find some rude awakenings in the outside job world. Training, empowerment and team-building programs were cut and never reinstated. Incentive and "random acts of kindness" programs were deleted.

15. Community Relations. The company was quite active in the Houston community for many of the right reasons but took its controls and influence too far. The company pushed many of its own pet agendas upon an unsuspecting community. It made too many charities dependent

upon the company, thus wielding more community control. By 2001, many charities that were still counting on pledged donations and found themselves left in a lurch (though it was also their fault for not casting other nets for funding and being too dependent upon Enron). This circumstance had occurred years before, when Enron diverted pledged charity and community funds into high-gloss events, such as the 1991 Economic Summit and the 1992 Republican convention.

16. Customers. They could have asked more questions, could have demanded further accountability. The customers are being hurt the most by the collapse and need to communicate their stories better to the public.

17. Wall Street Analysts. They too could have asked more questions and could have demanded further accountability over the years of Enron's growth and boom. Some analysts who asked the tough questions were scorned or scapegoated by Enron. One must question why one company could wield such control over the investment community and what powers Wall Street had acquiesced in order for such power to grow. One must also ask why weren't regular reviews conducted by underwriters and why were not annual reports more properly screened.

18. The SEC. The commission could have asked more questions, could have demanded further accountability. However, since deregulation, it has not been compelled to do so.

19. The Government. Nobody knew or kept their eyes on Enron until the scandals hit the front pages. Bureaucratic agencies quickly distanced themselves from funding issues or responsibilities in letting such a catastrophe occur. The U.S. government had deregulated too many industries over the years, thus having the effect of allowing loopholes and marketplace-unfriendly situations to occur. In my opinion, Congress should look at re-regulating certain industries (oil and gas, utilities, airlines, banking, trucking, broadcasting). Long before congressional hearings were held, the government could have asked more questions and could have demanded further accountability.

Chapter 11

BUSINESS MOVING FORWARD FROM THE DIRTY SIDE OF THE RECESSION

T he economy and business climate were on the dirty side of the recession in the years 2011-2015. Recognizing the damages done will result in healthier run companies for the future.

This is comparable to what is called the "dirty side" of a storm, hurricane or other weather created disaster. During those cleanup periods, the infrastructure rebuilds and optimistically moves forward by correcting certain damages done by the storms.

Signs are that our economy has somewhat recovered from the second worst recession in history. Many companies kept their heads in the sand during the economic downturn, fully intending to return to business as usual.

What happened in the recession of 2008-2010 was that many businesses went under. In my professional opinion, 25% of those that faded away probably should have. A great many frail companies were not on firm foundations and had abdicated their abilities to improve and serve customer bases.

As fallout from the recession, many people were thrown into the workforce. Many fell into jobs for which they were not suited. Many downsized and out-of-work people were forced to reinvent themselves.

Many became "consultants" of one sort or another. Many fell victim to corporate failures. Services and websites sprung up to capitalize upon the avalanche of new entrepreneurs. Some sites offered the platform to become a consultant with a national firm by paying them subscription fees. The already inflated world of "reputation management" websites lured people into buying advertising in order to create the facade of being a "consultant."

Distinctions must be drawn into three consulting categories (and percentages of their occurrence in the marketplace):

1.   Vendors selling products that were produced by others. Those who sell their own produced works are designated as subcontractors. (82.99%)
2.   Consultants conduct programs designed by their companies, in repetitive motion. Their work is off-the-shelf, conforms to an established mode of operation, contains original thought and draws precedents from experience. (17%)
3.   High level strategists create all knowledge in their consulting. It is original, customized to the client and contains creativity and insight not available elsewhere. (.01%)

As one distinguishes past vendors and subcontractors, there are six types within the 18% which constitute consultants (with their percentages in the marketplace):

1.   Those who still lead in an industry and have specific niche expertise. (13.5%)
2.   Those who were downsized, out-placed or decided not to stay in the corporate fold and evolved into consulting. (28%)
3.   Out of work people who hang out consulting shingles in between jobs. (32%)
4.   Freelancers and moonlighters, whose consultancy may or may not relate to their day jobs. (16%)

5. Veteran consultants who were trained for and have a track record in actual consulting. That's what they have done for most of their careers. (2%)

6. Sadly, there is another category: opportunists who masquerade as consultants, entrepreneurs who disguise their selling as consulting, people who routinely change niches as the dollars go. (8.5%)

Clients are confused and under-educated, not able to discern the "real deal" consultants from the hype. That is why those of us who are veterans write these articles, speak and advise on best practices. Enlightened clients hire real consultants and get great value, as opposed to companies who fall prey to under-prepared resources.

There are five generations in workforce, more than any time in our history. Each generation has different working styles and must be considered according to their attributes. Age discrimination for workers over 40 is rampant and cruel.

Workplace illiteracy is higher than ever before. 50% of employees in the business world are considered functionally illiterate.

Society must not be lulled into a false sense of security right now,. The recovery phase of the recession has been steady and real. Much of the damage was done and will take years to fix. This could cause the next recession.

I believe that small business is resilient and will try its best to stay on firm grounding. Wise entrepreneurs will bring in qualified mentors, as opposed to wannabe consultants. Cool heads will prevail, and small business will recover and prosper.

Small business has learned many lessons from the recession. While some will still fight change and adhere to the same processes that got them into trouble, I see great opportunities for forward-focused businesses.

The biggest source of growth and increased opportunities in today's business climate lie in the way that individuals and companies work together.

It is becoming increasingly rare to find an individual or organization that has not yet been required to team with others. Lone rangers and sole-source providers simply cannot succeed in competitive environments and global economies. Those who benefit from collaborations, rather than become the victim of them, will log the biggest successes in business years ahead.

Just as empowerment, team building and other processes apply to formal organizational structures, then the teaming of independents can likewise benefit from the concepts. There are rules of protocol that support and protect partnerships, having a direct relationship to those who profit most. Professionals who succeed the most are the products of mentoring. The mentor is a resource for business trends, societal issues and opportunities. The mentor becomes a role model, offering insights about their own life-career. This reflection shows the mentee levels of thinking and perception which were not previously available. The mentor is an advocate for progress and change. Such work empowers the mentee to hear, accept, believe and get results. The sharing of trust and ideas leads to developing business philosophies.

Chapter 12

ROADBLOCKS TO GROWTH, OPPORTUNITIES MISSED

C ompanies come and go. Not every startup is destined to make it. Yet, in this era of super-hype about tech and dot.com companies, unrealistic expectations precluded most of their successes from the beginning.

The hype now is that the bubble burst. Former dot.com owners are crying that they were stripped of their entitled riches. Employees who were promised stock options came away without still knowing what it takes to build a real business.

The e-commerce and dot.com wars have more than their share of casualties because their players never had the artillery and mindset to play seriously in the first place. Overt marketing hype led to an unwatchful marketplace, which always wakes up to the realities of business eventually.

Technology companies must now learn the lessons that steady-growth companies in other industries absorbed. Actually, most companies still have not truly learned the lessons. Thus, most businesses are at frequent "crossroads," where turns have deep implications and far-reaching.

I advised several technology companies during their gravy years. I tried to warn them about the things that would get them into trouble:

- Focusing upon technology, not upon running a business.
- Maintaining too much of an entrepreneur and family business mindset.
- Branding before being a real company.
- Their system's inability to deal with any kind of disruption.
- Each side picks their favorite numbers for "success" because they really do not know.
- Not comprehending the business you're really in.
- Venturing too far from your areas of expertise.
- Thinking that the rules of corporate protocol did not apply to them.
- Misplaced priorities and timelines.
- Making financial yardsticks the only barometers.
- Wrong relationships with investors, letting the "angels" call too many of the shots.
- Getting bad advice from the wrong people, mainly other tech professionals.
- Rationalizing excuses, "the rules have changed."
- Feeling entitled to success and exemptions from business realities.
- Copycats of others' perceived successes.
- Working long and hard, but not necessarily smart.
- Failure to contextualize the product, business, marketplace and bigger picture.
- Inability to plan.
- Refusal to change.

Most of these pitfalls are common to so many industries. They simply were focused upon tech companies from 1994-2000 because they were the latest flavor. Some heeded the advice of myself and others, but many did not avail themselves.

Reasons why some want to grow beyond their current boundaries:

1. Prove to someone else that they can do it.
2. Strong quest for revenue and profits.

3. Corporate arrogance and ego, based upon power and influence (as well as money).
4. Sincere desire to put expertise into new arena.
5. Really have talents, resources and adaptabilities beyond what they're known for.
6. Diversifying as part of a plan of expansion, selling off and re-growing subsidiaries.
7. The marketplace dictates change as part of the company's global being.

Circumstances under which they expand include:

1. Advantageous location became available.
2. Someone wanted to sell out. It was a great deal that was tough to pass up.
3. Can't sit still and must conquer new horizons.
4. Think they can make more money, amass more power.
5. Desire to edge out a competitor or dominate another industry.
6. Create jobs for existing employees (new challenges, new opportunities).
7. Part of their growth strategy to go public, offering stock as a diversified company.

This is what often happens as a result of unplanned growth:

1. The original business gets shoved to the back burner.
2. The new business thrust gets proportionately more than its share of attention.
3. Capitalization is stretched beyond limits, and operations advance in a cash-poor mode.
4. Morale wavers and becomes uneven, per operating unit and division.
5. Attempts to bring consistency and uniformity drive further wedges into the operation.
6. Something has to give: people, financial resources, competitive edge, company vision.
7. The company expands and subsequently contracts without strategic planning.

7 Defeating Signs for Growth Companies

1. Systems are not in place to handle rapid growth … perhaps never were.

2. Their only interest is in booking more new business, rather than taking care of what they've already got.

3. Management is relying upon financial people as the primary source of advice, while ignoring the rest of the picture (90%).

4. Team empowerment suffers. Morale is low or uneven. Commitment from workers drops because no corporate culture was created or sustained.

5. Customer service suffers during fast-growth periods. They have to back-pedal and recover customer confidence by doing surveys. Even with results of deteriorating customer service, growth-track companies pay lip service to really fixing their own problems.

6. People do not have the same Vision as the company founder … who has likely not taken enough time to fully develop a Vision and obtain buy-in from others.

7. Company founder remains arrogant and complacent, losing touch with marketplace realities and changing conditions.

Everything we are in business stems from what we've been taught or not taught to date. A career is all about devoting resources to amplifying talents and abilities, with relevancy toward a viable end result.

Business evolution is an amalgamation of thoughts, technologies, approaches and commitment of the people, asking such tough questions as:

1. What would you like for you and your organization to become?

2. How important is it to build an organization well, rather than constantly spend time in managing conflict?

3. Who are the customers?

4. Do successful corporations operate without a strategy-vision?

5. Do you and your organization presently have a strategy-vision?

6. Are businesses really looking for creative ideas? Why?

7. If no change occurs, is the research and self-reflection worth anything?

Failure to prepare for the future spells certain death for businesses and industries in which they function. The same analogies apply to personal lives, careers and Body of Work. Greater business awareness and heightened self-awareness are compatible and part of a holistic journey of growth.

Chapter 13

100 KEY QUESTIONS FOR BUSINESS

Setting the Stage to Paint a Big Picture, for Companies to Survive and Thrive

I n order to tackle the challenges of the future, one must assess the current company position. One must presuppose that little or no strategic planning was previously done. After all, only 2% of the businesses in the world actually have functioning strategic plans.

This means the 98% of the companies in the world have no real strategic plan. They may have sales quotas or financial projections, but those are not fully authentic strategic plans. Is it any wonder that so many businesses steer off course or never really make their journeys?

Research and "what if" scenario building are the cornerstones for effective strategic planning. As company leaders, we weigh circumstances and situations. Then we formulate workable strategies. Always, we measure the results.

This book is about building successful Big Picture strategies to navigate business in the New Order. With turbulence and accelerated changes, the opportunities for survival and long-term success are quite varied.

In this prelude chapter, I ask 100 key questions that challenge business. We question what was conducted in the past, welcome opportunities for the future and hopefully widen the scope of the planning that your organization will hence be conducting.

These 100 thought provoking and stimulating questions cover all aspects of business operation. The goal is to widen the scope of scenario planning for the future.

Some people ask a lot of questions. Some don't ask enough of the right ones at the right times. Some are inquisitive in such a way as to seek true answers. Some go far beyond the obvious in order to glean keen insights between the lines of the answers.

The best way to build an organization or a career is to investigate the facts, uncover the needs and get others to articulate what they would consider good approaches to problems and opportunities. Wise businesses employ research and customer relations techniques to stay ahead of the curve. Understanding what is being said enables further research. With the facts in place, a pattern of strategic organizational growth will emerge.

Great planning starts with blank sheets of paper and an open mind for what will be formulated. Rather than just rekindle past budgets, quotas and outputs, truly visionary planning examines the reasons why the business exists. Then it tackles the heart and soul of the organization, the manner in which it moves forward and its core values.

By asking the tough, obvious and creative questions, we seek to paint scenarios by which the business will weather uncertainty.

100 Questions for Taking Hold of the Future

When the forces of change and the resistors of progress clash, who usually prevails?

Who are the forces of change in your company and industry?

Who are the resistors of progress?

How much have you or your company changed within the last year? How? In what ways?

If not, are you proud of your company simply staying the same, while others changed?

Don't you know that those who steadfastly rebuke change become social-business dinosaurs?

To what do you ascribe the success of your competition?

Who really is your competition?

How will your company establish its own Point of Difference?

What is your company's most important asset? Who placed the value on it? What was their basis?

Why might others want the assets of your organization?

How might they prepared to benefit from your failures?

Should your members be players in the world market?

What constitutes excellence?

Who are your company's stakeholders?

How should customers factor into management styles and decisions?

How can business become more ethical?

How might the ethical things that you do be communicated to your stakeholders?

What constitutes a leader?

Are leaders born or made?

What are the differences between an executive and a leader?

What leadership qualities were you taught? What weren't you taught?

What are the most important things that executives are not taught on their way up the ladder?

Why do executives fail to go the distance and fall from the ladder?

What qualities of greatness do you embody?

Who were your role models?

Aren't many lapses in corporate credibility due to lack of true leadership?

How much do you study forces outside your organization that could affect your livelihood?

How loyal are your present employees?

How many employees take pride in their work and see themselves as part of the Big Picture?

How many employees are drains to the company assets?

What are the costs of replacing and training workers?

How many generations are presently in the workforce? How do they differ?

Wouldn't it be nice if people would focus more upon the positives than the negatives?

How might you best showcase your accomplishments?

How do you benchmark those accomplishments?

If problems outweigh accomplishments, how will you turn that tide?

Have you attended a management retreat during the past year?

Might some fresh approaches work for your business?

Where do you expect to be in another 10 years? How will your company get there?

If you don't plan for the future, what will likely happen?

What expertise do consultants have, outside of their core business experience?

Have you been burned in the past by consultants? Why did it happen?

When was the last time that you failed? What did you learn from it?

Isn't success a natural outgrowth of failure?

When was the last time that you were truly successful at something?

Why were you so successful at what you accomplished?

What are the ingredients of success?

How can we learn from the shortcomings and failures of others?

What are the most important things that you learned in life?

Who were your teachers and mentors?

What did they teach you that you use now?

How long can band aid surgery be applied to an organization and really stick?

What is the Big Picture of your business? Who paints it? Who should also be included?

Shouldn't Strategic Planning be conducted to assure long-term business success?

What valuable lessons did you learn from competitors, colleagues and consultants?

Where have you been in the last 20 years, and what were your professional accomplishments?

How many successes were attributable to you?

If the ideas were not yours, whose brain power enabled your company to succeed?

Have you thanked your business collaborators lately? If not, when?

Are there plans for crisis management or preparedness?

Outside of the term "mission statement," what are the components of a Strategic Plan?

How far behind the trends can a company stay and yet still survive?

How cyclical are business trends?

Where are the bright young professionals of tomorrow coming from?

How are you insuring that new talents will be trained properly and allowed to blossom?

Who is really in charge of your organization? Who runs whom?

Have you been taught ways to manage change, rather than becoming a victim of it?

When the organization does not progressively grow, who are the losers?

What are the costs of an under-empowered and undereducated workforce?

How does a company on the downslide patch its problems?

How many companies have you seen fail because they did all the wrong things?

How are you keeping it from happening to your organization?

Specifically, what pro-active things are you doing? When? With whom?

What are your goals for the next 10 years?

How do you define goals?

How will your company be accountable in reaching those goals?

If you don't champion a pro-active direction for your organization, who will take the initiative?

Where's the end game?

Is there really an end game, or isn't business a continuum, weathering crises?

What are the worst crises that could beset your company?

How prepared is your organization to manage crises that inevitably occur?

What constitutes corporate Vision?

Isn't change wonderful?

Who is directly responsible for your failures and successes?

This book addresses these 100 penetrating, thought-provoking and pertinent questions. It does so with wider-scope perspectives than do business textbooks and other niche-focused writings. It embraces each micro-niche of business and redefines each from the Big Picture perspective.

The Big Picture is an ongoing process of re-examining the small pieces, redefining each business function and growing concepts of the business itself.

Good companies do not set out to go bad. Most of them do not properly set out. By living from day to day, they deal with problems as they come up. Thus, it costs six times more to function this way than if proper planning and creative visioning had transpired.

Toward the end of this book will appear 100 Ways to Master the Big Picture, summarizing the essence of perspectives posed herein.

7 Levels of Answers Given to Questions

1. Easy, Obvious Ones. Based upon the only information available, assumptions, conclusions, innuendo or hearsay. Sometimes, answers are just enough to get rid of someone or to discourage them from asking deeper questions or conducting more substantial research.

2. Knee-Jerk, Shoot from the Hip. Based upon surface conclusions or generalities. Quoting other people, mass media or popular sayings. Not based upon original thought or investigation of the facts or circumstances.

3. Party Line, Politically Correct. Bureaucracies like to give out pat answers that cover their obligation to respond, but they are not saying much. Some answers echo company policies and wishes (either actual or perceived as just enough to avoid blame). Some are targeted at certain audiences.

4. Tell People What They Want to Hear. These are phony and are usually justified in the mind of the person giving the answers. The sophisticated questioner will pursue further. After the stock answer, ask for what they really think or believe.

5. Factual, Complete Explanations. Rich on content, backup descriptions and inviting further questions.

6. Answers That Get Them Thinking Further. Offer what you do with the information and the longer implications.

7. Deep Wisdom. Having been there, considered the situation and offering insights into the deeper aspects of your question. These are the rare people worth listening to.

7 Levels of Research

1. Gossip, Hearsay. Third-hand. Because someone else said it, then we believe it. Such companies are marked by long gossip grapevines. Triangulation of distorted facts tends to perpetuate the inaccuracies.

2. Ego. Third-hand. These folks see, hear, interpret and believe what they want. They conduct research to validate points of value, justify past mistakes, scapegoat messengers of change or avoid confronting marketplace realities. Sometimes, they buy research that is skewed, prejudicial or subjective.

3. Niche. Secondary research is often conducted, with material culled from existing documents, sources, libraries, media clippings, etc. The companies further investigate industries in which they do business, studying journals and interviewing stakeholders. Their goal is to learn, absorb and apply the material learned.

4. Comparison. A more in-depth study of secondary research looks at trends and views other companies, learning from each. Interest from this spurs the company to commission its own primary research, to get grasps upon why things occur and how their company can benefit.

5. Imposed by Conditions. Market conditions have changed, and we needed to understand the implications. Outside influences forced the company to carefully re-examine its position. This impetus for conducting research is really a blessing in disguise. Societal trends must be viewed as indicators for business growth.

6. Planning. This is primary research, commissioned and conducted with the full support of top management. Sophisticated planning should account for 15% of an organization's full picture. Research-savvy executives know this, and their company likely has a research and development division. The company that does not plan has no way of achieving staying power. Responding to crises is a good way to get in the research-and-planning habit. The more focused study that is done, the more the company wants to do more of it.

7. Change, Growth. This future-focused group of companies makes a priority of utilizing experts who are versed in corporate strategy, not just in processes. These rare companies look at the Big Picture. All decisions

are based upon internal and external considerations. This insures longevity for the organization and assures higher value for its products-services.

7 Levels of What Companies Do with Research

1. Deny or Refute. Skeptical folks fail to see the merit, study the possibilities or commission further research. They do not invest in research because they may be afraid of its findings. Perhaps the process intimidates them. Perhaps they had one unpleasant experience with research previously. These folks will oppose research and sabotage its conducting.

2. Nothing. In this case, research was conducted so the company could say they had done so, perhaps to fulfill a grant, court order or government mandate. Such research unfortunately sits on a shelf.

3. See Value and Merit. These executives have read case studies of where research helped other organizations. They see trends in opportunities and, therefore, give research an open mind.

4. Want to Know and Learn More. They realize that it's more than just facts and statistics. These companies find the true worth of research in the interpretation. Insights gleaned will lead to good opportunities. Knowledge workers tend to embrace change and vision more readily and regularly.

5. Do Something with It. These folks put the findings to good use. They see applicability of the studied material to their increased ability to do business.

6. Want to Do More and Evolve the Business to Higher Plateaus. These organizations would not consider making major changes without first researching the prospects, affected spheres of the business and potential after-effects. They are very research-savvy and understand the many tiers of study that can impact their operations.

7. Change-Growth. These forward-thinking organizations have achieve great advantages by managing knowledge. Research has made impacts upon processes and projects. Now, company management employs research in formulating policies, strategies and benchmarks of success.

What Would Happen If These Things Occurred in Your Business?

The Big Picture of Business explores the path by which companies can learn from the mistakes of others and focus to the future through strategic planning.

The ideal company could hopefully make the following answers to questions posed above, per categories on The Business Tree™, including:

1.   The business you're in. You're in the best business-industry, produce a good product-service and always lead the pack. Customers get what they cannot really get elsewhere.

2.   Running the business. The size of your company is necessary to do the job demanded. Operations are sound, professional and productive. Demonstrated integrity and dependability assure customers and stakeholders that you will use your size and influence rightly. You employ state-of-the-art technology and are in the vanguard of your industry.

3.   Financial. Keeping the cash register ringing is not the only reason for being in business. You always give customers their money's worth. Your charges are fair and reasonable. Business is run economically and efficiently, with excellent accounting procedures, payables-receivables practices and cash management.

4.   People. Your company is people-friendly. Executives possess good people skills. Staff is empowered, likeable and competent. Employees demonstrate initiative and use their best judgment, with authority to make the decisions they should make. You provide a good place to work. You offer a promising career and future for people with ideas and talent. Your people do a good day's work for a day's pay.

5.   Business Development. Always research and serve the marketplace. Customer service is efficient and excellent, by your standards and by the publics. You are sensitive to customers' needs and are flexible and human in meeting them.

6.   Body of Knowledge. There is a sound understanding of the relationship of each business function to the other. You maintain a well-earned reputation and are awake to company obligations. You contribute much to the economy. You provide leadership for progress, rather than following along. You develop-champion the tools to change.

7. The Big Picture. Approach business as a Body of Work, a lifetime track record of accomplishments. You have and regularly update-benchmark a strategy for the future, shared company Vision, ethics, Big Picture thinking and "walk the talk."

Chapter 14

RESPONSIBILITIES AND STAKEHOLDERS OF BUSINESS AND PROFESSIONAL ASSOCIATIONS

E very major profession has an association to make it a better profession, champion its cause, bring members together and advocate concerns that benefit the profession and its customers. The truly effective associations make profound impacts upon business and society through their consistent and pro-active works.

American trade and professional associations currently employ more than 500,000 people (almost as many as the airline industry).

Associations contribute $48 billion to the annual national economy, raised through member dues and non-dues income and spent on member services, programs, activities and materials.

There presently exist more than 23,000 national associations and an additional 64,000 regional, state and local associations (not including local chapters). Association members donate more than 300 million hours of service time per year, conservatively worth $3.3 billion.

Associations have responsibilities to plan where they're going and how they're changing. The art and professionalism with which it is done has a direct relationship to the association's ability to grow, serve members, build a competitive advantage, influence external' constituencies, combat negative interference, obtain credible third-party endorsement and establish a bank of goodwill.

Members derive great benefits from services, interactions with other members and shifts in thinking that they derive through programs and conferences.

The mark of a profession is its commitment to professional enhancement of its members.

Associations, What They Are and All They Must Do

The reasons for the existence of business-professional associations, per categories on The Business Tree, include:

1. The business you're in
   - Stay abreast of issues reflecting the core business.
   - Enlighten on changing ways in which the core business is conducted.
   - Demonstrate that association members are the "cream of the crop" of the industry.
2. Running the business
   - Establish a favorable arena in which to do business.
   - Help members to develop necessary tools, techniques and resources to do business more successfully.
   - Enlighten members on new ways of doing business.
   - Lead by example. The manner in which the association is run is indicative of how the profession is run.
3. Financial
   - Offer expertise in the economics of running a business.
   - Demonstrate fiduciary responsibility to members.
   - Offer financial incentives, discounts and group buying power to members.
4. People
   - Interaction with colleagues, associates and mentors.
   - Training and professional development programs.

- Enlightenment on people skills aspects of doing business successfully.
- Empowerment of members to volunteer within the association.

5. Business development
    - Establish a favorable image for the industry.
    - Motivate the public to respond to and actively support the association's efforts.
    - Provide the public with information that it would not otherwise access.
    - Stimulate association members to think well of themselves and, in turn, create positive public perceptions of each other.
    - Help sell association products/services to members and non-members.
    - Promote the association's membership growth and retention.

6. Body of Knowledge
    - Research trends that will change the way in which the industry does business.
    - Offer members an understanding of all components of their profession and industry, how all interrelate and the importance of Big Picture thinking.
    - Reflection upon strengths, weaknesses, opportunities and threats, assuring greater success through due diligence steps.

7. The Big Picture
    - Plan for the future of the profession, industry and climate in which members do business.
    - Help members to be more successfully than they would have been on their own.
    - Advocate Strategic Planning and Visioning to member organizations, as well as to the association.

Many Have a Stake

For associations, there are many stakeholders with whom one must interface:
- Volunteer leadership.
- Association staff.
- The membership.
- Prospective members.

- Clients and prospects for members' products/services.
- Public officials and regulatory agencies important to the association.
- Appropriate educators and students.
- Other related associations.
- Suppliers of products/services to the association's members.
- Non-member prospective customers for association products/services.
- Other interested publics.

Utilize these seven basic strategies to assure the association's growth and success:

1. Analyze the challenges for members and programs to meet needs.
2. Define all operational strengths and problem areas.
3. Identify the association's and profession's pertinent stakeholders.
4. Set goals and objectives.
5. Write and regularly update a full Strategic Plan.
6. Develop a Vision for the profession, replacing micro processes with Big Picture thinking. Encourage members to think" outside the box."
7. Routinely evaluate the progress and successes of each activity, methodology, process, policy and vision.

Tell Members and the Marketplace Who You Are and What You Do

Methods of internal communications to association members include:

- Correspondence from association leadership to the membership.
- Computerized mailings via database and electronic mail.
- Other computer communications.
- Journals.
- Internet web site.
- White papers on topical, controversial or emergency issues.
- Membership surveys.
- Regularly scheduled association meetings.
- Seminars, conferences and other professional development offerings.
- Pamphlets, flyers and brochures.
- Training and informational tapes (video and audio).
- Government relations monitoring and advocacy.

- Communications media of sections or special interest groups.
- Receptions, tours, open houses and field trips.
- Mailings with dues statements.
- Think tanks from segments within the membership.
- The annual report.
- The annual meeting.

Methods of external communications to desired constituencies include:
- Newsletters, bulletins, trade and technical publications.
- News coverage, features and interviews in mass media.
- Video productions.
- Direct mailings.
- Form letters, memos.
- Conventions, exhibitions, meetings and workshops.
- Competitions and awards presentations.
- Trade exhibits at other shows.
- Providing of PR, advertising and marketing materials—resources for members.
- Representation before government agencies.
- Monitoring of legislation and regulatory actions which affect the association.
- Crisis management communications program.
- Industry image awareness advertising.
- Coalitions of other trade associations, assembled to address specific issues.
- Opinion panels or community advisory committees.
- Market surveys, opinion research polls and other services to facilitate consumer representation.
- Speaking engagements by industry leaders at high-profile conventions, seminars, workshops and business forums.
- Public service projects.
- Internet website.
- Written, verbal and non-verbal communications by association staff members.
- Personal contacts, telephone conversations, letters.

Visioning Reassessment

Periodically, each professional association must reappraise its current standing and future direction. Development of a new Strategic Vision is appropriate after the first two waves of leadership have become inactive and newer members have "gone through the chairs" of leadership positions.

Conditions which mandate a Visioning Reassessment may include:

- Membership is static, with little growth.
- Older members are rarely active and rarely consulted.
- New ideas get quickly shot down.
- Agendas of current board members drive programs.
- Research into member needs has not been conducted recently.
- Research into issues reflecting the association's stakeholders has not been conducted.
- The organization is not now what it started out to be.
- There seems to be a need to change the direction of the organization.
- No Vision was actually created. The organization just rolled with the flow.
- Paid management is not performing optimally.
- Paid management is not presenting the proper image of the association's industry.
- There is a need to step up growth and member services.
- Board members need to be trained further on being board members.
- Individuals are more concerned about their own areas than for the overall organization.
- The environment in which the organization competes is rapidly changing.

Why associations must utilize strategic planning:
- Competition for dollars, volunteer time and interest from members is keen.
- Members demand value in exchange for their dues. A well-perceived industry is the most comprehendible value.
- Planning helps associations to redefine their focus, streamline services and serve newly emerging areas. Marketing serves to keep the association ahead of industry trends.

- By failing to embrace proper imaging, the association fails to maximize its resources.

How to achieve effective public perception for associations:

- Retain professional strategic planning counsel to review past activities and design a plan for future actions.
- Designate one board member to oversee Visioning, recruit committee members and liaison with outside professional counsel.
- Make public relations a key responsibility for the executive director and officers.
- Keep focusing upon the mission statement, and update the strategic plan.
- Understand that effective marketing begins and remains at the top of the organization.
- Stylize all planning as pro-active, rather than reactive.
- Planning-visioning must be factored into every major policy decision by the board.
- Know the limitations of volunteers and staff members.
- Realize the relationship of retaining outside counsel toward the long-term success of the association.
- Budget for strategic planning.
- Look for corporate sponsorship and outside underwriting. Make special member assessments for special activities.
- Realize your comfort level with Visioning will increase with time. If you have not already embarked upon such an effort, please do so, or risk being left behind.

Chapter 15

PEOPLE IN ORGANIZATIONS, THE WORK FORCE

7 Dynamics of People in Organizations

1.   Education-Growth. Want to earn a living. Think that the company exists to be all things for them. Not yet focused upon their own goals, let alone the company's vision. Believes there is a fast-forward button to riches and success, without paying dues.

2.   Evolution. Education helps workers to choose and pursue a job niche. Contributions toward the work process are noticed-rewarded. Person sees an end result, begins seeking opportunities and viewing job in the longer term. Workers influence the attitudes of others. Still do not identify with management or its objectives.

3.   Experience Gathering. Learns better ways of performing tasks, procedures and assignments. Understands what works for the company and their own role in the process. Begins path of professional development, fine-tuning of skills and questing for more.

4.   Grooming. Experience with teams, trade-professional associations and the continuing education process. Mentorship occurs. Leadership skills begin to be developed.

5.   Seasoning. Professionalism is exhibited, transforming the worker from a job mindset to that of a career. Empowerment experiences bear the fruits of success. People skills are developed. Take lead roles in contributing to the organization's overall good.

6.   Meaningful Contributions. The cream rises to the top, in terms of attitude, ambition, drive and dedication toward company vision (as opposed to the Peter Principle). Commitments toward career longevity, mentorship of others, organizational development and contributions outside the organization are made and kept.

7.   Body of Knowledge. Is a leader in their field of expertise, the company, the industry and the communities in which they do business. Directly contributes to company vision. Committed to further knowledge curve for the rest of their life (rather than becoming complacent or stuck in the past). Knows that paying one's dues never stops, even at the senior stage of one's career. Is a champion for change, progress through accomplishment and leadership development.

7 Basic Categories of the Work Force

1.   People who only do the things necessary to get by. Just a series of jobs … no more, no less.

2.   People who are managed by others to meet quotas, schedules, procedures and statistics. People who do and make things.

3.   Administrative, managerial support. Keep the boat afloat. Push paper, systems, technology. Process is the driving force.

4.   System upholders. Don't rock the boat. Maintain the status quo. Resist change. Surround with like minds. Motivated by survival.

5.   People who sell something. Most companies have revenue-sales as their primary objective and measurement. To them, everything else is really secondary.

6.   People in transition. Forced by circumstances to change (career obsolescence, down-sizing, marketplace factors). Some voluntarily

effected changes, to achieve balance or new direction in life. Some do better in newer environments. Others cannot weather changes (too tied to staid corporate orientations).

7. Idealists ... out to do meaningful things. Deeply committed to accomplishing something special ... beyond basic job requirements. Adapt to and benefit from change. Learn to take risks. Motivated by factors other than money.

Classifications of Jobs and Workers

1. Unskilled Labor
2. Basic Jobs
3. Apprentices
4. Semi-skilled Labor
5. Helpers
6. Servers
7. Entry-Level Worker
8. Base-Level Sellers (door-to-door, telephone, clerks and checkers, retail sales)
9. Support Staff
10. Journeyman laborer
11. Technician
12. Administrative
13. Entry-Level Professional
14. Mid-Level Worker
15. Mid-Level Sellers (consumer services, multi-level marketing, retailers, vendors)
16. Tradesman, Skill Provider
17. Craftsman, Arts and Humanities Provider
18. Science-Technology Provider
19. Mid-Manager
20. Mid-Level Professional
21. Career Worker
22. Professional Sellers (business-to-business, professional and financial services)

23. Career Manager
24. Career Professional
25. Consultants (for every level to this point)
26. Senior Professional
27. Executive
28. Seasoned Professional
29. Beyond the Level of Professional
30. Knowledge Creator—Inspiring Force—Thinker—Wisdom Resource

7 Plateaus of Work Ethic

1. Just Enough to Get By. Getting paid is the objective. Don't know or have not learned anything further.
2. Taking Advantage of the System. Coffee break mentality. Abuse sick day policies, health benefits, etc. "Never gonna be" syndrome.
3. Inside the Box. Follow the rules but never consider formulating them. Subscribe to the philosophy: "There are no wise decisions … only activities carried out according to company procedures."
4. Don't Rock the Boat. Interested in remaining gainfully employed. Look forward in the short-term to the next paid vacation, in the long-term toward retirement.
5. Professional Is As Professional Does. Daily behaviors, achievements speak for themselves. Consistent in approaches. Never stop learning and growing.
6. Change Agent. Either forced by circumstances to change (career obsolescence, down-sizing, marketplace factors) or thrive upon change. As time progresses, become a mentor and champion for change.
7. Deep Commitments to Body of Work, Professionalism, Ethics. Don't know what a coffee break, sick day or vacation is. Give their lives, souls, expertise to careers … and the lifetime results show positively. Profound influence.

7 Dilemmas and Challenges of Business Owners and CEOs

1. The business you're in. What the company started out as is not what it is now. Not sure why and how to fully adapt. Not sure if others will run

it the same way. Concerned what will happen to the business under new management.

2. Running the business. Still thinking like the profession for which they were educated-trained, not like an organizational head. They embody the "lonely at the top" syndrome. They are uncomfortable in administrating but not willing to relinquish full control. Either assume that all employees are fully capable of running the business (and remain aloof from them) or don't give them enough rein-resources to do their jobs, becoming a micro-manager and watchdog.

3. Financial. If interest is only on financial gain and profit, will lose sight of the other reasons for being and staying in business.

4. People. Don't spend enough time with employees, then wonder why they're not an empowered team. Delegate away most people skills responsibilities. Don't fully communicate company Vision. Don't put enough resources toward training.

5. Business Development. Don't participate enough in sales, marketing and promotions. Abdicate duties to others. Lose sight of the marketplace.

6. Body of Knowledge. Understand one or two phases of company operations, without a relationship of each branch to the other. Don't participate holistically with Branches 1-5. Don't develop-champion the tools to change.

7. The Big Picture. Don't have a current strategy for the future. Still sticking to a partial past blueprint. May have never crafted or articulated a shared company Vision, with input from others. Fear change, without understanding how or why to master it. Advocate certain behaviors for others in the company but don't always "walk the talk." Unclear about where to proceed next.

7 Stages in the Making of a CEO

1. Education-Growth. Acquiring a profession, knowledge base and perspective. Values and work ethics instilled by family, environment and workplace.

2. Evolution. Pursuing a career. Paying substantial dues. Acting as though they will one day be management. Thinking as a manager, not as a

worker. Learning and doing the things it will take to assume management responsibility. Doesn't expect status overnight.

3.   Experience Gathering. Understands that careers evolve. Learning from successes and failures, experiences, training and assimilation. Was a good "will be," taking time in early career to steadily blossom. Being mentored by others. Measure own output and expect to be measured as a profit center to the company.

4.   Grooming. Learning to seize-create opportunities. Thinking like the boss. Accelerated commitment to training and professional development. Developing people skills. Has grown as a person and as a professional and quests for more enlightenment. Learn to pace and remain in their chosen career for the long-run. Don't expect that someone else will be the rescuer or cut corners in the path to artificial success. Contribute to the bottom line, directly and indirectly.

5.   Seasoning. Has paid dues and knows that, as the years go by, one's dues paying accelerates, rather than decreases. Realizes there are no quick fixes. Has sets of standards, marketplace sensitivity-predictability. Finds a truthful blend of perception and reality, with sturdy emphasis upon substance, rather than style. Comfortable making decisions, delegating. Acts as a mentor to still others. Sees this continuum as "continuous quality improvement."

6.   Meaningful Contributions. Sense of perspective that the more you know, the more you realize what you don't know. Learns to manage change, rather than falling victim to it. Learns from failures, reframing them as opportunities. Learns to expect, predict, understand and relish success. Champions planning, leadership for progress.

7.   Body of Work. They are continually acquiring visionary perception, Big Picture durability for the long-run. Study and comprehend the subtleties of life. Never stop learning, growing and doing.

7 Biggest Mistakes Made by Heads of Companies

1.   Out of touch with core product-service. Either remain in the mindset for which originally trained (losing touch with new products) or has

reoriented strictly as an executive (focusing on internal operations). Executives must keep current, balanced and changing.

2. People are trouble. Thinking that everyone else needs to be fixed. Executives need only edict that underlings be fixed, without participating in the process.

3. Bean counter mentality. Focused only upon the bottom line, whatever it takes to maximize it. Listens only to financial people as sources of information and consultation.

4. Inability to listen, seek truths and analyze. Get advice from the wrong people. Seek validation and affirmation from advisors, not truths and ideas.

5. Lack of customer service orientation. Don't get involved with customers, delegating full responsibilities for customers elsewhere and then wonder what happened.

6. Corporate arrogance. They set and believe their own image. Their agenda should become that of the company. Others are expected to conform, or they're out. Doesn't want full scrutiny-accountability of "the image" because it may be inaccurate or untrue.

7. Clueless about The Big Picture. Have problems with change management. Have the obligation and responsibility to see and deal with things as they are, not as they would like them to be. Otherwise, operating with blinders is letting the entire organization down.

7 Biggest Blind Spots for Middle Managers

1. Single-track professional development. What they learned in college is what they should do for the balance of their careers.

2. Non-leadership development. Expend only company resources but never out of their own pocket. They volunteer in the community only on company time, when and where the company directs.

3. Bureaucratic obsessions. Process is everything. They were developed to be a spear carrier, not as a leader. Decline to contribute original ideas, for fear of criticism.

4. Non-communicative. You don't know them as individuals, where they stand and what they believe. This is sad because many good ideas are going denied within them.

5. Too identified with the job. Believe that staffing corporate tables at charity dinners, paid vacations and job perks constitute job fulfillment. When downsized, they go into "consulting" and are not suited because they know a portion of only one corporate culture.

6. Always a bride's maid syndrome. They do not see themselves as top management. They see their jobs existing to filter truths, shade perceptions, flatter the boss and build internal fiefdoms.

7. Lost the dream … or never did develop it. Managers (like companies) must develop career track plans. Just getting by and "remaining gainfully employed" do not constitute a plan. If staying in a job means giving up dreams, then it is just a job, not a career.

7 Biggest Mistakes Made by Young People at the Beginning of Their Careers

1. Desires. Want status that others have. Primary career motivation is money and the power it can bring. Want to be paid for everything they do. Don't learn how to be a joiner and, thus, cannot ascend as a leader.

2. Attitude. Believe that riches and success are due them. Say they are trying hard when they're not. Use, abuse and knowingly waste time of others. Always have an excuse.

3. Work Ethic. Want a job, not a career. Learn to cover tracks and justify excuses. Always looking somewhere else, without appreciating the opportunities at hand.

4. Education, Training, Professional Development. Unwillingness to learn. Seeking to be a carbon copy of someone else. Failure to pursue professional development. Think their academic credentials make them superior to persons in other professions. Clueless as to what business ethics or quality management principles are all about.

5. People Skills. Failure to develop people skills. Lack of upbringing and discipline sabotages their business life. Failure to show proper respect

to elders. It's always someone else's fault. Inability to identify their own shortcomings or limitations for what they are.

6. Organizational Savvy. Failure to pay sufficient dues. Many assume that they are a senior member of the profession, when in fact they never mastered being an effective junior, let alone mastering the middle career years. They exhibited a failure to learn pro-active attitude, positive marketplace grammar, etiquette, business savvy or common courtesies.

7. Body of Work. Won't go the distance or see career as a long-term set of challenges. Maintain the "I can do that" mentality, challenging seasoned professionals. Failure to understand either the Big Picture or the small pieces needed to implement it.

7 Most Significant Things that Managers Are Not Taught on Their Way Up

1. Know Where You Are Going. Develop, update and maintain a career growth document. Keep a diary of lessons learned but not soon forgotten. Learn the reasons for success and, more importantly, from failure.

2. Truth and Ethics. If you do not "walk the talk," who will? Realize that very little of what happens to you in business is personal. Find common meeting grounds with colleagues. The only workable solution is a win-win (or as close to it as can be negotiated).

3. Professional Enrichment. Early formal education is but a starting point. Study trends in business, in your industry and, more importantly, in the industries of your customers. There is no professional who does not have one or more "customers." The person who believes otherwise is not a real professional.

4. People Skills Mastery. There is no profession that does not have to educate others about what it does. The process of communicating must be developed. It is the only way to address conflicts, facilitate win-win solutions and further organizational goals.

5. Mentorship and Stewardship. We are products of those who believe in us. Find role models and set out to be one yourself. To get, you must give.

6. Going the Distance. Career and life are not a short stint. Do what it takes to run the decathalon. Set personal and professional goals, standards and accountability.

7. Standing for Something. Making money is not enough. You must do something worth leaving behind, mentoring to others and of recognizable substance. Your views of professionalism must be known.

7 Levels of Executive

1. Wanna-be. Want to ascend. Focused more upon status, rather than paying dues. Likely will not make it because not inclined toward "going the distance."

2. Entry-level. Training and education got them there. Desire the chance to work and contribute. Results and company teamwork will prove their worth.

3. Worker Who Advances. Starts at the bottom and advances through the ranks. This person is to be admired for overcoming internal obstacles, as well as attitudes and limitations of co-workers on the way up.

4. Industry Expertise, Skills, Knowledge. Mid-level managers with non-core training and credentials which are necessary for company operation. Brought from outside the company. Valuable resources, though may carry baggage from past corporate cultures.

5. Management Track. Persons recruited and developed by the company, augmented by those who advance within. These get the largest degree of professional nourishment. While considering themselves the luckiest on The Organization Tree, they have responsibilities to communicate, mentor others and set standards for other executives.

6. Senior Level. Mostly self-taught. Good at what they do. Advanced career status in the eras before quality improvement, empowerment, marketplace partnering and other modern business concepts. Though at the top, they must avoid getting trapped into past mindsets.

7. Beyond the Level of Executive. Senior advisor, routinely advancing the organization's Body of Knowledge. Big Picture proponent and

champion. Vision inspiration to management, shareholders and other constituencies.

7 Measures of a Successful Executive

1. Education and Training. Properly trained for organization at the time of joining. Remains ahead of the curve via accelerated professional development, reading, networking and skills enhancement. Emphasis throughout career upon leadership development and training on all five major branches of The Business Tree.

2. Company Contributions. Participates in empowerment and teambuilding programs. Sophisticated understanding of company internal dynamics. They are not content to rest upon past laurels. They maintain an annual increased level of goals, output and accountability.

3. Marketplace Value. They are valued as a profit center to the profession and its industry. They are comfortable in taking risks and making decisions. Worth more than salary to the company. Savvy contributor toward the company's marketing, customer service and business growth efforts.

4. Executive Development. Understands the executive mentality, attitude and level of achievements (as opposed to worker bees and mid-managers). Possesses quest for knowledge, leadership abilities and contribution toward overall Vision of the organization.

5. Mentorship Contributions Has contributed toward professional development of employees, advocating responsibilities to mentor others and set standards for other executives.

6. Leadership Outside the Company. Active in professional and associations, serving as an officer. Serves on business task forces, chamber committees and coalitions with customers and business partners. Active in community service, setting example for employees.

7. Body of Work, Body of Knowledge. Knows that treating symptoms of problems is not enough. Seeks to correct organizational root causes. Big Picture proponent and champion. Makes mark on company, career and marketplace that no other can effect.

Each Role Matters. The Value of Support Staff

Every person in the company matters to its success. Every job is important, as is filling them with the best people for each job. The art and skill of being great support staff is a cornerstone of business success.

From pop culture, think of the great role models that we grew up watching: Della Street was the loyal secretary to Perry Mason. She knew what everyone was thinking and was the glue to the cases. She was the model for executive assistants and office managers everywhere.

The CEO is made stronger with a good C-suite team. Ed McMahon was TV's premier second banana. He worked as assistant, announcer, sponsor commercial pitchman and sketch narrator to Johnny Carson throughout their 29-year run on NBC-TV's "Tonight Show." They had previously worked together on a game show, "Who Do You Trust" on ABC-TV. Bandleaders on the late-night are vital #3 characters on the show, including "Tonight Show" venerable talents such as Doc Severinsen, Skitch Henderson, Paul Shaffer and The Roots band.

The movie star heroes had buddies to help them navigate the adventures. John Wayne and Roy Rogers had Gabby Hayes. Gene Autry had Pat Buttram.

TV show stars had great support casts. Lucille Ball and Desi Arnaz had Vivian Vance and William Frawley as Ethel & Fred Mertz. This historic teaming became the formula for most other TV sitcoms. Shows like "The Mary Tyler Moore Show," "30 Rock," "The Office" and others had expanded ensemble casts.

Some performers made careers as supporting players. Ann B. Davis was Schultzy on "The Bob Cummings Show" and Alice on "The Brady Bunch."

Back characters on TV shows included restaurant and bar operators, where the stars went top relax. There were friendly, familiar places such as Cheers bar, Arnold's Drive-In on "Happy Days," the Krusty Krab on "SpongeBob Square Pants," Dale's Diner on "The Roy Rogers Show" and other homey places. In the business world are those staff people who make us feel more like family. Therefore, our loyalty to the company rises, and we are more productive.

Still other back characters bring cohesion to the enterprise. On "Gilligan's Island," those glue-adhesive characters were the Professor Roy Hinkley and Mary Ann Summers. Those vital employees in the business world might include the IT guy, the receptionist, the mailroom manager, the ethics adviser and the secretary to the Board of Directors.

Great executives know the value of crediting support figures for the business success. Lt. Columbo was always quoting his wife as basis for testing hypotheses, though the character was never shown. Newspaper publisher Perry White was always upstaged by his employees, notably Clark Kent/Superman. Al Roker does the weather on "The Today Show," and he is also the motivating segment host as well. Nobody turns letters like Vanna White, making her essential to the legacy of "Wheel of Fortune."

And then there were those mentors behind the scene who were responsible for lots of creativity. The Beatles had George Martin as their producer. Steven Spielberg had John Williams as music composer for his films.

A host of people make the CEO look good. Further, they transform the company to greater plateaus. Warmly recognize the contributions of executive assistants, trusted advisers, mentors, support staff, future leaders, adjuncts, vendors and outside stakeholders.

Here are some characteristics of support personnel and rising stars who will make it as professionals and business leaders:

- Act as though they will one day be management.
- Think as a manager, not as a worker.
- Learn and do the things it will take to assume management responsibility.
- Be mentored by others.
- Act as a mentor to still others.
- Don't expect status overnight.
- Measure their output and expect to be measured as a profit center to the company.
- Learn to pace and be in the chosen career for the long-run.
- Don't expect that someone else will be the rescuer or enable you to cut corners in the path toward artificial success.
- Learn from failures, reframing them as opportunities.
- Learn to expect, predict, understand and relish success.
- Behave as a gracious winner.
- Acquire visionary perception.
- Study and utilize marketing and business development techniques.
- Contribute to the bottom line, directly and indirectly.

Chapter 16

MANAGEMENT STYLES

O rganizations should coordinate management skills into its overall corporate strategy, in order to satisfy customer needs profitably, draw together the components for practical strategies and implement strategic requirements to impact the business. This is my review of how management styles have evolved.

In the period that predated scientific management, the Captain of Industry style prevailed. Prior to 1885, the kings of industry were rulers, as had been land barons of earlier years. Policies were dictated, and people complied. Some captains were notoriously ruthless. Others like Rockefeller, Carnegie and Ford channeled their wealth and power into giving back to the communities. It was an era of self-made millionaires and the people who toiled in their mills.

From 1885-1910, the labor movement gathered steam. Negotiations and collective bargaining focused on conditions for workers and physical plant environments. In this era, business fully segued from an agricultural-based economy to an industrial-based reality.

As a reaction to industrial reforms and the strength of unions, a Hard Nosed style of leadership was prominent from 1910-1939, management's attempt to take stronger hands, recapture some of the Captain of Industry style and build solidity into an economy plagued by the Depression. This is an important phase to remember because it is the mindset of addictive organizations.

The Human Relations style of management flourished from 1940-1964. Under it, people were managed. Processes were managed as collections of people. Employees began having greater says in the execution of policies. Yet, the rank and file employees at this point were not involved in creating policies, least of all strategies and methodologies.

Management by Objectives came into vogue in 1965 and was the prevailing leadership style until 1990. In this era, business started embracing formal planning. Other important components of business (training, marketing, research, team building and productivity) were all accomplished according to goals, objectives and tactics.

Most corporate leaders are two management styles behind. Those who matured in the era of the Human Relations style of management were still clinging to value systems of Hard Nosed. They were not just "old school." They went to the school that was torn down to build the old school.

Executives who were educated in the Management by Objectives era were still recalling value systems of their parents' generation before it. Baby boomers with a Depression-era frugality and value of tight resources are more likely to take a bean counter-focused approach to business. That's my concern that financial-only focus without regard to other corporate dynamics bespeaks of hostile takeovers, ill-advised rollups and corporate raider activity in search of acquiring existing books of business.

To follow through the premise, younger executives who were educated and came of age during the early years of Customer Focused Management had still not comprehended and embraced its tenets. As a result, the dot.com bust and subsequent financial scandals occurred. In a nutshell, the "new school" of managers did not think that corporate protocols and strategies related to them. The game was to just write the rules as they rolled along. Such thinking always invites disaster, as so many of their stockholders found out. Given that various management eras are still reflected in the new order of business, we must learn from each and move forward.

In 1991, Customer Focused Management became the standard. In a highly competitive business environment, every dynamic of a successful organization must be geared toward ultimate customers. Customer focused management goes far beyond just smiling, answering queries and communicating with buyers. It transcends service and quality. Every organization has customers, clients, stakeholders, financiers, volunteers, supporters or other categories of "affected constituencies."

Companies must change their focus from products and processes to the values shared with customers. Everyone with whom you conduct business is a customer or referral source of someone else. The service that we get from some people, we pass along to others. Customer service is a continuum of human behaviors, shared with those whom we meet.

Customers are the lifeblood of every business. Employees depend upon customers for their paychecks. Yet, you wouldn't know the correlation when poor customer service is rendered. Employees of many companies behave as though customers are a bother, do not heed their concerns and do not take suggestions for improvement.

There is no business that cannot undergo some improvement in its customer orientation. Being the recipient of bad service elsewhere must inspire us to do better for our own customers. The more that one sees poor customer service and customer neglect in other companies, we must avoid the pitfalls and traps in our own companies.

If problems are handled only through form letters, subordinates or call centers, then management is the real cause of the problem. Customer focused management begins and ends at top management. Management should speak personally with customers, to set a good example for employees. If management is complacent or non-participatory, then it will be reflected by behavior and actions of the employees.

Any company can benefit from having an advisory board, which is an objective and insightful source of sensitivity toward customer needs, interests and concerns. The successful business must put the customer into a co-destiny relationship.

Customers want to build relationships, and it is the obligation of the business to prove that it is worthy.

Customer focused management is the antithesis to the traits of bad business, such as the failure to deliver what was promised, bait and switch advertising and a failure to handle mistakes and complaints in a timely, equitable and customer-friendly manner. Customer focused management is dedicated to providing members with an opportunity to identify, document and establish best practices through benchmarking to increase value, efficiencies and profits.

Chapter 17

BOSSES AND EMPLOYEES

Management styles reflect human basic behaviors. Bosses and employees all reflect one of the four basic behavioral styles:

1.   **The Steady Relater.**

They want to maintain good relationships.

We're all in this together. So, let's work as a team.

They like to maintain the status quo and are reluctant to make changes.

They are drawn to helping professions, focusing upon relationships.

2.   **The Cautious Thinker.**

The overriding concern is for accuracy.

Can you provide documentation for the claims?

They focus first on each task at hand.

They move slowly and are self-contained.

They are technicians and are drawn toward exact sciences.

3.   **The Dominant Director.**

The need is to get the job done.

I want it done right, and I want it done now!

They need to make the decisions and be in charge.

They are managers of organizations and departments.

4.   **The Interactive Socializer.**

They want to be noticed.

Let me tell you what happened to me.

They love variety, hate routine and should be shown the Big Picture.

They need to be where the action is and choose creative, high profile professions.

Questions Bosses Ask

At some point, most of us have experienced either the "boss from hell" or the employee who just would not fit into the organization or the co-worker who persisted in digging his-her own grave.

What was wrong with those people? Why couldn't they get their acts together? Couldn't they realize that going with the flow would have been easier than against it?

Where were they standing when the brains and the people skills were handed out? And, why were our careers cursed by their getting in our paths?

Many people have banes of their professional existence, difficult bosses, employees and co-workers who make life miserable. We do not understand how they got to be that way, usually from being ill-prepared for the job at hand.

Lonely at the Top

Just as bosses are not properly schooled in supervising other people and juggling multiple roles, they suffer the "lonely at the top" syndrome. Heads of companies receive filtered information from within. They don't know which outside consultants to trust and, as a result, don't use the ones they should.

The process of walking through landmines causes most bosses to learn as they go. Few companies have the luxury of a long executive development curve. Thus, supervisors must compress their growth process, while getting maximum productivity out of their workers.

These truths exist in the workplace:

- Good bosses were good employees. They are consistent and have understanding for both roles.
- Bad bosses likely were not ideal employees. They too are consistent in career history.
- Poor people skills cloud any job performance and overshadow good technical skills.
- The worst bosses do not sustain long careers at the top. Their track record catches up with them, whether they choose to acknowledge it or not.
- Good workers don't automatically become good bosses.
- Just because someone is technically proficient or is an exemplary producer does not mean that he-she will transition to being a good boss. Very few great school teachers like becoming principals, for that reason. Good job performers are better left doing what they do best.
- Administrators, at all levels, need to be properly trained as such, not bumped up from the field to do something for which they have no inclination.
- At some point in our lives, we are better suited to be a boss than to be an employee.
- Leadership and executive development skills are steadily learned and continually sharpened. One course or a quick-read book will not instill them. The best leaders are prepared to go the distance.
- Being your own boss is yet another lesson. People who were downsized from a corporate environment suddenly enter the entrepreneurial world and find the transition to be tough.

Management Traps

The most common fatal flaws of supervisors include:

- Insensitivity and/or abrasiveness to employees.
- Tendency to over-manage.
- Inability to delegate.
- Inflexibility.
- Poor crisis management ... are reactive to problems, rather than being pro-active.
- Aloofness.

Bosses traditionally manage things so that workers will do things right. The preferable style is to lead people, so that they will do the right things.

Most workers do not perform up to standards because they are not fully told what is expected. 90% of mistakes are made because of wrong instructions. Failure to communicate and provide training on the front end proves more costly to business in the long-run.

Within the ranks of workers, chain reactions occur. Attitudes create other problems. They may be delegated tasks but are not held accountable. Responsibility rests upon employees, just as it does with their supervisors.

How to Get More

I use and recommend the acronym **SCORE** to motivate staff to perform their duties in the best possible manner:

- **S**eek suggestions.
- **C**omfort employees.
- **O**ffer opportunities.
- **R**eassure them.
- **E**ncourage risk taking.

The following suggestions are offered to maximize productivity:

- Set and maintain boundaries, while giving employees the latitude to add their own touches and, thus, invest themselves in their jobs.
- Set performance standards, giving reasons, tasks to perform and a vision of what "finished product" looks like.
- Assign priorities.
- Have starting and ending times for project assignments, rather than be nebulous.
- Identify your people's strengths and weaknesses.
- Pinpoint staff's strengths in relation to the company's strengths at the soonest possible point.

Employees should aspire to be leaders. Thus, they will become empowered employees and will be ready to assume supervisory duties, when appropriate. Effective leaders:

- Provide vision.
- Inspire commitment.
- Create strategies.
- Encourage, rather than push or force people to do things.
- Realize that, with a team effort, everyone's share of the pie grows.

In summation, as one climbs The Organization Tree (Career Track for Professionals), one must amass skills and knowledge, as well as the:

- Art of being a leader.
- Art of being a boss.
- Art of being a good team member.
- Art of interchanging roles, responsibilities, which is the mark of a truly valuable professional.

Why Employees Do Not Perform

1.   They don't know why they should do it.
2.   They don't know where to begin and end.
3.   They don't know what they are supposed to do.
4.   They don't know how to do it.
5.   They think they are doing it.
6.   They think their way is better than what the boss or the rules suggest.
7.   Something else is more important to them.
8.   They are not rewarded for doing … just punished for not doing.
9.   They are rewarded for not doing it … and punished for doing it.
10. They think they cannot do the tasks at hand or are not up to bigger challenges.

Why We Don't Get Profitable Action

1.   The organization does not plan for change or success.
2.   People do not identify with objectives of the organization. Just work for a paycheck.
3.   People are not empowered to feel important as contributors toward desired results.
4.   People are not sure where they fit into the overall structure and mission.

5. Follow-up systems are not implemented.
6. People do not clearly understand what they are expected to do.
7. Goals are either too large or non-communicated.
8. Managers do not set enough of an example.

How to Get Profitable Action

1. **OBJECTIVES**

   Know the organization's mission, goals, tactics and methods to achieve results.

2. **WHAT'S EXPECTED**

   Know job responsibilities, performance standards and contributions toward total effort.

3. **RULES, BOUNDARIES**

   Procedures, regulations, scope of work and ramifications are communicated.

4. **CONSISTENT DISCIPLINE**

   Support for correct actions. Accountability for mistakes. Fair, consistent supervision.

5. **HELP AVAILABLE**

   Training is provided. Latitude is given to exercise judgment. Support by management.

6. **FIT INTO NETWORK**

   Everyone expresses ideas and suggestions. People mentor others, learning from experiences.

7. **CHALLENGE**

   Empowerment to do something worthwhile.

Sample Position Results Oriented Job Description

Major Goal for my Job:

Key Results Area #1: Core Business Activities

Supporting Goal:

Performance Standards:

My job in the area of Core Business Activities will have been satisfactorily performed when:

1.

2.

3.

4.

Key Results Area #2: Administratively Running the Department/Providing the Service:

Supporting Goal:

Performance Standards:

My job in the area of Administratively Running the Department/Providing the Service will have been satisfactorily performed when:

1.

2.

3.

4.

Key Results Area #3: Fiduciary Responsibility/Financial Aspects of the Job

Supporting Goal:

Performance Standards:

My job in the area of Fiduciary Responsibility/Financial Aspects of the Job will have been satisfactorily performed when:

1.

2.

3.

4.

Key Results Area #4: Management Skills/Human Capital/People Activities

Supporting Goal:

Performance Standards:

My job in the area of Management Skills/Human Capital/People Activities will have been satisfactorily performed when:

1.

2.

3.

4.

Key Results Area #5: Business Development, Customer Service

Supporting Goal:

Performance Standards:

My job in the area of Customer Service will have been satisfactorily performed when:

1.

2.

3.

4.

Key Results Area #6: Personal-Professional Development

Supporting Goal:

Performance Standards:

My job in the area of Personal-Professional Development will have been satisfactorily performed when:

1.

2.

3.

4.

Key Results Area #7: The organization's overall vision, growth and strategies

Supporting Goal:

Performance Standards:

My job in the area of The agency's overall vision, growth and strategies will have been satisfactorily performed when:

1.

2.

3.

4.

Defining Performance Standards for Production Work:

Planning: schedule, expedite

Inventory: control, measure, purchase

Transportation: ship, receive

Maintenance: equipment, facilities

Defining Performance Standards for Technical Work:

Design: product, service

Research and Development: new products

Writing: procedures, manuals, systems, testing

Customer Relations: complaints, contracts, inspection, start-up, debug, install

Feasibility: studies, materials, processes

Quality: measure, rework, scrap, recapture, sustain, heighten

Defining Performance Standards for Financial Work:

Budgeting: develop, approve, control, report

Expenses: approve, control, remit, report

Accounts Receivable: bill, control, follow-up, report

Payroll: calculate, approve, submit, report

Defining Performance Standards for Management, Administrative Work:

Meetings: set up, run, attend, plan

Reports: generate, read, write, review

Correspondence: read, write, approve

Literature: read, write, business-to-business, consumer materials

Legal: get information, analyze, synthesize, testify, develop strategy

Security: set up, monitor, control, advocate

Planning: goals, objectives, strategy, vision, implementation, review, advocate

Organizing: structure, growth

Chapter 18

FINE WINE, AGED CHEESE
AND VALUABLE ANTIQUES

Professionals Who Go the Distance
Lifelong Learning and a Body of Work

A professional's career and their collected Body of Work encompass time, energy, resources, perseverance and lots of commitment in order to produce. This holds true for any company, institution and for any person.

The multiple parts of a successful company require care, attention, grooming and benchmarking. All branches must interact and contribute to the base of the organization. The base waters and feeds every part of the tree.

There are three key ingredients in developing deep leadership roots. Long-term success for the company and a healthy career for the individual are attributable to:

1.   The manner in which an organization or professional lives and conducts business on a daily basis. I symbolize this with the analogy Fine Wine.

2. The evolution, education, enrichment, professional development, training and life experiences that one amasses. This continuum is symbolized by the analogy Aged Cheese.

3. What of value is really accomplished and left behind. This shows that the business or person actually existed and contributed meaningfully to society, rather than just filling time and space on this earth. This is symbolized by the analogy Valuable Antiques.

Wine

Just because it is a bottled alcoholic beverage does not mean that it contains great wine. In the marketplace, there exist large quantities of fair wine, some bad wine and some good wine. There's very little great wine.

Defining what is "good" is a matter of judgment, perspective and prejudice. When one assigns the term "great," then the wine (used as an analogy for one's daily process of living and working) takes on rare proportions.

The general public is not exposed to the wine vineyard process and, thus, is not familiar with the characteristics of that special reserve:

- A good crop of grapes from which to draw.
- Skilled processes in picking and processing the grapes.
- Knowledge in the making of wine.
- Care for the industry, the product and the process (a defined Vision).
- Skilled technicians, who transfer the intent of the wine maker into the bottle.
- Packaging, distribution and marketing of the product.
- Reputation of the winery, steadily built and carefully preserved.
- An informed clientele, with the ability to appreciate and enjoy the wine.
- The right settings in which to showcase the product.
- A body of pleasurable and memorable experiences from which customers will build brand loyalty.
- A reinforced manufacturing process that assures consistency in all areas.
- Stated, refined strategies for the winery to remain in business, producing a quality product and maintaining clientele appreciation.

Cheese

We all eat and enjoy cheese, in some form. If it's a brand or flavor we recognize, we think it's good. When cheese is part of a favorite recipe, then it's an essential ingredient, though we might not eat it by itself.

The process of creating and curing the cheese (used as an analogy for the process of sharpening and amassing life and professional skills) is both an art and a science.

When it comes to cheese, people generally uphold these constants:

- Cheese is made from milk.
- It is manufactured in various places, utilizing various processes.
- Some sources of cheese making (Switzerland, Wisconsin) are acknowledged for their expertise.
- Cheese is wrapped and packaged in various forms: sliced, chunks, rounds, barrels.
- Sometimes, cheese is processed, liquefied, smoked, whipped, grated or otherwise reconfigured.
- Cheese is bought in stores where we regularly trade. Sometimes, we trade with specialty stores just to get that style or brand.
- It comes from packages that are neatly wrapped and arranged for eye appeal in a clean, well-lit and suitably refrigerated dairy case.
- Price is often a deciding factor in buying. Most people buy the cheapest brands.
- The flavor of cheese we buy depends upon the use we have for it … be it as an appetizer, as an ingredient in an ensemble dish, as a salad enhancement or just to munch on.
- Most often, we mix the cheese with something else.
- Various styles of cheese are often served at a time, or mixed into recipes.
- If it tastes good, we consume that flavor or brand again. If not, we will not likely give that flavor or brand another try.
- If guests like it, we will serve it again. If not, their preferences will influence ours, and, thus, the cheese will not reappear.
- If it is really good, we refer it to others … sometimes giving it as a gift.
- The better it appears to be (marketing, wrapping, price, place of purchase) affects our viewpoint on its quality.
- It is often served with wine, sometimes on antique trays or dishes.

Antiques

Antiques are rare, interesting, fanciful and out of the ordinary. They tend to stimulate affection, admiration and appreciation. They are generally thought of as joyful, artistic and quality-reflecting possessions that are in rare supply.

Everyone owns and buys possessions, including clothing, equipment, furniture and household items. A small percentage of the public views unique versions of these same items as antiques, creating a preferred place for them in their lives.

Antiques are perceived in different manners. The substance of antiques (used as an analogy for what one does-accomplishes with his-her life and organization) is that of the creator, not the seller or the collector.

Among the truisms of antiques are:

- Their quality and workmanship are set by the creator, with inspiration from diverse sources.
- Their market value is set by the seller, who often is a connoisseur or, at the least, has a profit motive in seeking its value increase.
- The purchase price is set by the buyer, who also believes that getting a bargain or making a long-term investment will enhance the value of the antique.
- The buyer appreciates collectibles as a whole and their own specialties in particular.
- The collector appreciates those who appreciate.
- As one attaches value to the unique, one finds value in other things around them.
- Appreciation for value becomes a quality of life ingredient.
- Definitions of antiques vary from collector to collector, depending upon interest. To one, it may be a rare painting. To another, it is custom-made furniture. To still another, it may be a Roy Rogers wristwatch, one of Elvis Presley's scarves or a Partridge Family lunchbox.
- Seeking out new and unique places to find antiques is great fun, and one seeks to include friends in the quest.
- The hunt is worth as much or more than the actual find.
- As friends take up sub-specialties in collecting and preserving, we support their passions and interests.

- Once one gets acclimated toward antiques, one does not "go back." As an interest, it becomes a "way of life."
- The nature of value continually changes and evolves.

Nourishing a Body of Work (Antique)

No company or individual sets out to create an antique (lifelong Body of Work). It just works out that way, depending upon such factors as:

- The crafting artist, as a person and a professional.
- The arsenal of tools which the creator has at hand.
- Combinations of experiences, training and assimilation which were gleaned by the artist.
- Unexpected twists, turns and situations which the crafter saw and seized upon.
- Vision for the project, from concept through execution.
- Sets of standards, with mediocrity not a rung on the ladder.
- An innate sense of perspective, with the reality that no such thing as perfection exists.
- Marketplace sensitive considered in the overall project, but not pandered to.
- Applications for the concept and durability of the product for the long-term.

The phenomena of people liking and admiring antiques, years after their creation, is like a successful wine and cheese party. But, this isn't why the wine and cheese were made.

There are many forces and outside influences who set standards for quality. Normally, it's the marketplace. Who should be the arbitrator and benchmark? You should. Your company will. Your family must.

7 Plateaus of Professionalism

1. Learning and Growing. Develop resources, skills and talents.
2. Early Accomplishments. Learn what works and why. Incorporate your own successes into the organization's portfolio of achievements.

3. Observe Lack of Professionalism in Others. Commit to sets of standards as to role, job, responsibilities, relationships. Take stands against mediocrity, sloppiness, poor work and low quality. Learn about the culture and mission of organizations.

4. Commitment to Career. Learn what constitutes excellence, and pursue it for the long-term. Enjoy well earned successes, sharing professional techniques with others.

5. Seasoning. Refining career with several levels of achievement, honors, recognition. Learn about planning, tactics, organizational development, systems improvement. Active decision maker, able to take risks.

6. Mentor-Leader-Advocate-Motivator. Finely develop skills in every aspect of the organization, beyond the scope of professional training. Amplify upon philosophies of others. Mentoring, creating and leading have become the primary emphasis for your career.

7. Beyond the Level of Professional. Never stop paying dues, learning and growing professionally. Distance runners tend to develop and share their own philosophies. Thus, a track record, unlike anything accomplished by any other individual, is established. Such valuable leaders contribute toward their organizations' philosophy, purpose, vision, quality of life, ethics and long-term growth.

Criteria for Assessing and Nurturing Professionalism

Fine Wine
Core Values
Ethics
Professionalism
Quality
Work with Colleagues
People Skills
Executive-Leadership Abilities
Collaborative Team Experience
References

Aged Cheese
    Expertise
    Talents, Skills
    Education and Training
    Resume
    Industries Served
    Business
    Marketplace Understanding
    Business Savvy

Valuable Antiques
    Track Record, Experience
    Accomplishments
    Case Studies
    Professional Reputation
    Body of Knowledge
    Original Ideas, Concepts
    Self-Created Expertise
    Vision
    Uniqueness
    Creativity
    Value-Added Contributions
    Substance

Characteristics of a Top Professional
- Understands that careers evolve.
- Prepares for the unexpected turns and benefit from change, rather than becoming the victim of it.
- Realizes there are no quick fixes in life and business.
- Finds a truthful blend of perception and reality ... with sturdy emphasis upon substance, rather than style.
- Has grown as a person and as a professional ... and quests for more enlightenment.

- Has succeeded and failed … and has learned from both.
- Was a good "will be," taking enough time in early career years to steadily blossom … realizing that "fine wine" status wouldn't come quickly.
- Has paid dues … and knows that, as the years go by, one's dues paying accelerates, rather than decreases.

Rising Stars in the Business World

Here are some characteristics of young people (rising stars) will make it as professionals and business leaders:

- Act as though they will one day be management.
- Think as a manager, not as a worker.
- Learn and do the things it will take to assume management responsibility.
- Be mentored by others.
- Act as a mentor to still others.
- Don't expect status overnight.
- Measure their output and expect to be measured as a profit center to the company.
- Learn to pace and be in the chosen career for the long-run.
- Don't expect that someone else will be the rescuer or enable you to cut corners in the path toward artificial success.
- Learn from failures, reframing them as opportunities.
- Learn to expect, predict, understand and relish success.
- Behave as a gracious winner.
- Acquire visionary perception.
- Study and utilize marketing and business development techniques.
- Contribute to the bottom line, directly and indirectly.
- Offer value-added service.
- Never stop paying dues and see this continuum as "continuous quality improvement."
- Study and comprehend the subtleties of life.
- Never stop learning, growing and doing. In short, never stop!

And, If They Don't

Here are the characteristics of "wanna-be's" who do not choose to view their apprenticeships as a mode to grow, viewing it as a burden or unnecessary time. They think the dues paying process is for others, never themselves. Such persons will undoubtedly become stuck in the land of "never-gonna-be" because they:

- Perennially wants the status that others have.
- Will not go the distance or see their career as a long-term set of challenges.
- Seek to become a carbon copy of someone else.
- Fail to do adequate research into their industry and its business challenges.
- Fail to pay sufficient dues.
- Want a job, not a career.
- Have poor people skills … and fail to improve them.
- Show an unwillingness to learn beyond just the sheepskin on the wall.
- Fail to show proper respect to their elders and superiors.
- Assume they're a senior member of the profession when they never mastered being an effective junior, let alone mastering the middle career years.
- Constantly whines and says they are trying when they are not.
- Use, abuse and knowingly waste the time of others.
- Always have an excuse.
- Skillfully learns to cover tracks and justify excuses.
- Contend that it's always someone else's fault.
- Maintain an "I can do that" mentality, challenging seasoned professionals.
- Don't learn how to be a joiner.
- Cannot ascend as a leader.
- Always looking somewhere else, without appreciating the opportunities at hand.

Differences Between a Career and a Job:
- Possession and nurturing of a dream.
- Maintains an interest in pursuing and achieving, versus just doing something.
- 20 hours a week. Top professionals are not clock watchers.
- Not knowing what a coffee break is.

- Working smarter hours, not necessarily longer.
- A career is not something that one retires from or puts on the shelf temporarily.
- Thinking like the boss, whether or not you are it at this present position.
- Money is not the dominant driving influence.
- Training and professional development are rewards, not punishments.
- The more you know, the more you realize what you don't know … and proceed to learn.

Truisms of a Career and Life

- Whatever measure you give will be the measure that you get back.
- There are no free lunches in life.
- The joy is in the journey, not in the final destination.
- The best destinations are not pre-determined in the beginning, but they evolve out of circumstances.
- Circumstances can always be strategized, for maximum effectiveness.
- You've got to give in order to get.
- Getting and having power are not the same thing.
- One cannot live entirely through work.
- One doesn't just work to live.
- As an integrated process of life skills, career has its place.
- A body of work doesn't just happen. It's the culmination of a thoughtful, dedicated process, carefully strategized from some point forward.
- The objective is to begin that strategizing point sooner rather than later.

The Moment of Truth

There comes a point when the pieces fit. One becomes fully actualized and is able to approach their life's Body of Work. That moment comes after years of trial and error, experiences, insights, successes and failures.

Young people often think that they can "have it all" overnight. They don't know yet how much they don't know. Many aren't willing to pay sufficient dues to "get there."

As one matures, survives, life becomes a giant reflection. We appreciate the journey because we understand it much better. We know where we've gone because we know the twists and turns in the road there. Nobody, including ourselves, could have predicted every curve along the way.

However, some basic tenets charted our course. To understand those tenets is to make full value out of the years ahead. The best is usually yet to come.

Your output should be greater than the sum of your inputs. This is accomplished by reviewing the lessons of life, their contexts, their significance, their accountabilities, their shortcomings and their path toward charting your future.

Alas, all of us practice Futurism of one sort. It is not an esoteric concept. It is a potpourri of where we've been, why we've done well and what we're going to do about the lessons learned. That's the holistic, common sense approach to Futurism.

Chapter 19

THE BUSINESS LEADER
AS COMMUNITY LEADER

In eras following downturns and scandals, it is incumbent upon good companies to go the extra distance to be ethical and set good examples. Demonstrating visible caring for communities by company executives is the ultimate form of potlache.

No matter the size of the organization, goodwill must be banked. Every company must make deposits for those inevitable times in which withdrawals will be made.

To say that business and its communities do not affect each other, is short-sighted ... and will make business the loser every time. Business marries the community that it settles with. The community has to be given a reason to care for the business. Business owes its well-being and livelihood to its communities.

Business leaders have an obligation to serve on community boards and be very visible in the communities in which they do business. If done right, community stewardship builds executives into better leaders, as well as receiving deserved credit for the company. Civic service is the ultimate way to steer heir apparent executives toward the leadership track.

Communities are clusters of individuals, each with its own agenda. In order to be minimally successful, each company must know the components of its home community intimately. Each company has a business stake for doing its part. Community relations in reality is a function of self-interest, rather than just being a good citizen.

Companies should support off-duty involvement of employees in pro bono capacities but not take unfair credit. Volunteers are essential to community relations. Companies must show tangible evidence of supporting the community by assigning key executives to high-profile community assignments. Create a formal volunteer guild, and allow employees the latitude and creativity to contribute to the common good. Celebrate and reward their efforts.

Publicity and promotions should support effective community relations and not be the substitute or smokescreen for the process. Recognition is as desirable for the community as for the business. Good news shows progress and encourages others to participate.

The well-rounded community relations program embodies all elements: accessibility of company officials to citizens, participation by the company in business and civic activities, public service promotions, special events, plant communications materials and open houses, grassroots constituency building and good citizenry.

No entity can operate without affecting or being affected by its communities. Business must behave like a guest in its communities, never failing to give potlache or return courtesies. Community acceptance for one project does not mean than the job of community relations has been completed. It is not "insurance" that can be bought overnight. It is tied to the bottom line and must be treated accordingly, with the resources and expertise to do it effectively. It is a bond of trust that, if violated, will haunt the business. If steadily built, the trust can be exponentially parlayed into successful long-term business relationships.

Potlache

Potlache is the ultimate catalyst toward Customer Focused Management. It means extra gifts, beyond value-added, visionary mindset and the ultimate achievement of the organization.

The word "potlache" is a native American expression, meaning "to give." For American Indians, the potlache was an immensely important winter ceremony featuring dancing, food and gift giving. Potlache ceremonies were held to observe major life events. The native Americans would exchange gifts and properties to show wealth and status. Instead of the guests bringing gifts to the family, the family gave gifts to the guests.

Colonists settled and started doing things their own way, without first investigating local customs. They alienated many of the natives. Thus, the cultural differences widened. The more diverse we become, the more we really need to learn from and about others. The practice of doing so creates an understanding that spawns better loyalty.

When one gives ceremonial gifts, one gets extra value because of the spirit of the action. The more you give, the more you ultimately get back in return. Reciprocation becomes an esteemed social ceremony. It elevates the givers to higher levels of esteem in the eyes of the recipients.

Potlache is a higher level of understanding of the business that breeds loyalty and longer-term support. It leads to increased quality, better resource management, higher employee productivity, reduced operating costs, improved cash management, better management overall and enhanced customer loyalty and retention.

Community Relations

The well-rounded community relations program embodies all elements: accessibility of company officials to citizens, participation by the company in business and civic activities, public service promotions, special events, plant communications materials and open houses, grassroots constituency building and good citizenry.

Never stop evaluating. Facts, values, circumstances and community composition are forever changing. The same community relations posture will not last forever. Use research and follow-up techniques to reassess the position, assure continuity and move in a forward motion.

Companies need community relations at all times:

- Prior to coming into locales.
- Every year in which they do business there, in good and bad economic times.

- When they are leaving an area.
- Even after they have ceased operation in certain communities.

In today's economy, no business can operate without affecting or being affected by its communities. Business must behave like a guest in its communities ... never failing to show or return courtesies. Community acceptance for one project does not mean than the job of community relations has completed. Programs always shift into other gears ... breaking new ground.

Community relations is not "insurance" that can be bought overnight. It is tied to the bottom line and must be treated accordingly, with the resources and expertise to do it effectively. It is a bond of trust that, if violated, will haunt the business. If steadily built, the trust can be exponentially parlayed into successful long-term business relationships.

Material in this chapter is addressed in my previous book, "Non-Profit Legends."

Chapter 20

ANNIVERSARIES HONOR THE PAST
AND BUILD SUPPORT FOR THE FUTURE

A nniversaries are important milestones. Organizations reflect on their heritage and accomplishments. In doing so, they build and widen stakeholder bases, enabling organizations to grow for the future.

I've recommended anniversary celebrations to client companies before. In each case, the results were phenomenal, because they took the effort to mount anniversary celebrations. In 1978, I was advising Uniroyal Tire Company. They wanted to sponsor a 40th anniversary for Little League Baseball. My research revealed that their company had in fact founded LLB, which younger generations of management did not know.

In 1998, I advised the Disney corporation and reminded them that Walt Disney's 100th birthday in 2001 would offer great marketing and positioning opportunities. In 2007, I was advising the credit union industry of America, reminding them that their upcoming 100th anniversary in 2009 would provide outreach opportunities for chapter members around the country. This was news to them, and they jumped on it with relish. I'm the person who planted the ideas and strategy. Great organizations work tirelessly to celebrate and involve their customers.

When one reflects at changes, he-she sees directions for the future. Change is innovative. Customs come and go, and some should pass while others might well have stayed with us. The past is an excellent barometer for the future. One can always learn from the past, dust it off and reapply it. Living in the past is not good, nor is living in the present without wisdom of the past.

Here are some recent celebrations that drew acclaim and participation: the Civil Rights Act, 50th landmark anniversary. The Beatles coming to America, 50th anniversary. "The Star Spangled Banner" by Francis Scott Key, 200th observance, "Alice in Wonderland" by Lewis Carroll, 150th, "Star Trek," 50th. Sir Isaac Newton discovering gravity, 350th. NASA lunar landing, 50th gala. Suez Canal, 150th anniversary.

There are seven kinds of anniversary reunions that may be observed:

1. Pleasurable. Seeing an old friend who has done well, moved in a new direction and is genuinely happy to see you too. These include chance meetings, reasons to reconnect and a concerted effort by one party to stay in the loop.

2. Painful. Talking to someone who has not moved forward. It's like the conversation you had with them 15 years ago simply resumed. They talk only about past matters and don't want to hear what you're doing now. These include people with whom you once worked, old romances, former neighbors and networkers who keep turning up like bad pennies and colleagues from another day and time.

3. Mandated. Meetings, receptions, etc. Sometimes, they're pleasurable, such as retirement parties, open houses, community service functions. Other times, they're painful, such as funerals or attending a bankruptcy creditors' meeting.

4. Instructional. See what has progressed and who have changed. Hear the success stories. High school reunions fit into this category, their value depending upon the mindset you take with you to the occasion.

5.   Reflect Upon the Past. Reconnecting with old friends, former colleagues and citizens for whom you have great respect. This is an excellent way to share each other's progress and give understanding for courses of choice.

6.   Benchmarking. Good opportunities to compare successes, case studies, methodologies, learning curves and insights. When "the best" connects with "the best," this is highly energizing and inspires your future success.

7.   Goal Inspiring. The synergy of your present and theirs inspires the future. Good thinkers are rare. Stay in contact with those whom you know, admire and respect. It will benefit all involved.

7 Levels of Learning from the Past:

1.   Re-reading, reviewing and finding new nuggets in old files.
2.   Applying old pop culture toward today.
3.   Review case studies and their patterns for repeating themselves.
4.   Discern the differences between trends and fads.
5.   Learn from successes and three times more from failures.
6.   Transition your focus from information to knowledge.
7.   Apply thinking processes to be truly innovative.

When we see how far we have come, it gives further direction for the future. Ideas make the future happen. Technology is but one tool of the trade. Futurism is about people, ideas and societal evolution, not fads and gimmicks. The marketplace tells us what they want, if we listen carefully. We also have an obligation to give them what they need.

Apply history to yourself. The past repeats itself. History is not something boring that you once studied in school. It tracks both vision and blind spots for human beings. History can be a wise mentor and help you to avoid making critical mistakes.

Chapter 21

BRANDING

**Many Companies Over-Represent to Sell Something
and Believe Their Own Word Games**

I t is both comical and sad to analyze certain promotional hype that one hears. Some companies claim that purchasing their product is the "be all, end all" panacea for life's dilemmas. If only you will buy their version of "The Answer," then you can surely fast-forward your way to instant riches, success and an easy life.

This is not written to take swipes at responsible branding, marketing and advertising. More than 80% of what one sees and hears is clever, informative, research-based, sensibly executed and intended to orient target audiences toward marketplaces. Advertising fulfills many essential niche needs.

This is written to address the bigger issue that some companies believe the hype that they are issuing. One most often hears inflated misrepresentations, false perceptions and over-statements via such contexts as:

- Corporate image spots that appear on TV news shows.
- Business-to-business publication advertising.
- Self-promotional brochures.
- Direct mailings to niche audiences.
- Catalogs.
- Cause-related marketing materials.

Some companies are downright parsimonious about themselves. Some either skillfully lie to get what they think they want ... or may really believe themselves to be what they hype to publics who don't know any better.

Many consumers are gullible, "name" crazy and susceptible to grandiose claims. They take what is said at face value because they have not or don't care to develop abilities to discern what is hyped by others. They believe distortions faster than they believe facts, logic and reason.

This negatively impacts our society, which continually seeks button-pushing answers for life's complex problems without paying enough dues toward a truly successful life. Consumers naively believe misrepresentations, to the exclusion of organizations which are more conservative, yet substantive, in their informational offerings.

Many of the claims represent "copywriting" by people who don't know anything about corporate vision. Their words overstate, get into the media and are accepted by audiences as fact. By default, companies have the appearance of credibility based upon mis-representations.

Companies put too much of their public persona in the hands of marketers and should examine more closely the distorted messages and partial images which they put into the cyberspace. Our culture hears and believes the hype, without looking beyond the obvious. People come to expect easy answers for questions they haven't yet taken the time to formulate.

Here are some examples of the misleading and misrepresenting things one sees and hears in the Information Age:

"Achieve Perfection."
What they're really selling: Computer software.

My analysis: There is no such thing in life as perfection, as anyone who had led a meaningful life has learned. Continuous Quality Improvement is a higher level of thinking. Computer software is merely one tool out of many. It cannot single-handedly create quality.

"Solutions for a Small Planet."
What they're really selling: Internet access.
My analysis: It takes more than a keyboard to effect solutions. You need global thinkers, planning, visioning, human interaction, the ability to reason … and much more.

"Problem Solvers."
What they're really selling: Computer technicians.
My analysis: Yes they are, for less than one tenth of one percent of business issues.

"Helping You Achieve Your Future."
What they're really selling: Photocopying equipment.
My analysis: You achieve your own future, with the help of skilled advisors. Once you strategize your life's plan, it is a good idea to share photocopies of it with others.

"A Better Life for the People of ____."
What they're really selling: Electric power plants.
My analysis: Yes, but how community-responsive are the companies which sell equipment to public utilities. What is their commitment toward literacy, social services, health care, the environment, multicultural diversity and other key issues that really create a better life?

"Work Smarter, Not Harder."
What they're really selling: Computer software.
My analysis: Productivity software does no good unless one commits to change, alters behavioral traits and commits to time management. Then,

we move on toward the bigger issues which software is not capable of addressing: what you do with your time, what you contribute and how you grow-succeed.

"Tap the potential of companies focused on the future."

What they're really selling: Stock investments.

My analysis: The stock market looks primarily at profits ... one small part (1%) of the business picture. It must also focus upon people, products, processes, procedures and potential.

"How the Fortune 1000 Made Their Fortune."

What they're really selling: Paging equipment.

My analysis: Pagers were not invented when they made their fortunes. Communications is fundamental to maintaining, but technology is only as good as the people using it. The bigger question is: how accessible are the executives, and how is company vision articulated and shared? That's the kind of communications that really grows companies.

"Products for Healthy Living."

What they're really selling: Skin cream.

My analysis: An overstatement. Health care professionals rank other things higher on the list of priorities.

"Your Survival Could Depend On It."

What they're really selling: Home fire safety gear.

My analysis: Agreed, though I would include continuing education, self-fulfillment and the ability to plan one's future life to the equation.

"Change Your Hairstyle as Easily as You Change Your Mind."

What they're really selling: Ladies' hairpieces.

My analysis: Many people (women and men) have trouble changing both ... which still reflect the mindsets and self-images of their college days.

"Speak the Language of Business Success."

What they're really selling: Foreign language lessons.

My analysis: English is the international business language, and most people do not use it to best advantage. Workplace illiteracy is much more rampant than people even understand. Many managers have poor people skills, as well as poor verbal-written communications skills. Business writing and public speaking classes should be mandatory. The ability to communicate must be taught to all who wish to attain business success.

"Develop the Drive to Accomplish Anything."

What they're really selling: Motivational tapes.

My analysis: Agreed, in philosophy. They require human development, mentoring, knowledge enhancement and much more to be successful. Tapes alone are not enough. They may start or augment a path of self-growth and success. Tapes cannot take the place of reading.

"Insightful Advice for a Complex World."

What they're really selling: Banking.

My analysis: Financial planning does not constitute global thought on life. It's 1% of the total picture. Banks buy money wholesale and sell it to borrowers at retail rates. Banks are now trying to compete with financial planners and investment banking houses.

"Getting you back to the way things once were."

What they're really selling: Home owners' insurance.

My analysis: There is nothing more permanent and positive than change (which is 90% beneficial). Too many people spend much of their lives clinging to the past, fighting change and criticizing those who progress. While insurance is important, nothing should promise a return to the past. That plays into the hands of has-beens.

"Enhancing Your Life at Home."

What they're really selling: Outdoor signage.

My analysis: To facilitate enhancement, focus upon quality time with the family, hobbies, reading, exercise, gardening and entertaining guests.

"The Spirit of Excellence."

What they're really selling: Residential real estate.

My analysis: Price and location are the deciding factors in real estate. Knowledge of the agents is the next factor. While all companies should achieve excellence in what they do, no single organization embodies it all.

"Your opportunity of a lifetime is here. You owe it to yourself and your family to be successful."

What they're really selling: Multi-level marketing, home-based business.

My analysis: The language of infomercials often preys upon low-income and low-esteem people. It alleges that their scheme is the only true way to riches … which is a quick path toward a successful family life. Obviously, they are mixing messages to sell their programs. Life is a series of progressions, choices, dues-paying and self-earned successes. There is no substitution for diligence and hard work.

"Has All the Trappings of a Box Office Sensation."

What they're really selling: Trucks.

My analysis: That means that it's based upon flash, sizzle and hucksterism. This week's box office sensation will be forgotten soon enough. There's always another waiting to take its place. Why do TV newscasts devote so much valuable airtime to show box office grosses for movies? That's not news. Further, it reinforces the erroneous message that sales rankings are the primary measure of a company or product. Anybody who hangs their hat upon changeable, temporary rankings is headed for a fall. The public also loves to see celebrities, products, trends and cultural icons fall just as quickly as they rise. It's a sick phenomena. Nothing—not even reputable films—should be judged only by fickle box office ratings.

"Accelerate Your Business."

What they're really selling: Computer software.

My analysis: Not every company grows at the same rate. Database software does not make a company grow. It is a tool of people who put thought, planning, products and processes into perspective. Computer "consultants" are not business strategists. Their product is one out of hundreds of business tools and must, therefore, be kept into proper perspective.

"Improving Health Care in America."

What they're really selling: Data processing systems.

My analysis: Managing data and managing doctors (which is tough to do) are not the same thing. Non-core vendors do not and cannot improve the quality of a client's core business. Products and services assist the bureaucracy to do its job more efficiently but cannot claim credit for Big Picture success of a client's entire industry. In the case of health care, it's more of a societal phenomenon that goes beyond the controls of its industry, providers and vendors.

"Brewing solutions for a better environment."

What they're really selling: Packaged beverages.

My analysis: It is misleading to list the charities one has supported in one's history, especially to prove a deceiving point. When you're in the business of manufacturing and marketing packaged beverages, it is misleading to suggest that you're in the business of protecting the environment. Cause related marketing is wonderful, but a company that exploits one cause may paint a partial (and thus false) picture of itself.

"The Internet is fast becoming the greatest business revolution ever."

What they're really selling: Computer software.

My analysis: The Internet is a vehicle for sales and marketing. History tells us that revolutions are never fast. For terms like "greatest," try practical experience, learning, planning and human communication with colleagues … qualities which a sales vehicle cannot provide.

"The Bumpy Road to Success Made Smooth."

What they're really selling: Small business banking services.

My analysis: Banking, like computer hardware and software, is a tool of the trade ... not a driving force. Success is a long process, based upon how well one takes the turns. There are no shortcuts to true success.

Red Flag Expressions
When You Hear, Beware of False Claims!

Mission

Family Tradition

Fastest Growing

Caring

In One Easy Lesson

Better

#1 in Sales

World Class

Wealth and Riches

The Best

For All Your Needs

"Our Mission."

What they're really selling: Retail merchandise.

My analysis: Beware of that phrase in advertising. It's a sales ploy. Retailers are motivated by keeping the cash registers ringing. It's unlikely that sales people know what a Mission Statement and the Strategic Planning process are. To confuse sales and Big Picture messages is a travesty.

"Family Tradition."

What they're really selling: Usually retailers, restaurants, service companies.

My analysis: If the founder is still active in the business and is accessible to customers, then the reputation is upheld. Dysfunctional family-run businesses reflect dysfunctional families. Hiring blood relatives, in-laws and old friends is not always good business. A few pull their share, and others coast on the certainty of nepotism. Research shows the odds are against family businesses going past a second generation, for these and other reasons. Tradition is a red flag expression because it implies that change has not occurred. Nobody does things exactly as they did in the early days. To say they do is deceptive to customers, employees and the good family name. Tradition and maintaining the status quo are two different concepts. Real tradition is predicated upon change management and steady evolution of the business.

"Caring for the Community."
What they're really selling: Perceived corporate self-image.
My analysis: Television stations are notorious about producing and airing self-serving promotional campaigns. They "care" about the community. The bulk of their "caring" is to promote local newscasts, which are their most lucrative sources of advertising revenue.

They say they are facilitating community dialog. Most available public service time, instead of going to non-profit organizations, is sold to corporations. Cause-related marketing packages have the "feel-good" look of public service but are really disguised ad campaigns to promote corporate agendas and produce more revenues for the TV stations.

Newspapers brag about all they donate toward educating the community. What they're really "donating" is unsold ad space. They make up by increasing rates of advertisers ... offering cause-related marketing packages as incentives.

When one media insists upon having exclusive name rights to a special event, that's the kiss of death. For years, I've recommended to charities that they not put all their eggs in one basket. If one media is the "name sponsor," then that will negate coverage by other media. Charities rationalize that exclusivity gets them more intensive coverage than would a "shotgun publicity" approach, which is not true and has never been proven so.

Name media are also notorious about failing to give all the exposure that they promised ... citing advertising commitments as the overriding factor. This is truthful because media companies are firstly in the business of running advertising. Running programming and local news coverage is just the "wrap-around" to generate audiences for advertisers. At the bottom of the totem pole sits coverage of community activities ... unless they can sell advertising around it.

"In One Easy Lesson."

What they're really selling: A quick fix, or a quick way to get company buy-in.

My analysis: Meaningful strategy, improvement and change are not achieved via quick fixes. They also need not be long drawn-out processes. Reasonable timelines may be achieved. Company growth or success cannot be accomplished **In One Easy Lesson** because human beings require more than once to learn meaningful lessons ... plus the time and attention necessary to put lessons learned to good use.

"Better."

What they're really selling: Their way of producing and selling.

My analysis: Human behavior training tells us that judgmental qualifiers like "good, bad, mean, evil and better" are self-defeating. To be better is to slam someone else.

"#1 in Sales."

What they're really selling: You should buy from them, since so many others do.

My analysis: #1 is for now. Sales rankings constantly change. To buy only because a company hypes that they are #1 is not a valid reason. Buy what you want ... from a company that you respect. Also, if they're #1, you're just another sales statistic and customer service will suffer commensurately to the numbers behind whom you must stand in line.

"World Class."

What they're really selling: If you want to be associated with a winner, buy from them.

My analysis: The organization that claims "world class" is trying too hard to be put in the league of others. "World class" is not self-bestowed ... it is earned via a long track record.

"Wealth and Riches."

What they're really selling: Their product is all that you need.

My analysis: There are no shortcuts to wealth and riches. Nobody will give away their secrets. Pyramid marketing schemes take advantage of failed hopes and ungrounded wishes. As P.T. Barnum once said, "There's a sucker born every minute."

"The Best."

What they're really selling: Temporary rankings.

My analysis: There are too many ups and downs in business, without proclaiming yourself in a position for others to dispute or attack. Being successful in the long-run is much more admirable than being temporarily "the best."

"For All Your Needs."

What they're really selling: They exhibit the wanna-be syndrome.

My analysis: No product or service fulfills all of a customer's needs. To suggest otherwise is narrow-minded. The more self-assured business makes long lists of what it doesn't do. It knows and relishes its niche, without trying to be all things to all people.

Now, to Salute Good Examples of Slogans and, Thus, Company Posturing

As many misleading statements and campaigns there are, I would like to cite some of the ones that I respect. These prove that marketing can be compelling, thought provoking and intriguing at the same time. Here are some that I salute:

Better Grades Are Just the Beginning. Sylvan Learning Centers. This illustrates that continuous quality improvement is a process, not a quick fix. I heartily agree that learning is the key to everything else in life and that it must be planned and nurtured.

The Difference is Planning. Merrill Lynch. Agreed, although financial planning (a subset of Branch 3 on The Business Tree) constitutes less than 1% of full-scope organizational planning. If every consultant and vendor would advocate a cohesive approach to planning, directed toward a Big Picture, then organizations would run better and individuals would lead quality lives.

It's All in How You Look At It. *The New York Times*. Bravo. Very insightful. Perspective is everything … continually changing, reflective and powerful for our future.

Look and You See the World Around You. Investor Owned Light and Power Companies. If one ages gracefully, they become more perceptive and enjoy life better. Otherwise, they stagnate. The choice is up to the individual (and any organization, as well).

Silence is Acceptance. Public service campaign to facilitate discussions about drug abuse. Many families abdicate responsibilities for parenting to schools, the community or to anybody but themselves, Organizations reflect their own lack of training about people skills and management issues. They either cannot or won't try to teach what they were not taught. Managers tell employees what not to do and criticize them for being wrong. Yet, it's their fault because ground rules were not adequately communicated, nor has mentorship occurred. Doing nothing causes much more organizational damage than making mistakes while operating in good faith. Silence (followed by harsh criticism) is the worst way to communicate.

We Make Money the Old Fashioned Way. We Earn It. Smith Barney. Business is a process, not a sure thing. Companies which are prepared to "go the distance" will reap greater rewards, including financial.

Touches the Lives of Just About Everybody. General Electric. If more companies thought of the implications of what they do upon multiple constituencies, they would do a better job. Don't think in the "micro." Think more "macro" about who decisions and policies affect.

The Mantle of Greatness Cannot Be Earned in a Single Summer or in a Decade. Greatness is Earned Over an Entire Career. Rolex Watches. Yes, indeed. Too many people want the acclaim of their seniors but are not willing to do the things that their seniors did to get there. Wanna-be's generally will not go the distance because they don't take the time to amass skills for success. Those who achieve long-term do so because of a plan to succeed, commitment to their profession, people skills, community stewardship, participation in mentorship, ongoing professional development, self-fulfillment and a positive attitude.

Characteristics of Good Slogans-Campaigns and, thus, Company Philosophy

Focus upon the customer.

Honor the employees.

Show life as a process, not a quick fix.

Portray their company as a contributor, not a savior.

Clearly defines their niche.

Say things that inspire you to think.

Compatible with other communications.

Remain consistent with their products, services and track record.

Chapter 22

100 REASONS WHY GOOD BUSINESSES GO BAD

F ailure to take pro-active business strategies and steps becomes a habit in any organization. Let one thing slide, and another layer of problems will appear. It's easier and more comfortable to look the other way.

Organizations try to maintain the status quo, thinking it to be their best course, by finding greater comfort with the "same old, same old," rather than new concepts. Habits become described as "traditions" by the organizations denying the implications of change, hoping their problems will go away and focusing anywhere besides their own culpability with problems. Problems are seemingly swept under the carpet by blaming mistakes away, refusal to take personal accountability and failure to emphasize the positives.

There are costs attached to neglect, indecision and non-actions. Failure to take pro-active measures costs the organization exponentially each year by six.

You and your company will pay the bills for damage caused by inertia or lack of progress. Waste, spoilage, down-time and empty activities currently existing bring down productivity and profitability potential.

Lack of having a cohesive marketplace strategy means you're chasing too many of the wrong leads, prospects or markets, which sets the company back.

By sticking to "business as usual," even when it is clearly not what it used to be, companies began telling themselves the great lies which justify their refusal to change and believe them to be truisms.

Long-term expenses incurred by adopting quick fixes and applying band aid surgery to problems usually result in opening new ones. Possessing an inability to spot where the current and upcoming opportunities lie result in the company abdicating its marketplace to others. The company falls behind the competition … out of failure to change, grow and succeed, plus failure to recognize and reward the strengths within your own organization.

These are the 100 reasons why good organizations of all sizes go astray, categorized per each branch of The Business Tree™. Take the following test. Grade your company.

More than 40 bullet points checked is a failing score. Consider these negatives as opportunities to improve growth and success.

The Business You're In

1. Service is rendered, and products are designed-and manufactured the same way in which they always were.
2. Technical abilities and specialties are not further developed after the company's initial successes in creating their widget.
3. The presumption held is that, if it worked for the company founder(s), then it still works for the rest of the industry and all competitors within it.
4. Management doesn't see the need to use industry consultants or technical specialists.
5. Core business supplier relationships have not been examined or updated lately.
6. No investment has been made toward quality controls.
7. The company applies "band aid surgery" toward core business issues and problems … but only at such time they absolutely have to or are forced to.

Running the Business

8. The business continues to be run as they always have operated, citing the first way of doing things as a "tradition."

9. Top management subscribes to the philosophy, "If it ain't broke, don't fix it."

10. Lack of formal organizational structure leaves many company executives blamable but not accountable, with many unclear as to their roles and responsibilities.

11. Practices, procedures, operations, structure are not documented in writing, nor are they communicated to employees.

12. Measuring performance is not factored into the production continuum. Management asks, "Why bother to review everything? Let's just do it."

13. The physical plant is not regularly studied, updated or modified. Management contends, "It was good enough when we built it and still fits our needs."

14. Cost containment is the main driver of all process applications, technologies, equipment, supplies and systems.

15. Distribution standards are not documented, practiced or measured.

16. Time management is not observed, studied or utilized. The attitude is perpetuated, "When it's ready, it's ready."

17. The company continues to stockpile inventories. No efforts are made to reduce surplus or adopt practices such as "just in time delivery."

18. Management does not consult the lawyers until the company gets in trouble or sued.

19. The organization rarely outsources, if ever. The prevailing attitude is: "We have enough engineers and technicians working for us. Why pay others on the outside?"

20. Executives believe that computer software is the one and only answer to take care of all company problems and that computer consultants are expert business strategists.

21. No telecommunications system or strategy exists. "We already have telephones," they cry, as a rag-tag setup angers customers and diverts business.

22. The administrative function does not have a written, formal purchasing plan. "When we need something, just send out for it."

23. To cut expenses, repair and maintenance contracts are not held and are often not renewed.

24. Equipment is bought outright, rather than leased or financed.
25. Continuous quality improvement is not practiced. No consideration is given toward creating or implementing such a program.
26. The company applies "band aid surgery" toward process and operations facets ... but only at such time they absolutely have to or are forced to.

Financial

27. The belief is steadfastly held that every product must make a profit, at all times.
28. Few, if any, profits are plowed back into the business. Few long-term investments are made.
29. The company's book of assets are not adequately valued or managed.
30. Owners believe that the only reason for being in business is to make as much money for themselves as possible.
31. Cash flow, forecasting and budgeting are inconsistent, if monitored at all.
32. Policies with receivables are not formal, and squeaky wheels get the grease.
33. The business officer does not concern himself about equity and debt financing. The contention is that such things are only applicable to public companies.
34. The company doesn't call or consult the accounting firm until income tax season or audit time.
35. Banking and investing relationships are not fully valued and are perceived as free advice from vendors.
36. Creditor payments are drug out as long as possible, even paying past-due interest when charged. The game is to keep them waiting, using their money interest-free, without realizing the costs of administrative minutia.
37. The company has gotten a reputation for being slow-pay. The accounts payable officer never mediates differences with creditors until they sue, figuring that if one wears creditors down, they will hopefully go away.
38. Finance charges are paid at maximum rates. No attempt has been made to negotiate volume discounts.

39. The company buys the cheapest insurance, which leaves company employees under-covered, unnecessarily bothered by third-party red tape and not as focused on company loyalty as they could be.

40. Management does not see any relationship of benefits packages toward heightened employee productivity.

41. The company applies "band-aid surgery" toward financial dynamics ... but only at such time they absolutely have to or are forced to.

People

42. The corporate culture is slow paced, sluggish and without professionalism.

43. Employees are complacent and rarely carry the company banner forward. Low morale persists and builds upon itself.

44. Human resources does not pay recruiters and personnel firms. They run ads only when they need people to fill specific job titles.

45. Human resources hires only to fill vacant jobs, rather than match talent to potential company opportunities.

46. Top management does not see itself as needing to have People development, skills or team building responsibilities.

47. Human Resources department perceives that it knows what the company is all about ... is expected to take care of all problems, without top management intervening.

48. Only executives get bonuses. Others should be grateful to get a regular paycheck.

49. The boss takes the attitude, "Those people work for me. I don't work for them."

50. A regular paycheck is thought to be the only and best incentive for people to work.

51. Upon hiring, employees are handed nebulous job descriptions and are supposed to perform. If they don't, they're fired.

52. Management believes that troublesome employees are easily replaceable and does not realize the economic sense of saving productive workers.

53. Executives see themselves as being the heart of this company. "They do the real work, especially the ones whom the CEO brought on board."

54. The value of training is not understood, appreciated or related to employee performance or the bottom line. They ask, "Why spend money on professional development?"

55. The company develops and teaches all workshops and seminars with in-house talent. The value of outsourced training by niche experts is not comprehended.

56. Management does not know how to discern among or properly utilize business consultants. To cover its lack of analytical ability, it queries, "Why do consultants keep looking at how the organization operates? They cannot possibly know what we know."

57. Performance reviews are arbitrary and are never held with any regularity, nor are employees judged against viable corporate objectives.

58. Empowerment, team building and people skills programs are seen as necessary evils and are minimized.

59. The company applies band aid surgery toward people and their issues … but only at such time they absolutely have to or are forced to.

Business Development

60. The company does not have a clearly defined image or communications strategy.

61. Branding depends upon the boss' latest whim or whatever company he wants to copy.

62. The communications section manager is never in the planning or production loops, nor is asked to advise corporate management.

63. No formal, written or measurable sales plan exists. Goals are either unreasonably high or dangerously low.

64. Marketing and sales are viewed as the same thing and, thus, are lumped together in management's consciousness.

65. No formal marketing plan exists. Marketing is done either on a whim or after the fact..

66. The sales force is not valued and is seen as a necessary evil. "If sales slack off, then we fire people and go hire those who can sell."

67. Sales and marketing people are under-trained, under-managed and threatened with termination for not meeting quotas … always with an axe poised over their heads.

68. No formal written advertising program exists. The company runs ads, which is not

69. No formal written public relations program exists.

70. Advertising and public relations are viewed as the same thing and, thus, are lumped together in management's consciousness.

71. The cheapest possible promotional activities are utilized. Incentives, advertising specialties and customer appreciation items are not factored into the marketing budget.

72. All creative work is done in-house. No need to buy graphic, audio-visual, advertising, research or other promotional services is seen. Thus, expenses are incurred to fully staff a creative services department.

73. Top management does not see itself as needing to maintain or contribute to Business Development responsibilities.

74. Incorrect assumptions preclude an aggressive communications strategy. "The marketplace knows who we are. Why should we have to adapt?"

75. Marketing and sales are viewed only as necessary evils. Engineers and other core business practitioners disdain the concepts and refuse to cooperate with marketing and sales.

76. The company applies band aid surgery toward business development, but only at such time they absolutely have to or are forced to.

Body of Knowledge

77. The company maintains a false sense of success, rarely attributing the contributions of employees and scapegoating others for management's own shortcomings.

78. Critical faculties toward pro-active change become low, and, thus, the company remains stuck in a complacent mode.

79. Management has an inability to predict or stay ahead of trends. "Why worry about changing markets, opportunities, barriers, since we don't need to change?"

80. Decision makers never learn the lessons of failure or the true reasons for successes.

81. The company follows its industry, rather than leading. Product and service development take place after its competitors do the innovating.

82. Management keeps its head in the sand. The rationale is, "Nothing that goes on outside our company affects our business in any way."

83. There is an unwillingness to invest in research or to comprehend how it might impact corporate growth.

84. There is a reluctance to joint-venture or work with other companies. Some contend, "They just want to steal our customers."

85. It is believed that government agencies and regulators are to be avoided, feared, fought or ignored. The concept of collaboratively volunteer to work with them in achieving mutual goals is not on the radar.

86. Company leadership feels that it does not owe anything back to the communities in which it works, nor has the need to interface with them.

87. The company applies band aid surgery toward anything affecting the holistic operation of the company … but only at such time they absolutely have to or are forced to.

The Big Picture

88. Applying band aid surgery to problems keeps the company from ever having to create, face or benchmark against a Big Picture.

89. No Shared Vision is ever crafted, let alone articulated and followed.

90. Low corporate self-esteem persists.

91. The CEO remains isolated from creative, contrary or alternative viewpoints. "Why share ideas and philosophies with anybody else? I know what I'm doing." Corporate purges result from isolationism.

92. Creative business practices are not welcome, sought or achieved.

93. Strategic planning is viewed as a superfluous exercise that is only applicable to companies other than ours.

94. Strategic planning is done when the boss goes away for the weekend and comes back with a list of things to be executed by others.

95. The assumption is that one corporate culture is held equally by all employees. "Whatever the company thinks, so will all of its employees."

96. "Outside-the-box thinking does not apply to us, nor will be tolerated. What is it, anyway?"
97. "We do not engage in unethical practices. What is an ethics statement?"
98. "The quality process means doing things the way we've always done them, without deviation or interference by unwanted intruders. What is Continuous Quality Improvement, anyway?"
99. No crisis management, preparedness or prevention program exists. Management deals with each crisis as it comes up.
100. At best, change will be tolerated. Most resources have already been expended to fight and prevent change from occurring.

Tallying the High Cost of Doing Nothing

On a scale of 1-100, how did the company which you rated fare? If the total number of bullets checked exceeds 40, this means assured failure. 20-40 means barely getting by ... which is not acceptable in today's competitive economy.

Think of the changes and improvements necessary to get the organization to have less than 20 bullet points checked ... because that's what it will take to succeed.

Most of the statements quoted above are voiced by poorly run companies which are clueless about sophisticated growth skills. However, pro-active techniques for actualized company growth can be learned. An articulated, well-implemented vision will pre-empt and prevent many of the mistakes that companies make.

There are two choices, completely up to each organization: (1) The company that does not champion change will falter and die. (2) The company that capitalizes upon change (which is 90% beneficial) will grow and prosper.

As each company pursues the strategic planning process, a deeper understanding of the business develops. The company begins to address and master change, rather than becoming a victim of it.

Chapter 23

100 BIGGEST EXCUSES THEY USE

Euphemisms Most Often Heard
Rationales and Reasons Why Businesses Fail

S ome people and organizations go to great extremes to place spins, rationalize or save face in their business lives. Often, sweeping generalizations involve making far-fetched excuses or scapegoating someone else.

Criticizing others may be cloaked as a subtle or even polite dialog. Yet, behind these often-voiced expressions lie fallacies in reasoning, the wrong facts, jealousy, animosity, personal self-defeat or cluelessness of the speaker.

When people pose the following questions or statements, there often lurk sarcasm or hidden agendas behind the "seemingly innocent" comments.

Failing to make investments in future company success:

I'm building a new house right now. Just took a vacation. Got to send the kid to college.

(or some other personal reason)

224

Can't spend money on marketing my business to customers.

We just bought a bunch of equipment.

Well, we do have to pay taxes.

Have to make cuts everywhere else to pay for rising production costs.

We make a good product, and that should be enough.

Why must we spend time on things other than our core business?

We have a good company image. That's enough to sustain us.

We can dispense with all that employee training and professional development.

We just cannot afford to make the investments.

Rationalizing organizational setbacks:

We were growing too fast anyway.

It was time to pull in our reins and get back to basics.

We took a risk once, and it didn't work out.

This hasn't been our lucky year.

It's a tight economy. When things get better, then we'll expand.

If we didn't have so much (any) competition, then we would be on Easy Street.

That was caused by the previous management. We blame it all on them.

We're lean and mean now. We cut out all the fat.

Our people just need to work a little harder.

Those advocate groups did it to us again.

Economic forces beyond our control are at work.

But, we're still making money.

If our people would think more about what they're doing, then we would be successful.

That's our problem: people thinking but not doing, as well as people doing but not thinking.

Rationalizing poor service or quality:

You won't get it any better elsewhere. If you don't believe it, go try to find out.

We're number one in sales.

Our people were hired to do their jobs. They know what they're doing.

Nobody has complained about this issue before. The problem must be with you.

Quality is our middle name.

We've got the latest technology.

Our CSI rating never changes.

If you can do so much better, why don't you go try.

Put your money where your mouth is.

Profitability is all that matters.

Customers are a dime a dozen. They can be easily replaced.

We're running this business for us ... not for them.

We got an automated phone system to take care of all that.

Customer service is as good as it always was.

Quality is as good as it ever will be.

Blaming problems upon others:

Our consultant told us to do it.

We used to have a lot of business. Had a guy here who chased it off. (The "cash cow" switched companies.) Even though we don't have any business now, we still choose to blame him.

Oh, that's a bunch of media hype.

We're waiting to see what __(governmental entity)__ will do.

What's all this talk about organizational effectiveness? We're good at what we do. No need to

change things because some outsider says so.

People are expendable. If they don't like it, they can leave. Workers are easily replaced.

Our accountant says we cannot do that right now.

We've got to get to the base root of the problem, which is your attitude.

With your behavior, you'll either be very successful or end up in jail.

Our ad campaign backfired.

The devil made me do it.

We're too worried about _____ (some item in the news, the latest source of gossip).

Interest rates are too high.

Our lawyer can take care of any problems that arise. Until then, it's business as usual.

Ethics and standards are for chumps. Making the big bucks is all that matters.

Avoiding change, denying the need for change:

What worked before works now, and it always will.

Things will always stay the same here.

Once the PR crisis passes, things will get back to normal.

Can't change the weather or the world. So, why bother trying to change anything else.

That's just the way he-she is. Learn to live with it.

Our human resources department takes care of that.

We're afraid of litigation.

There's not a thing that we can do to change things. The status quo is perfectly acceptable.

That's the way the cookie crumbles. That's life. What are you going do about it?

Not engaging in planning for future operations:

So what are you going do about it?

There's too much talk about planning. We're just busy doing things.

We have a Mission Statement.

We're good.

All I have to do is dream. Dreams come true.

Our track record should speak for itself.

Money covers up a lot of ills.

We have annual sales projections.

My future is in your hands.

Your future is in my hands.

Good things happen to good people. It will be our turn soon.

Surely, things will work themselves out.

When They Say One Thing, It Really Means Something Else
It's our tradition.

The implication is that they've attained a plateau and no longer need to learn, grow or evolve. Just because something was done a couple of times, they are now calling it a "tradition." This is designed to stave off change or the need for re-evaluation.

Why can't you learn to compromise?

Do things their way.

What kind of training do you have to do this?

They're trying to either impress or intimidate you with credentials. Or, they may suggest that you're not properly trained to do what you already do successfully.

How did you get that project-assignment-client?

They figure that you must have known someone with an inside track. It couldn't have had much to do with your talent and expertise.

How do you get clients?

They want some fast-track answers so they can try them and receive direct benefit.

I want to be like ___ when I grow up.

They still have not found their own niche, self-esteem or purpose. They haven't learned yet that you cannot go through life as a carbon copy of someone else's public image.

Why don't you go write your life story?

They're uncomfortable with people who possess diverse accomplishments-talent-esteem. Some want to classify you as something you may have done well in the past but cannot acknowledge that you have moved forward. Some may poke holes at your body of work.

He's a good guy.

That person holds my beliefs, which are right and just. He-she is also someone from whom I want something or could benefit from association. People who are different are not to be acknowledged, accepted or tolerated. They're not good guys.

We don't have any problems here.

They're not willing to acknowledge problems truthfully. It's easier to scapegoat others who offer constructive criticism. A company or manager can only bury one's head in the sand for so long. After that, the truth of the messengers must be heard. Though constructive criticism and expert advising are tough to take at first, they are vital for continuous quality improvement.

You have my guarantee on it.

Customer service is presently at an all-time low. Companies will say anything to sell products, including building your "trust" in them. By having a commercial spokesperson issue a personal guarantee, you'll know they're one of the "good guys." This phrase is more a condemnation about the poor state of customer service than a slogan of a particular seller. It's an acknowledgement that the marketplace has profound problems with establishing-nurturing customer relationships and that trust is a novelty.

You have the education necessary to do the job. What more do you need?

Many managers throw employees into the water and expect them to swim, without giving lessons. They cannot and do not function in a mentor role because nobody did it for them (and likely didn't know how themselves). To turn bosses into coaches is a much-needed concept, but it cannot happen unless they want to become more than the supervisors they once had. Management by neglect is a continuum that proliferates the business culture. Managers do not know or won't admit to how much they don't know. Unless there's a desire to be something more, then the continuum will endure.

I took early retirement.

They may not have been viewed by their employer as long-term team players. They may not really have contributed toward company goals and may have been released for good reason.

I didn't want to work for that company anymore. They weren't up to my standards.

It wasn't a good fit, for one party or the other. Too often, people want to place blame for something that was not destined to work out in the long-run.

The Request for Proposals was subsequently withdrawn.

All they really wanted to do was garner ideas, methodologies and information from proposing firms. Public sector agencies are notorious about putting proposers through the ringer. A large percentage of Requests for Proposals are bogus processes and contain unfair criteria.

Your proposal was rejected because the committee thought it did not meet the requirements.

Selecting the "successful proposer" was probably an "in job." The bureaucrats had someone else in mind but went through the Request for Proposals process as a formality or perhaps to steal ideas from over-eager proposers. If your proposal was different or offered new or creative ideas, it threatened the status quo of the "committee."

We now have some year-end budget money to spend, but the project has to be finished ASAP.

A mid-manager wants to look good on his-her year-end performance review or to justify a bonus. Thus, they want a quick-sizzle project to help them shine. This project will not go well for the executing contractor because it is not sufficiently prepared or ill-timed.

We're not ready to do this project at this time.

A mid-manager went hunting for a project but could not secure enough funding. Perhaps, that person was never fully authorized to begin the project in the first place but will not admit it publicly.

We have all the help we need. Our present consultants are taking care of everything.

The company cannot really distinguish one "consultant" from another. May have been scammed by one consultant who says that they can "do it all." Their corporate culture likely does not really want to try new approaches and is afraid to seek out seasoned advice.

Can I have additional references?

If they didn't request references earlier, they are back-pedaling … trying to find a reason **not** to do the project. They are hoping the references will discredit or shoot the messenger of change. If they agree to work with you and request references after the fact, they may be afraid of what you represent, which may portend to changes in the way they do business.

He's not my type. There's no chemistry.

I think I can do better. He does not have the outward qualities that I consider attractive. Never mind the inner qualities because I'm only interested in external appearances and cannot handle a deep communication relationship anyway.

So, what do you think about ____?

They are playfully challenging your status as an expert in your field. In humor lies a large degree of sarcasm. They may be jealous of your fame or expertise. **So** is the red flag word.

Common Sense Retorts to Sweeping Generalizations

Here are some of the common mis-statements that people make. Some do so to avoid addressing the real business issues head-on. Others never had the rationales and their implications explained to them properly.

The savvy business executive or advisor will offer pro-active follow-ups. Trite statements should not just sit as they are made. By responding realistically and with an eye toward company improvement, you'll be doing colleagues a service. Examples:

This company reflects the character of its CEO.
Sadly, that's true, to extremes. Many companies are ego-driven. The wise CEO is one who listens to others, surrounds himself-herself with smart people and fosters a spirit of teamwork. A good company is not predicated upon one personality but, instead, has adopted a corporate culture that thinks and feels.

Our company has got the most up to date computer hardware and software.
Companies spend disproportionate amounts of money on technology and neglect their people, processes and policies. Technology represents less than 1% of an organization's pie chart. Technology should be addressed as a tool of the trade, he bigger issues being a cohesive plan of action and organizational vision.

We must be doing something right.
Some companies succeed in their early stages because of raw energy. Conditions change … as should the companies. We must encourage colleagues to honestly examine reasons for their initial success and caution them that Continuous Quality Improvement is necessary. Companies must always grow to "the next tier" and not rest upon laurels.

If it ain't broke, don't fix it.
This is probably the worst cop-out. There is no organization that is totally perfect and cannot stand some fine-tuning. The process of Continuous Quality Improvement is for good companies that want to get better and move forward, which is a sign of wisdom. To adhere to the belief that nothing needs fixing is sheer stupidity.

We are a very quality-oriented company.
Quality is as quality does. Some organizations pay considerable lip service to quality but are clueless as to what it really is, what it means or how it can be sustained. There is no single standard of quality. It is customized and is a continuous effort to plan, think, act and measure. Quality is neither a quick fix for problems nor a shortcut to success and riches.

Success speaks for itself.

People who have high sales love to crow. To them, monetary volume is the "definition" of success. You should do with business with them because they are a "winner," so they claim. In reality, no single market shift speaks completely for itself. Sales rankings vary, with various influencers. Many factors contribute toward long-term success, which is a road filled with ups and downs. Everything is subject to interpretation. Organizations must educate consumers, in a pro-active way, on how to best utilize their products-services.

Ways to Avoid Negative Euphemisms

- Put more emphasis upon substance, rather than flash and sizzle.
- Look outside the organization, instead of keeping your total focus internal.
- Challenge negative comments and make the accusers accountable for organizational progress.
- Keep communications open and continual.
- Refrain from making false representations.
- Abilities to think, reason, take risks and feel gut human instincts must all be nurtured.
- Take advise from all sources. Do your research. Get informed counsel from seasoned advisors.
- Document and comprehend reasons for successes. Cite case studies often.
- Empower the organization to embrace-embody the corporate culture.
- Learn to manage change, rather than become a victim of it.

Avoid the Pitfalls and Be Very Successful

Companies come and go. Not every startup is destined to make it. I have advised many companies during their gravy years. I tried to warn them about the things that would get them into trouble:

- Focusing upon technology and not upon running a business.
- Maintaining too much of an entrepreneur and family business mindset.
- Branding before being a real company.
- Their system's inability to deal with any kind of disruption.

- Each side picks their favorite numbers for "success" because they really do not know.
- Not fully comprehending the business you're really in.
- Venturing too far from your areas of expertise.
- Thinking that the rules of corporate protocol did not apply to them.
- Misplaced priorities and timelines.
- Making financial yardsticks the only barometers.
- Having the wrong relationships with investors, letting angels call too many of the shots.
- Getting bad advice from the wrong people, mainly other tech professionals.
- Rationalizing excuses, such as "the rules have changed."
- Feeling entitled to success and exemptions from business realities.
- Copycats of others' perceived successes.
- Working long and hard, but not necessarily smart.
- Failure to contextualize the product, business, marketplace and bigger picture.
- Inability to plan.
- Refusal to change.

Companies are collections of individuals who possess fatal flaws of thinking. They come from different backgrounds and are products of a pop culture that puts its priorities and glories in the wrong places. They embody a society that worships flash-and-sizzle over substance.

Reasons why some want to grow beyond their current boundaries:

1. Prove to someone else that they can do it.
2. Strong quest for revenue and profits.
3. Corporate arrogance and ego, based upon power and influence, as well as money.
4. Sincere desire to put expertise into new arena.
5. Really have talents, resources and adaptabilities beyond what they're known for.
6. Diversifying as part of a plan of expansion, selling off and re-growing subsidiaries.
7. The marketplace dictates change as part of the company's global being.

Circumstances under which they expand include:
1.   Advantageous location became available.
2.   Someone wanted to sell out. A great deal was too attractive to pass up.
3.   They cannot sit still and must conquer new horizons.
4.   Think they can make more money, amass more power.
5.   Desire to edge out a competitor or dominate another industry.
6.   Create jobs for existing employees (new challenges, new opportunities).
7.   Part of their growth strategy to go public, offering stock as a diversified company.

This is what often happens as a result of unplanned growth:
1.   The original business gets shoved to the back burner.
2.   The new business thrust gets proportionately more than its share of attention.
3.   Capitalization is stretched beyond limits, and operations advance in a cash-poor mode.
4.   Morale wavers and becomes uneven, per operating unit and division.
5.   Attempts to bring consistency and uniformity drive further wedges into the operation.
6.   Something has to give: people, financial resources, competitive edge, company vision.
7.   The company expands and subsequently contracts without strategic planning.

To those successful companies, I ask you to continue reflecting:
1.   What would you like for you and your organization to become?
2.   How important is it to build an organization well, rather than constantly spend time in managing conflict?
3.   Who are the customers?
4.   Do successful corporations operate without a strategy-vision?
5.   Do you and your organization presently have a strategy-vision?
6.   Are businesses really looking for creative ideas? Why?
7.   If no change occurs, is the research and self-reflection worth anything?

Failure to prepare for the future spells certain death for businesses and industries in which they function. The same analogies apply to personal lives, careers and Body of Work. Greater business awareness and heightened self-awareness are compatible and are fundamental parts of a holistic journey of business growth.

Chapter 24

ENTREPRENEURS' GUIDEPOSTS TO REAL BUSINESS SUCCESS

There are many romantic notions about entrepreneurship. There are many misconceptions.

People hear about entrepreneurism and think it is for them. They may not do much research or may think there are pots of gold at the end of the rainbow. They talk to other entrepreneurs and learn that it all about perseverance and building sweat-equity in companies.

The wise entrepreneurs have mentors, compensated for their advice, tenured in consulting and wise beyond reproach. Advisers are important to fitting the entrepreneurs to the right niche. Mentors draw out transferrable talents to apply to the appropriate entrepreneurial situation.

The corporate mindset does not necessarily transfer to small business. Just because someone took early retirement is not a reason to go into a startup business. People who worked for other people do not necessarily transfer to the entrepreneurial mode.

Those who have captained teams tend to make better collaborators and members of others' teams. Entrepreneur is as entrepreneur does

Make an equitable blend of ambition and desire: Fine-tuning one's career is an admirable and necessary process. It is quite illuminating. Imagine going back to reflect upon all you were taught. Along the way, you reapply old knowledge, find some new nuggets and create your own philosophies.

We were taught to be our best and have strong ambition to succeed. Unfortunately, we were not taught the best methods of working with others in achieving desired goals. We became a society of highly ambitious achievers without the full roster of resources to facilitate steady success.

Every company must and should put its best face forward for the public. The public perceptions of companies are called "credence goods" by economists. Every organization must educate outside publics about what they do and how they do it. This premise also holds true for each corporate operating unit and department. The whole of the business and each sub-set must always educate corporate opinion makers on how it functions and the skill with which the company operates.

Gaining confidence among stakeholders is crucial. Business relationships with customers, collaborators and other professionals are established to be long-term in duration. Each organization or should determine and craft its own corporate culture, character and personality, seeking to differentiate itself from others.

Every business, company or organization goes through cycles in its life. At any point, each program or business unit is in a different phase from others. The astute organization assesses the status of each program and orients its team members to meet constant changes and fluctuations.

I've talked with many entrepreneurs and founders of companies which rapidly grew from the seed of an idea they had. Most admitted enjoying the founding phase but lost interest shortly after giving birth. Over and over, they said, "When it stops being fun, I move on. "

After the initial honeymoon, you speak with them and hear rumblings like, "It isn't supposed to be this hard. Whatever happened to the old days? I'm ready to move on. This seems too much like running a business. I'm an idea person, and all this administrative stuff is a waste of my time. I should move on to other new projects."

When they come to me, they want the business to transition smoothly and still make the founders some money. They ask, "Are you the one who comes in here and makes this into a real business?" I reply, "No. After the caretakers come in and apply the wrong approaches to making something of your business, I'm the one who cleans up after them and starts the business over again." The reality is that I'm even better on the front end, helping business owners avoid the costly pitfalls attached to their losing interest and abdicating to the wrong people.

Entrepreneurial companies enjoy the early stage of success ... and wish things would stay as in the beginning. When "the fun ends," the hard work begins. There are no fast-forward buttons or skipping steps inn developing an effective organization, just as there are no shortcuts in formulating a career and Body of Work.

Questions to ask entrepreneurs:

1.   Do you have goals for the next year in writing?
2.   Are the long-range strategic planning and budgeting processes integrated?
3.   Are planning activities consolidated into a written organizational plan?
4.   Do you have a written analysis of organizational strengths and weaknesses?
5.   Do you have a detailed, written analysis of your market area?
6.   Do detailed action plans support each major strategy?
7.   Is there a Big Picture?

Chapter 25

THE BOOK OF ACRONYMS: NEW WAYS OF LOOKING AT FAMILIAR WORDS

Re-defining Key Business Terms by What They Potentially Represent

O rganizations are accustomed to looking at concepts and practices one way at a time. Clinging to obsolete definitions and viewpoints have a way of perpetuating companies into downward spirals.

By viewing from others' viewpoints on life, we find real nuggets of gold with which to redefine organizations. Companies that adopt new viewpoints and defy their conventional definitions will create new opportunities, organizational effectiveness, marketplaces and relationships.

As a Big Picture business strategist, I encourage clients toward adopting new ways of thinking about old processes, including those that brought past and enduring successes. Symbolic are these phrase definitions that I have created for familiar business words. I have created new acronyms for well-known business terms, in order to help us visualize opportunities differently.

My acronyms for

BUSINESS:
  Big-picture
  Understanding
  Symbiosis
  In
  Nomenclature,
  Economics,
  Systems, and
  Services

WORK:
  Windows of
  Opportunity,
  Requiring
  Know-how

GOALS:
  Getting
  Organized
  Allowing
  Lifeblood
  Systems

  Growth
  Opportunities
  And
  Legacy
  Support

THINK:
  To
  Have
  Ideas,
  New
  Keys

FAILURE:
  Finding
  Answers
  In
  Life,
  Utilizing
  Retrospective
  Enlightenment

SETBACK:
  See
  Experiences in
  Terms of
  Business
  Accomplishments,
  Commending
  Knowledge

SUCCESS:
  Sophisticated
  Utilizing of
  Conditions,
  Contributions,
  Energies,
  Strengths and
  Synergies

FEAR:
  Find
  Excellence
  After
  Reflection

  Formulating
  Energies
  Actions and
  Responsibilities

TECHNOLOGY:
  Teaching
  Excellence
  Can
  Have
  Numerous
  Outcomes on the
  Life
  Of the
  Global
  You

WEB:
  Worthwhile
  Economical
  Business

E- MAIL:
Enlightening
Marketplaces
And
Initiating
Links

PAST:
Perspectives
And
Systematic
Thoughts

FUTURISM:
Fully
Utilized
Thinking ...
Underscoring
Retrospective
Insights ...
Synergizing
Metholodogies

QUALITY:
Quintessential
Understanding of
Actions,
Linkages, and
Information
Taught to
You

AWARD:
Amazing
Wins
Are
Really
Deserved

PLANNING:
Process to
Learn
Alternatives,
Narratives,
Notations, and
Insights
Necessary for
Growth

TEAM:
Training and
Education ...
Always
Meaningful

VISION:
Valuable
Intelligence
Search
In
Organizational
Networks

Viewing
Ideas,
Systems,
Insights and
Occasional
Newness

STAR:
Super
Talent,
Acting
Responsibly

DECISION:
Duty for
Executives to
Communicate
Issues,
Symbolisms, and
Important
Organizational
Necessities

SPEECH:
Sophisticated
Presentation
Equates
Enlightenment,
Communication and
Harmony

ETHICS:
Enlightened
Thinking …
Holding
Ideologies,
Commitments,
Sensitivities

The purpose of any business is not just to make money. It is to be JUST:
- Committed to their customers.
- Respectful of their employees.
- Successful enough for the company to grow, pay its dues and continue growing.
- Upholding standards of quality and commitment.
- Focused through everything else we back to our customers.

Too often, one hears about what goes wrong in business relationships. From our viewpoint, if business is conducted honorably and professionally, then profitability and success flow from doing the right things, not from pursuing false goals.

The best successes are earned and learned. We should not take good fortune for granted. Business track records are earned by going the distance, reading the trends and continually changing.

As the years go by, one continues paying dues. Learning, experiencing and evaluating is the best process to achieve lasting success. The best dues yield nuggets of wisdom that couldn't have been earned any other way.

The smartest person is the one who knows what he-she does not know. With maturity comes the quest to learn more, understand the factors and apply newly acquired insights to higher purposes. The person who commits to a path of professional development never stops achieving … and profitably impacts his-her business relationships.

Language is food for the mind. Browse a dictionary, and you create new ideas. Words are fun and connect your business to tomorrow. Technology cannot take the place of human communication … only may add to it. Every opportunity should be taken to enhance literacy skills of employees and entire organization. The language of success is initially found in a dictionary.

My acronyms for

EDUCATION:
Standpoint of Students:
  Earning
  Distinction
  Usually
  Capitalizes
  After
  Training and
  Instruction
  Optimize
  Net-rewards

Standpoint of Teachers:
  Each
  Day
  Unleash
  Creativity
  After
  Teaching and
  Inspiration
  Occur
  Noticeably

MUSIC:
  Masterfully
  Utilizing
  Symbiosis,
  Imagination and
  Congruence

HEALTH:
  Honoring
  Excellence
  Allows
  Leadership
  Toward
  Humanity

IDEAS:
  Individualized
  Dimensions,
  Expectations,
  Analyses,
  Scenarios

FINANCE:
  Formulating
  Information,
  Notations
  And
  Newly
  Changing
  Efficiencies

RESEARCH:
  Reasoned
  Enlightenment,
  Seeking
  Education
  And
  Responsibly
  Connecting
  Hypotheses

TRUTH:
  Teach
  Realities
  Uniformly
  Through
  Harmony

COMMUNITY:
  Citizens
  Offering
  Missions,
  Metholodologies,
  Unification,
  Needs and
  Interconnections
  To
  You

MEETING:
Minds
Exercising
Effectiveness
Through
Ideas,
Negotiating
Goals

MONEY:
Mounting
Organizational
Necessities
Equal
Yields

BROKER:
Business
Resource for
Opportunities and
Keywords for
Economic
Rewards

SELL:
Skillfully
Explaining,
Linking
Language

Seeking
Enlightenment ...
Listening and
Learning

CHANGE:
Continually
Having
A
Natural
Guidepost
Effect

DIVERSITY:
Different
Ideas,
Visions,
Energies,
Realities,
Symbolisms and
Insights
Throughout
Yourself

ADVISOR:
A
Dedicated
Visionary
Inspires
Sophisticated
Organizational
Realities

LEARNING:
Legacy
Encompasses
All
Resource
Narratives ...
Introducing
Noticeable
Galvanization

KNOWLEDGE:
Kaleidoscopic
Nucleus
Of
Weighed
Learning ...
Embracing
Development,
Growth and
Effervescence

WISDOM:
We
Influence
Society
Due to
Our
Mastery

REWARDS:
Reap
Expectations
With
A
Resilient,
Durable
System

RESPECT:
Responsibilities
Epitomize
Sophisticated
Perspectives,
Earning
Commensurate
Truths

TRAINING:
Teaching
Radiant
And
Innovative
Nourishment
Inspires
Natural
Growth

LISTEN:
Language
In
Studying
The
Evident
Networks

PROBLEM:
Polarizing
Routine
Obstacles
By
Letting
Elegance
Materialize

SERVICE:
Securing
Excellence
Requires
Visualizing
Innovative
Customer
Effectiveness

PROGRESS:
Pursuing
Royal
Objective
Gages ...
Rewarding
Empowered
Super
Service

FORTUNE:
Future
Operations
Require
Teams
Understanding
Needs and
Expectations

INNOVATE:
Imagining
Niches and
Norms,
Optimizing
Valuable
Alliances,
Training and
Experiences

Every business, company or organization goes through cycles in its evolution. At any point, each program or business unit is in a different phase from others. The astute organization assesses the status of each branch on its **Business Tree™** and orients its management and team members to meet constant changes and fluctuations. Going "outside the box" to shift perceptions enables any company to think, plan and operate in productive new ways.

Characteristics of Creative Business Definitions, Company Philosophy
- Focus upon the customer.
- Honor the employees.
- Show business life as a continuous quality process (not a quick fix or rapid gain).
- Portray their company as a contributor (not a savior).
- Clearly define their niche (not trying to be all things).
- Say things that inspire you to think.
- Compatible with other company activities and behaviors.
- Remain consistent with their products, services and track record.

Acronyms Often Used

AM-FM	Amplitude Modulation—Frequency Modulation
AQS	Advanced Quality System
ATM	Automated Teller Machine, Asynchronous Transfer Mode
BASF	Baden Aniline and Soda Factory
BCR	Bar Code Reader
BLOB	Binary Large Object
BMW	Bavarian Motor Works
B2B	Business to Business
BVD	Bradley, Voorhies and Day
CAD	Computer Aided Design
CARE	Cooperative for Assistance and Relief Everywhere
CAT (scan)	Computerized Axial Tomography
CD	Compact Disc

COBOL	Common Business-Oriented Language
CONELRAD	Control of Electronic-magnetic Radiations
CRM	Customer Relationship Management
CVS	Customer Value Stores
DES	Data Encryption Standard
DNR	Do Not Resuscitate
DSL	Digital Subscriber Line
DVD	Digital Versatile Disc
EBAY	Echo Bay Trading Group
EBITDA	Earning Before Interests, Taxes, Depreciation and Amortization
EOD	End of Day, End of Discussion
EOT	End of Transmission
EPCOT	Experimental Prototype Community of Tomorrow
ESOP	Employee Stock Ownership Plan
ESSO	Standard Oil (Rockefeller-owned oil company, now Exxon)
ETA	Estimated Time of Arrival
FDIC	Federal Deposit Insurance Corporation
4G	Fourth Generation Mobile Telephone System
4-H	Head, Heart, Hands and Health
FUBAR	"Fouled" Up Beyond All Recognition
FYI	For Your Information
GAF	General Aniline and Film
GESTAPO	Geheime Staatspolizei (Lit. secret state police)
GIGO	Garbage In, Garbage Out
HTML	Hyper Text Mark-up Language
HTTP	Hyper Text Transfer Protocol
IBM	International Business Machines
INTEL	Integrated Electronics
IP	Internet Protocol

ISO	International Standards Organization
ISP	Internet Service Provider
JEEP	General Purpose Vehicle
JPEG	Joint Photographic Experts Group
JVC	Japan Victor Company
KGB	Komitet Gosudarstvennoy Bezopasnosti (Lit. Committee of State Security)
KLM	Koninklijke Luchtvaart Maatschappij (Lit. Royal Dutch Airline)
KPI	Key Performance Indicators
KRA	Key Results Area
LASER	Light Amplification by Stimulated Emission of Radiation
M&M	Mars & Murray
MG	Morris Garages
MGM	Metro, Goldwyn & Mayer (movie studio)
MO	Modus Operandi
MRI	Magnetic Resonance Imaging
MSRP	Manufacturer's Suggested Retail Price
NASCAR	National Association for Stock Car Racing
NIMBY	Not In My Back Yard
NOI	Net Operating Income
OTC	Over the Counter
PDF	Portable Document Format
POP	Point of Presence
POTS	Plain Old Telephone Service (basic service by local exchange telephone companies)
PSI	Pounds Per Square Inch
QANTAS	Queensland And Northern Territory Aerial Service
QED	Quod Erat Demonstrandum (Lit. Which was to be demonstrated)
QVC	Quality, Value and Convenience

RBI	Runs Batted In (baseball)
R&D	Research and Development
RFD	Rural-Free Delivery
RH	Rhesus Monkey Factor
RKO	Radio-Keith-Orpheum (movie studio)
ROI	Return on Investment
ROM	Read Only Memory
ROTC	Reserve Officers Training Corps
RSVP	Respondez S'il Vous Plait
SAAB	Svenska Aeroplan Ab. (Lit. Swedish Airplanes, Inc.)
SARS	Severe Acute Respiratory Syndrome
SCSI	Small Computer Serial Interface
SCUBA	Self Contained Underwater Breathing Apparatus
SEGA	Service Games of Japan
SEO	Search Engine Optimization
SHAZAM	From the names, Solomon, Hercules, Atlas, Zeus, Achilles and Mercury
SOWETCO	Southwest Township
STP	Scientifically Treated Petroleum, Standard Temperature and Pressure, Spanning Tree Protocol
SWAT	Special Weapons And Tactics
3M	Minnesota Mining & Manufacturing Co., Man, Machine, Material
TIFF	Tagged Image File Format
TNT	TriNitroToluene
UNICEF	United Nations International Children's Emergency Fund
USB	Universal Serial Bus
VHS	Video Home System
VLAS	Virtual Local Area Network
WC	Water Closet
WD-40	Water Displacement, Formula 40

WPA	Wi-Fi Protected Access
WWW	World Wide Web
YKK	Yoshida Kogyo Kabushiki Kaisha (Zipper Company)
ZIP Code	Zone Improvement Plan

Chapter 26

CUSTOMER SERVICE,
HOLD ON TO WHAT YOU'VE GOT

The Biggest Customer Service Mistakes that Damage and Lose Business

E veryone with whom you do business is a customer or referral source of someone else. The service that we get from some people, we pass along to others. Customer service is a continuum of human behaviors, shared with those whom we meet.

Customers are the lifeblood of every business. Employees depend upon customers for their paychecks. Yet, you wouldn't know the correlation when poor customer service is rendered. Employees of companies behave as though customers are a bother, do not heed their concerns and do not take suggestions for improvement.

There is no business that cannot improve its customer service. Every organization has customers, clients, stakeholders, financiers, volunteers, supporters or other categories of "affected constituency."

Every employee is a customer of someone else's company. Theoretically, being the recipient of bad service inspires us to do better for our customers. The more that one sees poor customer service and customer neglect in other companies, we avoid the pitfalls and traps in our own companies. Unfortunately, it doesn't work out that way.

Customer service begins and ends at top management. If management is complacent or non-participatory, then the same philosophy is held by employees who make products or render services.

If management insists upon Continuous Quality Improvement and demonstrates by its own actions, then service continually improves. All involved benefit from sensitivity toward customer needs, interests and concerns.

7 Reasons Why Nice People Don't Get Good Customer Service

1. Basic Knowledge of Good Service. Don't ask for it. Too naive toward flaws in the service provider's organization. Don't know alternatives to request or demand.
2. Don't Realize Own Buying Power. Not aware of customer status. Allow vendors to set the terms. Knuckle under to companies' promises, half-truths and lies.
3. Limited Exposure to Excellence. Don't know what is considered Excellence in service. Don't demand excellence. May not really want-desire excellence.
4. Buy the Company's Hype. Believe that because they are high-profile, they are a good company. Falsely equate marketing to goodwill or standards of quality.
5. Indifference. Too shy or lazy to stand their ground for custom rights. Don't bother to state their case or set boundaries. Settle for mediocrity because not up to demanding quality.
6. Continue Being Nice About It. Not willing to write letters, speak to supervisors or make demands. Prefer to play the martyr but not assert own position over vendors.
7. Continue to Accept Less Than the Best. Let problems continue without correction. Get upset but do not let people in authority know. Continue

going back to where shabby treatment was experienced. Rationalize the companies' mistakes away for them.

7 Ways to Lose Business, the Biggest Customer Service Mistakes Made

1. Forgetting Why You Are in Business. Failure to keep a clear focus upon the product, its marketplace, its customers and people who influence your company's ultimate success. Thinking too limited, applying "band aid surgery" and pursuing activity without a cohesive plan.

2. Failure to Retain Customers. Figuring that lost customers are easily replaceable. Retaining 2% more customers has the same effect upon the bottom line as cutting costs by 10%. A longtime customer is 2-3 times more profitable for the business than a recently added customer. Longtime customers make referrals, which reduce the company's marketing costs. Dissatisfied customers will tell 10-20 other people. Thus, the successful business must put the customer into a co-destiny relationship. Customers want to build relationships, and it is the obligation of the business to prove that it is worthy.

3. Deceiving the Customer. Failure to deliver what was promised. Bait and switch advertising. Failure to handle mistakes and complaints in a timely, equitable and customer-friendly manner. Unexpected or unauthorized charges. When the bill is substantially more than was quoted.

4. Order-Taking Mentality. When the person taking the order delegates to others to fulfill in his-her absence. Fill-in people rarely deliver as though their livelihood depended upon it.

5. Lack of Service Orientation. Don't post a CSI rating unless you and every member of your team really know what it means. There must be a commitment to maintain it. Consumer complaints must launch a genuine action to improve. To avoid customer concerns and do business as usual is a mockery of the quality process. Such a company does not have the right to flaunt its perceived CSI rating any longer.

6. Poorly Trained Employees. Employees mirror management's philosophy. If they're only concerned with the cash register ringing, without giving any more, than they do not have a right to keep customers or stay in

business. Workers in companies think and behave as though customers are necessary evils and tolerate them. This mindset kills any Vision or Big Picture thinking that company founders have built, as well as marketplace goodwill.

7. Lack of Participation by Management. If problems are handled through form letters, subordinates or ignored, then management is the real cause of the problem. Management must speak personally with customers, to achieve understanding and set a good example for employees.

Typical Excuses Given for Poor Customer Service

They always want to make themselves right and the customer wrong. To them, customers are a pain in the neck. You're supposed to understand their position and stop complaining.

Some of the worst rationalizations by service personnel:

- Don't blame me. I'm just doing what I was told.
- I'm not doing anything wrong.
- What's your problem?
- It's our policy to _____.
- Things are tough enough today. Like I really needed your problems.
- Come back another day. Things will be better.
- That's not my job. This isn't my work station. Wait until your assigned server gets here. This isn't my regular job. I'm just filling in. Those are the rules.
- What do you say when people gripe to you all day?
- Please understand that we have had a lot to do lately.
- That's the way it is.
- If you don't like it, then take your business elsewhere.
- Customers like you think you own the place. Where do you get off?
- I don't work for you. I work for the company.
- My boss is satisfied by the job I do.
- Looks like you woke up on the wrong side of the bed today.
- There is nothing wrong with our company. So, what's your problem?
- We're very busy at this time of year.
- We sell the best products at the best prices. That should speak for itself.

Even worse—setting the tone for bad service—are excuses voiced by their supervisors:

- We're very busy and understaffed right now. You must understand.
- I'm sorry that you feel that way. But, that's the way it is.
- I'm management, and our customer service people have the ability to behave as they wish. Not everything is the way that I would like it to be.
- What right do you have to complain? What are your credentials to judge the quality of service?
- The boss doesn't give us enough resources. We're doing the best we can.
- We always give quality service. I cannot understand why you feel otherwise.
- He's so good in other areas. I cannot change his behavior just because you say so.
- I have to work with him and cannot upset the boat. I will not say anything to him about this.
- He refers us so much business. He cannot be all that bad.
- That's management's policy, not mine.
- Why don't you go back to the clerk and settle your grievance.
- I understand that you have a problem.
- We're Number One in sales. We must be doing something right.
- Our customer service department handles all problems. See them.
- We're operating according to company policies and procedures.

7 Cardinal Rules of Customer Service

1. It is Politically Incorrect to Make the Customer Wrong. Service personnel cannot appear "right" at the customer's expense. They are there to serve and, more importantly, to collaborate in the customer's satisfaction.
2. Everyone Makes Mistakes. The mark of Quality is how you handle them. Learn the art of diagnosing problems, taking customer input and effecting workable solutions.
3. Sales and Service Are Not the Same Package. People with sales expertise must develop customer service orientation. Know the difference, and train on both.
4. Businesses Live or Die By the Customers. If you think otherwise, you do not have the right to remain in business.

5. Attitude Affects Everything in Business. Customers and other stakeholders know when it is sincere. They support a company that tries harder and resent one that does not.

6. Service is Nurtured, Not Edicted. It doesn't just happen. Good customer service is the end product of experience and training. Employees must want to participate and continually improve. Consistency, resources and support assure the company's success.

7. Corporate Arrogance is Unacceptable. Management has the obligation and responsibility to see and deal with things as they are, not as they would like them to be. Otherwise, they are fooling themselves and letting customers and the entire organization down.

Or Else, Tally the Damages and Lose Customers

Heed these business truisms:

- Having annual sales projections does not substitute a customer service program.
- Training for employees is not a panacea for necessary long-term strategic planning.
- Having a bottom-line-only mentality.
- Squeezing every extra dollar, as if it's your God-given right to pursue greed.
- Failure to really listen to customers.
- Inability to read and hear between the lines.
- Condescension toward customers.
- Sloppy administrative handling of customer paperwork.
- Failure to initiate communications with the customer.
- Keeping the customer waiting unnecessarily.
- Giving the customer unsatisfactory explanations for things not done in a timely manner.
- When the customer has to prod your company to get action.
- Lying to the customer.
- Making the customer wrong.
- Never giving the customer anything value-added.
- Management pays lip service to quality but does not "walk the talk."

- Company vision is not fully articulated, nor communicated and understood by all within the organization.
- Employees do not have a clue about the subtleties and sophistications of life, especially when their customer base is upscale.
- Taking inappropriate actions to repair the damage.
- Getting advice from the wrong consultants.

Major concerns which every company must address to improve customer service:

- Hold On to What You've Got, what you think you've got and what you've actually got. Understanding what the marketplace thinks you've got, in relation to customer needs.
- Keeping What You've Earned, what you think you've earned and what you've actually earned.
- Comprehending How Companies Lose Their Business.
- Asking Yourself, "When is Enough Growth Really Enough?"
- Unmanaged Growth is Not Good Growth.
- Learning What it Takes to Really Stay in Business.
- Excellence and Partnering with the Customer ("Potlache," a Step Beyond Value-Added).

Chapter 27

NETWORKING

A Primer in Relationship Building and Resource Allocation

T his chapter has taken 100,000 hours of my life to write. From wasted and mis-spent time come perspective and wisdom.

Networking can be and should be a wonderful thing. In theory, you meet people, share ideas and grow richer for the experience. Indirectly, it enhances the climate in which business is done. Ostensibly, all participants benefit from the synergy.

If one is growing from networking and all parties benefit, it works well. Unfortunately, one can get caught in a trap of being on the short end of the equation. One can wake up, realize their energy has been zapped and experience setbacks in their business because he-she was spending disproportionate time on networking.

These pointers are offered to help manage time and resources. Business organizations are like trees. They seemingly look the same from day to day and will live forever. To the untrained eye, most resemble each other. After all, they are just trees (companies)!

This essay is not to discourage networking. Instead, it stimulates questions about your own wants, desires, experiences, gains, losses and changing perspectives in the game of "give and take."

By curbing old behavior patterns, you may feel less-used and get more out of future networking. By analyzing the true motives for networking (yours and other people's), one can avoid hurt feelings and letdowns. By approaching the process with a realistic attitude, positive outcomes of future efforts will pay better dividends.

Categories of Networking

Professional Networkers. For some people, it is their job to network, on behalf of their companies. They are given salaries, expense accounts, support staff and a company machine which sees business development and lobbying value in their work. These people jockey for favor with the power structures and are accorded community standing based upon the reputation-value of their company. People defer to them because of the wealth of their companies. They regularly squire stakeholders to charity events at corporate-purchased tables. None of their community stewardship comes out of their own pockets. Some of these people get the "big head" and think of themselves as local celebrities. They get a rude awakening when they leave their job.

Hobbyist Networkers. These people want to get involved, partly for business and partly to interface with the community. When they network, it means dollars, resources and time out of their own pockets. They exchange ideas, swap cards, engage in base-level volunteer work and participate in several concurrent networks. They are also valued according to the reputation of their companies, directly commensurate to how much money they give to charities and business organizations. In-kind donations (especially their time) are not valued as highly as money. It is unfair to stack them against professional networkers, but the community does. Since many are small business people, solo practitioners, sales force members and entrepreneurs, they make great sacrifices to network, usually much more than the payoff.

Niche Networkers. These people may have started with the shotgun effect but have narrowed down. They network through trade associations, chambers of commerce, leads groups, conventions and other sources which are primarily devoted to business. They staff committees and events, hoping to generate more leads. The longer they network, the better they get at niche marketing. They learn that one cannot be all things to all people.

Social Networkers. Business networking receptions became the "singles bars" of the 1980s and 1990s. Breakfast clubs carved their own niche, a balance of business, community and social networking. The same holds true with the "rubber chicken circuit" (clubs, associations and coalitions of networking groups). Just like the 1970s nightclub scene, people went into situations indiscriminately looking. They wanted to get something but were not quite sure what. Some really believed a chance meeting in a bar would produce Mr. or Ms. Right. They came out unfulfilled because they didn't really have clear objectives going in. The same is true with networking. The ideal customer doesn't "discover you" across a crowded room.

Wanna-Be Networkers. These people try to network anywhere and everywhere. They are in your face, at every turn. Their sense of accomplishment is in the quantity of business cards collected, lunches arranged and referral calls generated-completed. They network for the sake of networking, rarely with targeted purpose. Their opening line is: "What do you do?" Sizing you in terms of immediate benefit to them, they either probe further or move on. Usually, they are selling something and focus upon one of the niches listed above.

The Kind of Networking That Doesn't Really Exist. This is the category where we seniors ache to have exist. Sadly, it doesn't. Senior executives do not really have networks of our own. Our junior staff members populate the trade associations, chambers of commerce and service organizations. Top executives isolate themselves from people with differing opinions. They say they crave roundtables with fellow seasoned executives but rarely attend. Inevitably, when high-level forums are organized, the juniors, mid-managers and self-marketers infiltrate and take over ... which chases us away. Veteran executives meet on the charity party circuit, in board meetings and sometimes socially. Some commercial programs cater to this market but are usually populated by entrepreneurs on the way up. In the main, the top corporate strata is without an effective mechanism to network, share high-level ideas-experiences, get stimulated to overcome burnout and move toward higher plateaus. That's why many senior business leaders wear down or retire earlier than they should.

Red Flags in the Network

I Knew You When. They see you as they once did. They connect with the old commonalities and find it hard to see the evolution that you have made. Try to enlighten them, and they convert it all back to their old frame of reference, with questions like "Do you still talk to X?" or "Whatever happened to Y?" or "Remember the time when Z happened?"

Gurus of Networking. These are often the worst violators of the process. They want you to be there for them and those whom they refer to you. Yet, try to get something meaningful out of them. When you set boundaries to your free access, they cut you out of their network. That's not entirely bad, since you were likely peripheral to it in the first place.

Who Do You Know Who … In networking, the person who wants something stands three or four steps away from their ultimate target. As a member of the network, you are usually one of several conduits in their quest. It's tough to not be consulted as an expert, but rather as a step on someone else's journey.

You Once Did ___. Now I Want ___. Just because you once spoke to their business club, attended a workshop with them or served on a volunteer committee, they keep coming back to you for free work. To them, there is no statute of limitations on free access to your time, influence, resources or abilities.

X Says I Can Pick Your Brain. X probably gave your name to get rid of them. X doesn't really value your time or would have asked in advance if you could be periodically referred. Try referring callers back to X as really being the "best person" for them to consult. Tell them that X is far too modest and is your expert in that area. That will stop X from referring unsolicited nuisance callers.

If You ___, It Will Lead to Business. They always say that so you will volunteer to help their pet cause or serve their momentary need. People wave any carrot that will help to get what they want, think they need or wish they had. Entrepreneurs and service providers are easy targets to entice with the promise or glimmer of future business. Tell the networker that you will do what they ask … but only in reciprocation after the business transpires. Request a "show of good faith" gesture from them in the first place.

Adopt My Interests. It'll Be Good for You. This is the previous ploy with a new coat of paint. These people couch their requests in terms of your benefit. They just know that supporting their interests will get you somewhere and quickly add that it will be fun, as well. Don't be fooled. The same requests go out to all whom they approach.

Feeding Egos in Hopes of Getting Somewhere. Many people do things to get noticed by others, in hopes they can do something for us. So, we serve on their volunteer committees, convinced they will think well of us ... enough to speak well of us to still others. The problem is "they" want to be noticed by others and only want committee members to support their agenda. You will likely be perceived as a conduit or support mechanism to their causes and objectives.

Circuitous Routes to Get What You Think You Want. Many of us do things for reasons for which we are not quite sure. Spending time networking or volunteering for projects seems like a good idea at the time. Surely benefits will accrue. I'm not saying that people should create agendas for every act or action. However, one must recognize and curb patterns of doing things for nebulous reasons, from which nebulous outcomes always emanate.

Have You Got a Card? That means they will be calling you for their own networking purposes. If you don't want to get their calls, either say you are out of cards or tell them the truth ... that you're trying to cut down on networking activity. They'll move on to someone else. Most of the time, they're not after you. Any warm body will do. Being completely upfront about setting your boundaries helps you feel better and deters future unsolicited calls.

Hard Core Clueless. Some people simply don't know or care where you're coming from. They are self-serving networkers and offer nothing for you. There is no converting them to your more enlightened way of thinking and operating. Spot them and avoid them.

People Who Refer You for Freebies But Not for Business

I once agreed to meet to discuss serving on a non-profit board with an influential business executive, whose account I sought for my company. He had been using a pale-by-comparison, low-expertise competitor, and I thought he surely would want to grade up to the best. By knowing and working with me, he would discern excellence, switch his business to my company and be better off for it.

In the get-acquainted meeting, the executive explained that he did not mix business with volunteer work. He stated that I was a good person to serve on the board and give away my time, yet the incumbent agency had his business. That was his belief, and he wouldn't change it. Curiously, his own business was predicated upon community goodwill, and he owed his fortune to the public appearance of being a good citizen.

So why, then, should I waste my time serving on his board? He started dangling carrots of potential business from other board members. I fell for the bait and regretted it after the first board meeting. Other members had like minds to the executive who recruited me. They had their network of business resources and referrals, and I was not part of it.

I gracefully bowed out, citing the press of business and over-commitment to other volunteer work. The board member took it as a slap in the face, proclaiming that we would never get any work from him. After all, it was my job to curry community favor. How dare I meet to consider volunteering and then pull out? He found other warm bodies. Curiously, that charity has been clouded by public investigations of questionable ethics and dubious fund-raising practices. I sensed that at the time., which was the other reason why I walked away.

Lesson Learned: Set boundaries up front. Tell them that you only volunteer on committees of people who have the willingness and actually do business with each other, if that's your objective for participating. Let it be known that your volunteer time is a reward to those who support your company … not a prerequisite to being considered. Remind inquirers that you must be successful in your business first … in order to be in a position to give back to the community.

They Don't Care What You Think. Just Do What They Want

Public officials are notorious for this. They make it clear that you are important to them. Once you give a contribution or volunteer time to their initial campaign, you are pigeon-holed on the solicitation mailing list. Then, it is hard to convert to another level in their minds.

Public officials spend your contributions hiring young, inexperienced staff members and rely upon them for advice. They pay great sums to so-called "political consultants" but will not consider asking CEOs and seasoned business executives for meaningful policy advice. And the consultants with whom they contract are usually out-of-towners or those who have not "paid their dues" to the community.

Try offering your advice-counsel, and it falls on deaf ears. Try to get them to open doors or somehow return the favors. You'll quickly see how they aren't available, forgot that they owed you a return courtesy and resent being asked for "quid pro quo." Only money or volunteer time are wanted, thank you. Even though they decline or avoid you, the fund raiser invitations keep coming in the mail.

Lesson Learned: Set boundaries up front. Tell political candidates how you expect and are willing to be utilized. Give expertise on the front end, not money. If you want to be their advisor, tell them so. Don't expect them to read your mind, after the fact.

Caring When Others Don't

Some people will always go the extra distance for their organizations. They are consummate professionals and give their all to the company. They pursue professional development on their own time, bear personal monies to further the job, participate in community and volunteer activities and serve on committees. They have perfect attendance, rarely use all vacation days and don't know what a coffee break is.

Yet, many of their colleagues do the bare minimum to get by. These people learned the Peter Principle and enjoy the same pay and benefits as those who knock themselves out. And they always take more days off. The system allows them to continue, without accountability or the stimulation to try harder.

The active few say they are setting an example by which others will follow. Who? When? Why should the non-involved join the active few, at this late date?

Those of us who have been the "active few" in our organizations did not understand why the "non-active many" did not behave accordingly. We sometimes begrudged the others for not doing their share. Yet, we kept on being active … as if it were a mission to the death.

Lesson Learned: Understand your true motives for going the distance. If you're really doing it for your own enjoyment and fulfillment, you're rare. Realities dictate that we all do some things for the good of the company, the job, the community and others. Keep it in balance. Don't cheat yourself because you are spending energies on the "non-active many," mostly people who could care less.

How Quickly They Forget

Some people are creative and innovative. They craft concepts and then turn them over to others to implement or perpetuate. Recipients of other people's achievements will try to mold them as their own, injecting their touch. Often, it's not as good as the original creation. The more that people tinker with the concept, it gets watered down. Egos of the latters won't allow them to consult or involve the originator. In time, the latters will claim it as their brainchild and will not acknowledge the innovator.

I recall creating at least 30 such concepts that took circuitous and downward paths after turning them over to others. Sometimes, my only involvement was destined to be on the front end … giving concepts to fresh faces, with the chance to blossom and grow. Sometimes, the recipient organizations were so ungrateful for the innovation or clueless as to its value that I backed away. Sometimes, the concepts were only meant as one-time projects or to have short-term lives, though others chose to milk a good thing beyond its effectiveness.

It's tough to create and watch others butcher your idea. That makes it hard to market the concept as your creation.

Lesson Learned: If you are creating ideas and projects and intend to use them as case studies and for business development, get written documentation from authoritative people concerning your creation. Ask for thank-you letters and send to others who will influence the benefits you seek to reap. Apply for awards, where appropriate. Be recognized at their board meetings and other public forums. A pat on the back or congratulations after an event can be quickly rescinded, when they choose to forget your contributions. Get documentation in writing, asking them to acknowledge what you did, how you did it and the long-term implications for what you created.

Cut the Weeds. Focus on Priorities and Strategy. Avoid the Time Zappers.

One of the by-products of being high-profile is that you get hangers-on. Most mean well and want to associate with someone successful. Some are groupies, and some are outright users. The art is to discern and marginalize the weeds from your path.

One mean-weller kept hounding me. He wanted to introduce me to people to form "strategic partnerships." Turns out that they were people with their hands out, thinking that somebody (anybody) could magically open doors for them. I tried to set boundaries with that person. He would not respect perimeters.

One of his "strategic partners" called me and conferenced in the introducer. This was not a scheduled conference call, and I felt blind-sighted. Neither one asked if this was a good time to talk or apologized for calling with no warning. In a rapid-fire sales delivery, he proceeded to talk, starting out selling stock in a venture, then shifting from one idea to the next. I patiently listened and tried to get away. This person had already called me weeks before but could not remember who I was or what I was all about. This was a "dial and smile" sales call, and it was one-sided and self-focused, all about him.

The caller then announced that he had a time commitment and that I had one minute to state my case. I explained that they had called me and that I could not tell my "story" in one minute. I said that if he did not remember talking to me before, then that was the problem. He challenged that it was my obligation to "make a difference," defined as me giving time and money to his pet causes. I suggested that they turn their attentions elsewhere. The caller then got hyper and talked all over me. I stated that I wasn't interested in his projects and needed to end the call.

People who hound and use you in business are out for whatever they can get, from whomever they can get it. If you resist, they will go on to the next warm body. This is why I have a problem with networking: some are users and others are used by them, while others don't know what they are doing.

One must be resolute in protecting their most valuable and limited commodities: time, knowledge and resources. Weeds are everywhere, crying "gimme." One can never cut all of the weeds down because they re-grow elsewhere. I've learned the hard way the value of prioritizing time and focusing on the people and projects that matter.

Cut the weeds by seeing your time for networking and volunteering as a commodity. Budget it each year. Examine and benchmark the reasons and results. Set boundaries, and offer your time on an "a la carte" basis. Associate with those who feel similarly. Show and demonstrate respect for each other's time. Be careful not to pro-bono yourself to death.

Questions to Ask About Networking:

- Is the person making the request a true friend, a business associate or just an acquaintance? Who are they to you, and what would you like for them to be?
- Will there be outcomes or paybacks for the other person? Will there be outcomes or paybacks for you? If there's a discrepancy in these answers, how do you feel about it?
- Are there networking situations which are beneficial for all parties? If so, analyze them, so that you can align with those situations, rather than the fruitless ones?
- What types of "wild goose chases" have you pursued in your networking career? Analyze them by category, to see patterns.
- Is the person requesting something of you willing to offer something first?
- Are the people truly communicating when they network? Or, are hidden agendas the reason for networking? Without communicating wants, it is tough to achieve outcomes.
- How much time away from business can you take? How does it compare with the business you can or will generate?

Concluding Thoughts on Networking:

- Networking is a Two-Way Proposition.
- Associate with those who feel similarly.
- Show and Demonstrate Respect for Each Other's Time.
- Be Careful Not to Pro-Bono Yourself to Death.
- Budget Your Networking Time. See your time for networking and volunteering as a commodity. Budget it each year. Examine and benchmark the reasons and results.
- Set boundaries, and offer your time on an "a la carte" basis.

Chapter 28

DOING YOUR BEST WORK ON DEADLINES

Mobilizing the Energy for Best Business Success

W e recently had some live TV musical play extravaganza on television after a 50-year hiatus. The production was "The Sound of Music," starring Carrie Underwood. This TV special got a lot of attention because it was unique live, just like opening night of the Broadway show on which it was based. This inspired an annual live Broadway revival on NBC-TV in early December each year: "Peter Pan," "The Wiz," "Hairspray," "Jesus Christ, Superstar" and "Bye, Bye, Birdie."

Truth is that throughout the 1950s (the Golden Age of Television), there were comparable live TV extravaganzas on the air every night of the decade.

Many of them were consistently great. They were live, in real time. They had top talent behind them. They were well rehearsed. They had the adrenaline of "going live," and they shined with luster.

Among those crown jewel TV moments were:

- "Our Town," starring Frank Sinatra, Paul Newman and Eva Marie Saint.
- "Requiem for a Heavyweight," the premiere of "Playhouse 90." It was written by Rod Sterling and starred Jack Palance and Ed Wynn.
- "The Petrified Forest," starring Humphrey Bogart, Lauren Bacall and Henry Fonda. In it, Bogey reprised the 1930's Broadway hit and movie that launched his career.
- "The Ford 50th Anniversary," a two-hour musical starring Ethel Merman and Mary Martin. This was the first TV special and set the tone for thousands of others since.
- The first Beatles appearance on the "Ed Sullivan Show," where the whole world was watching. The Beatles topped that by composing "All You Need is Love" while they performed it on a global telecast.

I have those any other live TV gems on DVD. I watch them to experience the magical energy of live performances.

Many of us remember writing the college theme paper the night before it was due. We recall compiling the case notes or sales projections just before the presentation meeting.

The truth is that we do some of our best work under pressure. We might think that the chaos and delays of life are always with us, but we handle them better when on tight time frames.

Before you know it, you're on deadline again. Even though the tasks mount up, you have a knack for performing magnificently under deadline, stress and high expectations.

This is not meant to suggest putting off sequential steps and daily tasks. Learn when deadline crunch time is best to accomplish the optimum business objectives.

I'm a big advocate of Strategic Planning and Visioning. Every company needs it but rarely conducts the process because they're knee-deep in daily minutia.

I know from experience that planning while going through the "alligators" is the most effective way to conduct the process. By seeing the daily changes resulting from the planning, companies are poised to rise above the current daily crises. I recommend that diversity audits, quality control reviews, ethics programs and other important regimen be conducted as part of Strategic Planning, rather than as stand-alone, distracting and energy diverting activities.

Those of us who grew up working on typewriters know how to master the medium. You had to get your ideas on paper correctly the first time, without typographical errors and with great clarity. The first time that I worked on a computer was when I was 40 years old. I took that typewriter mentality with me when I had to compose a brochure and do the desktop publishing graphics in the same two-hour window where I was learning how to work on a computer.

There were years where I kept the typewriter on the work station next to the computer. When I had five minutes to write a cohesive memo and fax it off to the client, I wrote it on the typewriter. Though I wrote all my books on computers, I wrote the modern technology chapters on the typewriter, to make points to myself that the readers could never have grasped.

In mounting your next strategic Planning process for your company, go back and analyze what elements from the past can be rejuvenated as your future. That's a trademarked concept that I call Yesterdayism.

With planning and organizing, you can meet and beat most deadlines without working in a pressure cooker. Don't work and worry yourself into exhaustion over every detail. Sometimes it makes sense to move the deadline to the 11th hour. Having too much time to get projects accomplished tends to breed procrastination.

Here are my final take-aways on the subject of doing your best work when on last-minute deadlines:

- Learn what working style goes best with you.
- Care about deadlines.
- Prioritize the real deadlines, apart from the artificial or self-imposed ones.
- Review the work that you've done on tight deadlines. Analyze what makes it different.
- Know your own strengths and limitations.
- Work on your own timetable.
- When working with teams, determine the best compromise working tempo.
- Get your "to do lists" in order.
- Evaluate your progress.
- Remove the distractions to doing your best-focused work.
- Ready…Set…Be productive.

This chapter was written in one hour, at 11:00 p.m. on a Saturday night, just before the impending deadline to turn in the manuscript for this book.

Chapter 29

100 WAYS TO MASTER THE BIG PICTURE

L ooking holistically at the organization, then down to each part as a contributing factor to the Big Picture and again back to the larger scope is our recommendation for running creative, effective and profitable companies.

Alas, the Big Picture is an ongoing process of re-examining the small pieces, redefining each business function and growing concepts of the business itself.

People's formative years influence their business careers. Heroes and role models of movies, TV shows, literature and music are forever held in our hearts. Whether consciously or not, we mirror our role models in everyday business life. When the chips are down, that pop culture mentorship which we previously received really comes to our rescue. Deep inside, Roy Rogers and Dale Evans, Sky King, The Lone Ranger, Captain Midnight, Robin Hood, Zorro and others live within us.

Great scriptwriters and songwriters have stuck with us. Our views of humanity were shaped by folk and pop songs that we heard. The sense of purpose, dedication to an end result and relishing of victory bring to mind many adventure films, westerns and epic dramas of our youth. We were taught and believe that good things come to those who wait, good people get rewarded and evil defeats itself. Whether we articulate them to others, we carry inward values, ethics, quests and senses of dramatic conclusion.

Good companies do not set out to go bad. Most of them just do not properly set out. By living from day to day, they deal with problems as they come up. Thus, it costs six times more to function this way than if proper planning and creative visioning had transpired. Companies sandbag themselves by doing nothing. Doing anything—even making a few mistakes—is better than doing nothing. I've spent more than 35 years of my career in trying to explain that concept to otherwise reasonable people who simply stick their heads in the sand.

Read and learn from case studies of failure and success. Understand why decisions were made, conditions affecting them and the ramifications of actions and non-actions. Think like the boss and the workers. Learn to see company activities from multi-sides.

Research and stay current on front-burner issues affecting the climate and opportunities in which key corporate executives function. Stimulate "outside-the-box" thinking. Build customer coalitions. Distinguish your company from the pack.

There are many sophisticated and subtle topics which will bite you when you least expect it. Developing a consciousness, commitment and mastery of many areas makes for a Gold Medal winning company. These topics include: Grooming Emerging Executives, The New International Workplace, Multicultural Diversity, Team Building, Executive Development, How to Turn Every Member of Your Company into a Profit Center, Corporate Imaging. Employees are all at different phases of the career. Some believe that they have learned it all and resist change. The best managers integrate learning and communication into everything the company does.

Capturing and building a shared Vision for your company is not an option. It is essential. Existing and thriving in the future is predicated upon putting quality, empowerment, crisis management and other concepts into daily practice ... not viewing these as esoteric topics.

The Big Picture approach will accomplish many necessary business objectives:

1. Establishment of prestige and a favorable company image and its benefits.
2. Promotions of products and sales.
3. Good will of the employees.
4. Prevention of and solutions to labor problems.
5. Fostering the good will of communities in which the company has units.
6. Good will of the stockholders, board of directors, and owners.
7. Mechanisms for overcoming misconceptions and prejudices.
8. Good will of suppliers.
9. Good will of government.
10. Good will of the rest of your industry.
11. Attraction of other valuable collaborators into the industry.
12. Ability of your company to attract the best personnel.
13. Education of the public to the purposes and scope of the product.
14. Education of key stakeholders to the company's points of view.
15. Good will of customers (and their friends and colleagues).
16. Obtaining public recognition for the social and economic contributions that the company makes to communities in which it does business.
17. Reducing excessive competition within the industry.

Expected Results of Big Picture Planning

18. Your service is efficient and excellent, by your standards and by the publics. You are sensitive to the public's needs, and you are flexible and human in meeting them.
19. Your employees are professional and competent. They demonstrate initiative and use their best judgment, with authority to make the decisions they should make.
20. You have a good reputation and are awake to community obligations. You contribute much to the economy. You provide leadership for progress, rather than following along.
21. You always give your customers their money's worth. Your charges are fair and reasonable.
22. You employ state-of-the-art technology and are in the vanguard of your industry.

23. You provide a good place to work. You offer a promising career and future for people with ideas and initiative. Your people do a day's work for a day's pay.

24. The size of your organization is necessary to do the job demanded of you. Your integrity and dependability make the public confident that you will use your size and influence rightly.

Widening the Scope of Focus for Your Company

25. Learn how and why things happened.

26. Benefit from change, rather than become a victim of it.

27. Avoid making the same costly mistakes as we did last time, or as our competitors do.

28. Show ourselves and our organizations the ways toward success.

29. Continually seek to find, create and streamline the methodologies and devise better mousetraps.

30. By reinventing people and organizations, we reach the challenges of the future, rather than becoming baffled and eclipsed by changes.

31. Profit from all forms of knowledge.

Truisms of Business, Careers and Life

32. The strongest barriers are those that people set against each other.

33. There are no villains in this comic book, just us puppets.

34. Forever is one step behind you. Tomorrow is right over here.

35. Keep your mind here, now.

36. We only tease the people whom we love.

37. Old hatreds die very slowly.

38. If you make a good first impression, you make a good friendship.

39. The longer you stay apart, the less chance there will be for understanding. Mediating problems sooner will yield solutions.

40. The most arduous part of seeking the truth is deciding if you really want to know it.

41. You don't learn every answer by simply asking. Yet, you should never get out of the habit.

42. A misdirected quest for power creates deadly results.

43. We all have our specialties. You have yours. I happen to be working on something that could help you.

44. A person's life is the sum of his-her achievements. Be sure that the sum isn't reduced to zero by some rash act.

45. A large part of being a hero is being in the right place at the right time.

46. The real art is to communicate when nobody knows what the messages are.

47. You've got to have a unique product worthy of the marketplace.

48. You've got to have something to trade in exchange for others supporting you.

49. Class is a person's way.

50. Vision is an organization's way.

51. Corporate culture is the methodology by which they successfully accomplish Vision.

Big Picture Success is Earned and Learned

52. People don't know how much they don't know. The enlightenment comes from the joys of discovery, applicability of ideas and realized success.

53. Wise men and women listen and amass differing viewpoints as basis for developing informed opinions.

54. In order to learn from mistakes, one must: (1) Distance one's self from one's actions. (2) Become self-critical. (3) Recognize that actions have consequences. (4) Begin accepting responsibility for the consequences. (5) Learn how to eliminate errors. (6) Learn how to learn from mistakes. (7) Accepts fallibility, becomes open to critical feedback and modifies actions accordingly.

55. Invest in a system that requires less band aid surgery.

56. Get balance among investments in each branch of the company as a whole.

57. It's not whether you stay in business but how that matters.

58. "It takes an entire village to raise a child." (African proverb)

59. Management must think like a marathon, not like a sprint. Develop markers of achievement along the way.

60. Everyone in your organization has and must learn the role they play. They must bring strategies to their roles which are in concert with the strategies of the organization. Each part of the team must develop, maintain and refine strategies.

61. When you point a finger at someone, three fingers point back at you. We criticize others for those traits that we dislike most about ourselves but are unwilling to confront.

62. Young people engage in negative behavior because that is what they see in adults and authority figures and try to emulate.

63. The company must take collective responsibility for its whole and its parts. If you are building a house, and the nail breaks, do you stop building the house or change the nail?

64. There are no simple solutions to complex problems. When someone offers your organization a quick fix, beware.

65. In truly successful business collaborations, your success is my success. There are concurrent failures, opportunities, learning curves, wealth and inspirations.

Nuggets of Gold

66. There is a difference between political necessity and private opinion. Outwardly, we must adopt, embrace and communicate the party line. Privately, we must see it for what it is, live with it and continue to keep our own counsel.

67. It is difficult to solve a problem when the cause is unknown, denied or downplayed.

68. There is nothing on this earth that does not change.

69. Nothing is "made possible by technology." Thought processes, creativity, thinking, reasoning and commitments to action make things possible. Technology tools of the trade are utilized on a per-task basis.

70. Some say, "don't settle for second best." Who is to say what is second best? Setting unrealistic standards or unnecessarily low standards obscures one from the nuggets of gold in the middle.

71. Every business or organization goes through cycles in its life. At any point, each program is in a different phase from others. The astute

organization assesses the status of each program and orients its team members to meet constant change and fluctuation.

72. Understanding where one has been provides disciplined thinking about the organization, its environment and its future.

73. By identification of conflicts and reinforcement of team building and cohesion, the organization has a vehicle for monitoring organizational progress.

Managing Change

74. Effective change management beats the alternative. Organizations and professionals who become stuck in ruts and stubbornly cling to the past are dinosaurs, which the marketplace will pass by.

75. Change is 90% beneficial. So why do people fight what's in their best interest? Change management is an art, not a death sentence.

76. Professionals, specialists and technicians owe their careers and livelihoods to change. Because they are educated and experienced at new techniques, they have market power.

77. Change is not as high-risk as some people fear. Failure to change costs the company six times more. Lost business, opportunity costs and product failures are signs of neglect, poor management, failure to plan, anticipate and grow the company.

78. Those who champion change advance their companies and careers. It accelerates the learning curve and success ratio. Those who do not get on the bandwagon will not last in the company. Those who excel develop leadership skills, empowered teams and efficiencies.

79. Change helps you do business in the present and helps plan for the future. Without mastering the challenges of a changing world, companies will not be optimally successful.

80. The company-organization which manages change remains successful, ahead of the competition and is a business-industry leader. Meanwhile, other companies will have become victims of change because they stood by and did nothing.

Mining Ideas for Tomorrow, Your Own Wisdom Bank

81. It has been said by several philosophers, "A man who knows he is a man doesn't have to keep proving it." Too many people never really mature because they chase the wrong goals.

82. I was advising a community visioning program, and backers wanted to call the city "world class." I discouraged that because it would perennially put the city in a come-from-behind position. Organizations which call themselves "world class" are forever in a wanna-be mode. They try too hard to be compared to something else.

83. There are some people who view a career as a long-distance run, accumulating in a long-term Body of Work. Each job and project is approached as an important piece of the mosaic.

84. Some people see their job as an end, not a means, mechanism or mobility builder. Their identity is wrapped around one company. For those people, the company is a trysting place, not a corporate family. They are called One Hit Wonders. It tickles me when people use the term "re-inventing yourself." That implies that something may not have worked, and the individual started over. Many one hit wonders were just that because they had only one hit in them. No successful individual or organization should be tied to only one small distinction.

85. Much of the history of America is based upon marketers promoting the next great thing, just around the bend. For an investment, wealth and riches will be yours, so they say.

86. Perspective is the most changeable part of doing business. Understand from where you came, and it will indicate where you may be headed. Spend more time analyzing it. That is where solutions for problems present themselves. Through deep insight into your perspective comes the route toward success. Without perspective, you never make the journey. No quick fix on earth will make the journey for you.

87. The best part about being "older but wiser" lies in how much insight has been accumulated. We see where we've really learned. We analyze those activities that were so important to us at one time ... but which never brought fruit.

88. None of us is born with sophisticated, finely tuned senses and viewpoints for life. We muddle through life, try our best and get hit in the gut several times. Thus, we learn, amass knowledge and turn most experiences into an enlightened life-like perspective that moves us "to the next tier." Such a perspective is what makes seasoned executives valuable in the business marketplace.

89. Re-programming business from the quick fix syndrome to the Big Picture vantage takes as long as it took to get in that frame of mind. Things learned through a long, hard process must be de-learned via methodical steps.

90. The biggest problem with our society, in a capsule sentence: People with one set of experiences, values, wants and perceptions make mis-targeted attempts to communicate with others in trying to get what they want and need.

91. By dealing with the unexpected, preferably before it occurs, companies can bank public goodwill that may be useful later. Playing catch-up means that you have lost the game. It is the responsibility of corporate management to become duly educated about crisis management and preparedness.

92. People and organizations spend disproportionate amounts of time trying to be or look like someone else … or what they think others look like. Until one becomes one's own best, the futile trail continues.

93. Live your life as an exclamation, not an explanation.

94. People don't make fools of us. We do it to ourselves. Pride, lack of clear perspective and inflated self-image cause us to act foolishly.

95. It takes more courage to pursue a compromise than to pursue an extremist position. Conciliation and reason must be pursued. The skill with which they are approached often spells the difference between total success and political suicide.

96. Mediocrity represents the path of easiest journey. Too many people and organizations take it. Never consider this an option.

97. Freedom is not free. There are always costs attached.

98. Vision + caring + commitment + implementation + follow-through = a successful company. If any of the elements are missing, the equation

does not add up. An incomplete equation constitutes a company which will falter and fail.

99. It's amazing how many people are shocked at hearing the truth but are not quite as discerning about hearing lies and deceit. Fight for and with the truth. Truth is not always easy to recognize and not always pretty.

100. Mathematical formula: Take what you don't want to believe. Add what you have to believe. You come up with amazing answers. Expect the best, but prepare for the worst. There is no plan that is fool-proof. The little pictures—the mosaics—make up The Big Picture of business.

ABOUT THE AUTHOR

Hank Moore is an internationally known business advisor, speaker and author. He is a Big Picture strategist, with original, cutting-edge ideas for creating, implementing and sustaining corporate growth throughout every sector of the organization.

He is a Futurist and Corporate Strategist™, with four trademarked concepts of business, heralded for ways to remediate corporate damage, enhance productivity and facilitate better business.

Hank Moore is the highest level of business overview expert and is in that rarified circle of experts such as Peter Drucker, Tom Peters, Steven Covey, Peter Senge and W. Edwards Deming.

Hank Moore has presented Think Tanks for five U.S. Presidents. He has spoken at six Economic Summits. As a Corporate Strategist™, he speaks and advises companies about growth strategies, visioning, planning, executive-leadership development, futurism and the Big Picture issues affecting the business climate. He conducts independent performance reviews and Executive Think Tanks nationally, with the result being the companies' destinies being charted.

The Business Tree™ is his trademarked approach to growing, strengthening and evolving business, while mastering change. Business visionary Peter Drucker termed Hank Moore's Business Tree™ as the most original business model of the past 50 years.

Mr. Moore has provided senior level advising services for more than 5,000 client organizations (including 100 of the Fortune 500), companies in transition (startup, re-engineering, mergers, going public), public sector entities, professional associations and non-profit organizations. He has worked with all major industries over a 40-year career. He advises at the Executive Committee and board levels, providing Big Picture ideas.

He has overseen 400 strategic plans and corporate visioning processes. He has conducted 500+ performance reviews of organizations. He is a mentor to senior management. This scope of wisdom is utilized by CEOs and board members.

Types of speaking engagements which Hank Moore presents include:

- Conference opening Futurism keynote.
- Corporate planning retreats.
- Ethics and Corporate Responsibility speeches.
- University—college Commencement addresses.
- Business Think Tanks.
- International business conferences.
- Non-profit and public sector planning retreats.

In his speeches and in consulting, Hank Moore addresses aspects of business that only one who has overseen them for a living can address:

- Trends, challenges and opportunities for the future of business.
- Big Picture viewpoint.
- Creative idea generation.
- Ethics and corporate responsibility.
- Changing and refining corporate cultures.
- Strategic Planning.
- Marketplace repositioning.
- Community stewardship.
- Visioning.
- Crisis management and preparedness.
- Growth Strategies programs.
- Board of Directors development.
- Stakeholder accountability.
- Executive Think Tanks.
- Performance reviews.
- Non-profit consultation.
- Business trends that will affect the organization.
- Encouraging pockets of support and progress thus far.

- Inspiring attendees as to the importance of their public trust roles.
- Making pertinent recommendations on strategy development.

Hank Moore has authored a series of internationally published books:
- *The Business Tree*™ (with multiple international editions)
- *Pop Icons and Business Legends*
- *The Big Picture of Business*
- *Non-Profit Legends*
- *The High Cost of Doing Nothing: Why good businesses go bad.*
- *Houston Legends*
- *The Classic Television Reference*
- *Power Stars to Light the Flames: The Business Visionaries and You.*
- *The Future Has Moved … and Left No Forwarding Address.*
- *The $50,000 Business Makeover.*
- Plus monograph series for the *Library of Congress Business Section, Harvard School of Business, Strategy Driven* and many publications and websites.

Follow Hank Moore on:
Facebook: http://www.facebook.com/hank.moore.10
Linkedin: http://www.linkedin.com/profile/view?id=43004647&trk=tab_pro
Twitter: https://twitter.com/hankmoore4218
YouTube: https://www.youtube.com/watch?v=vELOvp-Kljg
Pin Interest: http://www.pinterest.com/hankmoore10/
Google+: https://plus.google.com/u/0/112201360763207336890/posts
Skill Pages: http://www.skillpages.com/hank.moore
Atlantic Speakers Bureau: http://atlanticspeakersbureau.com/hank-moore/
Business Speakers Network: http://directory.espeakers.com/buss/viewspeaker16988
Silver Fox Advisors: http://silverfox.org/content.php?page=Hank_Moore
Facebook business page: https://www.facebook.com/hankmoore.author/?fref=ts

Additional materials may be found on Hank Moore's website:
www.hankmoore.com

OTHER WRITINGS BY HANK MOORE

Digest of Excerpts From the Author's Other Books

Books by Hank Moore:

1. *The Business Tree*™.
2. *The High Cost of Doing Nothing: Why Good Businesses Go Bad.*
3. *The Classic Television Reference.*
4. *Power Stars to Light the Flame: The Business Visionaries and You.*
5. *The Future Has Moved ... and Left No Forwarding Address.*
6. *The $50,000 Business Makeover.*
7. *Non-Profit Legends.*
8. *Harvard Business Review Monograph Series.*
9. *Library of Congress Archive Series.*
10. *Strategy Driven Business Monograph Series.*
11. Articles in such other diverse media as *Rolling Stone, Wall Street Journal, TV Guide, Wharton Business Review,* the *London Times, Huffington Post, Journal of Education, Training Magazine, Fast Company, Reader's Digest, TV-Radio Mirror, The Alcalde,* the *Washington Post* and others.

From *The Business Tree*™

It seems so basic and so simple: Look at the whole of the organization, then at the parts as components of the whole and back to the bigger picture.

I advocate planning ahead and taking the widest possible view, very common-sense and utilizing a series of bite-sized chunks of business growth activity. This is the approach to clients that I have taken as a senior business advisor for 40 years. Even in times of crisis or when working on small projects, I use every opportunity to inspire clients look at their Big Pictures. The typical reaction is that my approach makes sense, and why haven't others taken it before.

The Big Picture can and does exist, though companies have not found it for their own applications very often. Organizations know that such a context is out there, but most search in vein for partial answers to a puzzling mosaic of business activity. The result, most often, is that organizations spin their wheels on inactivity, without crystallizing the right balance that might inspire success.

Obsession with certain pieces, comfort levels with other pieces and lack of artistic flair (business savvy) keep the work in progress but not resulting in a finished masterpiece.

Businesses rarely start the day with every intention of focusing upon the Big Picture. They don't get that far. It is too easy to get bogged down with minutia. This book and my advising activities are predicated upon educating the pitfalls of narrow focus and enlightening organizations on the rewards of widening the view.

Should every business become Big Picture focused? Yes. My job is to widen the frame of reference as much as possible. Under a health care model, I am the internist, a diagnostician who knows about the parts and makes informed judgments about the whole. This enables the specialists to then be more successful in their treatments, knowing that they stem from an accurate diagnosis and prescription.

Alas, the Big Picture of business is a continuing realignment of current conditions, diced with opportunities. The result will be creative new variations. Masterpieces can be continually evolving works in progress.

From *Power Stars to Light the Flame*

These are the stages in the evolution of ideas, concepts and philosophies:

1.   Information, Data. There is more information available now than ever before. Most of it is biased and slanted by vendors with something to sell. There exists much data, without interpretation. Technology purveys information but cannot do the analytical thinking.

2.   Perception. Appearance of data leads to initial perceptions, usually influenced by the media in which the information exists. To many people and organizations, perception is reality because they do not delve any further, and their learning stops at this point.

3.   Opinion. Determined more by events-processes than words. Verbal statements are more important when people are suggestible and need interpretation from a credible source. Opinion does not anticipate emergencies, only reacts to them. Many perceptions and opinions are self-focused and affected by self-esteem. Once self-interest becomes involved, opinions do not change easily.

4.   Ideas and Beliefs. Formulated ideas emerge, as people-organizations learn to hold their own outside their shells. Two-way communication ensues, whereby opinion inputs and outputs will craft ideas and beliefs. As people become more aware of their own learning, they tally their inventory of knowledge. Patterns of beliefs emerge, based upon education, experiences and environment.

5.   Systems of Thought and Ideologies. Insights start emerging at this plateau. Connect beliefs with available resources and personal expertise. Measure results and evaluate outcomes of activities, using existing opinion, ideas and beliefs. Actions are taken which benchmark success and accountability to stakeholders.

6.   Core value. Shaped by ideas, beliefs, systems of thought and ideologies. Becomes what the person or organization stands for. Leaders have conviction, commitment and ownership, able to change and adapt. Behavioral modification from the old ways of thinking has transpired.

7.   Company-Career-Life Vision. This is an enlightened plateau that few achieve. They are able to disseminate information, perceptions and opinions for what they really are. This level is wisdom focused, a quest to employ ideologies and core values for benefit of all in the organization. People are committed to thriving upon change.

From *The High Cost of Doing Nothing*

Each year, one-third of the U.S. Gross National Product goes toward cleaning up problems, damages and otherwise high costs of doing either nothing or doing the wrong things.

On the average, it costs six times the investment of preventive strategies to correct business problems (compounded per annum and exponentially increasing each year). In some industries, the figure is as high as 30 times ... six is the mean average.

Human beings as we are, none of us do everything perfectly on the front end. There always must exist a learning curve. Research shows that we learn three times more from failures than from successes. The mark of a quality organization is how it corrects mistakes and prevents them from recurring.

Running a profitable and efficient organization means effectively remediating damage before it accrues. Processes and methodologies for researching, planning, executing and benchmarking activities will reduce that pile of costly coins from stacking up.

Doing nothing becomes a way of life. It's amazing how many individuals and companies live with their heads in the sand. Never mind planning for tomorrow ... we'll just deal with problems as they occur. This mindset, of course, invites and tends to multiply trouble.

There are seven costly categories of doing nothing, doing far too little or doing the wrong things in business:

1. Waste, spoilage, poor controls, lack of employee motivation.
2. Rework, product recalls, make-good for inferior work, excess overhead.
3. Poor controls on quality, under-capitalization, under-utilization of resources.
4. Damage control, crisis management mode.
5. Recovery, restoration, repairing wrong actions, turnover, damaged company reputation.
6. Retooling, restarting, inertia, anti-change philosophy, expenses caused by quick fixes.
7. Opportunity costs, diversifying beyond company expertise, lack of an articulated vision.

From *The Classic Television Reference*

Most of us have fantasized the possibility of our parents being other people. Sometimes, idolized parents were those who already were attached to our friends. Most often, role models were symbols of people we didn't know ... but wanted to be like.

Businesses operate the same way as individuals. What looks good on the outside is what we must have and become. Tactics are commonly devised to get what we perceive that someone else has and look like what we assume they appear to be. The process of chasing the perception becomes an obsession for businesses of all sizes until reality sets in.

With the advent of television in the 1950s, it was natural that TV families would be held up as ideals. We jokingly wonder how June Cleaver could do the housework in her fancy dress, high heels and pearls. We just knew that Harriet Nelson would make more delicious meals than our own mothers did.

The families on TV situation comedies were all white, middle-class, carried traditional family structures and were mostly based in mythical small towns.

The realities behind the facades now make for fascinating insights:

Harriet Nelson could not really cook. She had grown up in hotels and was accustomed to ordering room service.

Ozzie Nelson had no job on TV, and his wife didn't work outside the home. No explanation was ever made about their means of support. Though his character appeared light on screen, Ozzie Nelson was the true guru of that show. In my mind, he stands with Desi Arnaz as one of the behind-the-scenes geniuses of TV.

There was dysfunctional behavior, even though we didn't recognize it as such. When Danny Thomas yelled at his kids and spit coffee on the living room floor, it was couched in wisecracks.

Women were stereotyped. Many TV wives appeared to be subservient ... yet pursued their own pro-active courses. Laura Petrie always got her way. Lucy Ricardo pursued hi-jinx. And mother did really "know best," though society would not quite position it that way in the 1950s. Nonetheless, women learned subtle ways to master the system, within the context of good humor.

While Western sheriffs won at the shootouts, the issues of good versus bad were overly simplistic. Life is mostly shades of gray, which tough strength does not work well against.

Behind the guns and action, the Westerns really did teach lessons of empowerment and team building. On "Wagon Train" and "Rawhide," people had no choice but to get along and work together. As a team, they fought the elements and usually won.

Gangsters always got their just deserves in movies and on cop TV shows. We were taught that crime does not pay … and were shown the price for violating property and safety. Jack Webb, Broderick Crawford and other tough cops put the baddies in their place, in no uncertain terms.

Many of us wonder why values like these are not taught now. Where is society headed, we wonder. Where are the new heroes coming from?

We now realize that many of our childhood idols had demons of their own. Keeping up appearances and being interchangeably confused with their on-screen characters led many a performer toward personal abuse, career burnout and eventual ruin.

Not many taught us about going the distance. Too many actors and singers had short-term careers. That was the design of the system. In business, we must not follow pop culture and train ourselves to last, prosper and get better with age.

As we get older and more cynical, society tends to shoot down its media heroes and watches them stumble and fall, sometimes with interest and joy. We don't expect any of them to measure up to past pedestal status. When one falls from grace, we may either repudiate our past allegiance or justify unrealistic ways to keep them perched up on high.

Having met many major performers and media heroes, I know that raw talent does not directly translate to business savvy and people skills. The Paul McCartney's of the world who successfully embody it all are few and far between.

One of my first career idols was Dick Clark, another man who is smart and accomplished in many facets. He had just debuted on "American Bandstand." I was in the fifth grade and started working at a radio station, determined to be Texas' answer to Dick Clark.

A mentor reminded me that none of us should go through life as a carbon copy of someone else. We can admire and embody their qualities but must carve out a uniqueness all our own. Good advice from a 24-year-old Bill Moyers, who stands for me as an ever-contemporary role model.

Corporate executives do not get a rulebook when the job title is awarded. They are usually promoted on the basis technical expertise, team player status, loyalty and perceived long-term value to the company. They are told to assume a role and then draw upon their memory bank of role models.

Top executives have few role models in equivalent positions. Thus, they get bad advice from the wrong consultants. In the quest to be a top business leader, one quickly reviews how poorly corporate executives were portrayed to the mass culture.

J.R. Ewing ("Dallas") sold every member of his family and work force down the river. He is hardly a CEO role model, though many "good old boys" think how he operated was perfectly acceptable.

Alan Brady ("Dick Van Dyke Show") practiced nepotism with his brother-in-law, Mel Cooley. Brady yelled at everyone and was especially abusive to Mel, in front of others. Creativity was determined by his will. All were expected to parrot his "vision."

Lou Grant ("Mary Tyler Moore Show") was brash, threatened termination, asked pervasive questions and sometimes dated co-workers.

Charlie Townsend ("Charlie's Angels") was never around. He left his staff to their own devices and to supervise themselves. The reasons most employees do not perform as expected is that they are given insufficient direction and time with a mentor, not knowing what is expected of them.

It was never revealed where John Beresford Tipton ("The Millionaire") earned all that money that he gave away to total strangers.

Economic accountability was never a consideration in TV families. They lived well, but we rarely saw the relationship between workplace output to family quality of life. How did Mike Brady ("The Brady Bunch") afford to feed a family of eight, especially with his wife staying at home and not working? He seemed to stay at home much more than the average successful architect.

In reality, most TV lead characters were the employees of someone else. The boss was the brunt of the jokes. Fear of being disciplined was openly communicated to viewers as part of the territory in earning one's way in life.

Ralph Kramden ("The Honeymooners") was not considered to become a supervisor, nor a leader. He exhibited a defeatist attitude that probably kept him from being successful.

Certain characters did their jobs in such a way as that the bosses fell in love with them and eventually married them. Witness Katy Holstrum ("The Farmer's Daughter"), Agent 99 ("Get Smart") and Jeannie ("I Dream of Jeannie"). At one time, some women went into business with such an unrealistic view.

We never saw psychologist Bob Hartley ("Bob Newhart Show") conferring with colleagues, attending professional symposia, authoring academic papers or seeking professional help himself. When he wasn't in session, he was joking with the receptionist and the dentist.

Editor Perry White ("Superman") threatened young Jimmy Olsen, "Don't call me chief," when mentoring the eager reporter would have amplified Olsen's service to The Daily Planet. Alas, Olsen was always a tagalong and did not develop as a seasoned reporter, stalling his career.

Marshal Simon Cord (played by Henry Fonda) was always out of town. His "Deputy" (played by Allen Case) was a shopkeeper, who became the town's part-time law and order by default. Part-time jobs and careers are not the same thing.

Money was rarely an issue. We rarely saw families just scraping by, as were most Americans. "The Real McCoy's" were farmers … with wealth in spirit and positive will.

There were unexplained quirks, showing insufficient resources necessary to do business. All the detectives on "77 Sunset Strip" drove the same car (a Ford convertible). How did the others get around and earn their livelihood, if a car was essential equipment?

Steve McGarrett ("Hawaii Five-0") drove the same car (a 1967 Mercury Monterey) year after year. With his arrest record, why didn't the department upgrade his equipment?

Jim Anderson was an insurance agent on "Father Knows Best." Yet, he never made evening calls … only working days. Thus, he couldn't sell that many policies and missed his marketplace … not being available at peak times that his customers were.

Ricky Ricardo worked in a nightclub and always went to work during the day, usually being home most evenings. Try to figure that one!

From *Houston Legends*

Houston represents many things to many people. This is where we live and work, where we are educated and entertained, where culture and community pride are stimulated and where we learn some lessons in living together with others.

Houston is a growth community. It has seen industries emerge and mature. It boasts generations of healthy families. It encompasses lifestyles, cultures and opportunity that no other world-class city can match.

Yet, when you look at Houston, it is a collection of neighborhoods, business districts and quality lifestyles. Houston embodies many growing communities, the confluence being an international hub for this nation. Creative partnerships account for Houston's documented growth.

As the city lives the 21st Century, we celebrate the historical, utilize state-of-the art technology and reflect changing social needs will always be at the forefront of the future. With a sense of pride, reflection and optimism for the future, Houston's business is dedicated to identifying, meeting and serving every need of our community.

Houston is a collection of neighborhoods, cultures and families. Communities which grow and prosper will analyze and serve the needs of present generations. While honoring the heritage, we carefully plan for the future. Whether in the global sense or on the blocks on which we live, layers of generations comprise our essence.

Every community is a collection of lifestyles, inspired through the structures in which they take place are centers of synergy.

Houston leaders are contributing to the quality of life and encompass the needs and activities of Houstonians.

From *Pop Icons and Business Legends*

Great scriptwriters and songwriters have stuck with us. Our views of humanity were shaped by folk and pop songs. The sense of purpose, dedication to an end result and relishing of victory bring to mind many adventure films, westerns and epic dramas of our youth. We were taught and believe that good things come to those who wait, that good people get rewarded and that evil defeats itself. Whether we articulate them to others, we carry inward values, ethics, quests and senses of dramatic conclusion.

Corporate executives do not get a rulebook when the job title is awarded. They are usually promoted on the basis technical expertise, team player status, loyalty and perceived long-term value to the company. They are told to assume a role and then draw upon their memory bank of role models.

Top executives have few role models in equivalent positions. Thus, they get bad advice from the wrong consultants. In the quest to be a top business leader, one quickly reviews how poorly corporate executives were portrayed to the mass culture:

- J.R. Ewing ("Dallas") sold every member of his family and work force down the river. He is hardly a CEO role model, though many "good old boys" think how he operated was perfectly acceptable.
- Alan Brady ("Dick Van Dyke Show") practiced nepotism with his brother-in-law, Mel Cooley. Brady yelled at everyone and was especially abusive to Mel, in front of others. Creativity was determined by his will. All were expected to parrot his "vision."
- Lou Grant ("Mary Tyler Moore Show") drank on the job, was brash, threatened termination, asked pervasive questions and sometimes dated co-workers.
- Charlie Townsend ("Charlie's Angels") was never around. He left his staff to their own devices and to supervise themselves. The reasons most employees do not perform as expected is they are given insufficient direction and time with a mentor, not knowing what is expected of them.
- It was never revealed where John Beresford Tipton ("The Millionaire") earned all that money that he gave away to total strangers, in order to study their behaviors.
- Economic accountability was not a consideration in TV families. They lived well, but we rarely saw the relationship between workplace output to quality of life. How did Mike Brady ("The Brady Bunch") afford to feed a family of eight, especially with his wife staying at home and not working? He seemed to stay at home much more than the average successful architect.

In reality, most TV lead characters were the employees of someone else. The boss was the brunt of the jokes. Fear of being disciplined was openly communicated to viewers as part of the territory in earning one's way in life. For example:

- Ralph Kramden ("The Honeymooners") was not considered to become a supervisor, nor a leader. He exhibited a defeatist attitude that probably kept him from being successful.

- Certain characters did their jobs in such a way as that the bosses fell in love with them and eventually married them. Witness Katy Holstrum ("The Farmer's Daughter"), Agent 99 ("Get Smart") and Jeannie ("I Dream of Jeannie"). At one time, some women went into business with such an unrealistic view.

- Then, there were those who fostered the notion of "do as I say, not as I do." For example:

- We never saw psychologist Bob Hartley ("Bob Newhart Show") conferring with colleagues, attending professional symposia, authoring academic papers or seeking professional help himself. When he wasn't in session, he was joking with the receptionist and the dentist.

- Editor Perry White ("Superman") threatened young Jimmy Olsen, "Don't call me chief," when mentoring the eager reporter would have amplified Olsen's service to The Daily Planet. Alas, Olsen was always a tagalong and did not develop as a seasoned reporter, stalling his career.

- Marshal Simon Cord (played by Henry Fonda) was always out of town. His "Deputy" (played by Allen Case) was a shop keeper, who became the town's part-time law and order by default. Part-time jobs and careers are not the same thing.

Money was rarely an issue. We rarely saw families just scraping by, as were most Americans. "The Real McCoy's" were farmers … with wealth in spirit and positive will.

There were unexplained quirks, showing insufficient resources necessary to do business:

- All the detectives on "77 Sunset Strip" drove the same car (a Ford convertible). How did the others get around and earn their livelihood, if a car was essential equipment?
- Steve McGarrett ("Hawaii Five-0") drove the same car (a 1967 Mercury Monterey) year after year. With his arrest record, why didn't the department upgrade his equipment?
- Jim Anderson was an insurance agent on "Father Knows Best." Yet, he never made evening calls ... only working days. Thus, he couldn't sell that many policies and missed his marketplace ... not being available at peak times that his customers were.
- Ricky Ricardo worked in a nightclub and always went to work during the day, usually being home most evenings. Try to figure that one!

From *Non-Profit Legends*

The successful volunteer leaves a mark, having done something in a way that others could not have done it. That's the way that I look at diversity, a concept that we must champion daily in our own unique ways.

One does not render pro-bono hours just to get acclaim. That's nice, after the fact. The real thrill was knowing that those few hours helped save lives.

The true heroes of our communities volunteer because it feels good. Volunteers also help alleviate problems in communities. We do not volunteer just to get awards. However, periodic recognition inspires the unsung heroes to chant a little more vibrantly the next time.

Community relations is action-oriented and should include one of these forms:

1. Creating something necessary that did not exist before.
2. Eliminating something that poses a problem.
3. Developing the means for self-determination.
4. Including citizens who are in need.
5. Sharing professional and technical expertise.
6. Tutoring, counseling and training.
7. Repairing, upgrading or restoring.
8. Promotion of the community to outside constituencies.
9. Moving others toward action.

The well-rounded community relations program embodies all elements: accessibility of company officials to citizens, participation by the company in business and civic activities, public service promotions, special events, plant communications materials and open houses, grassroots constituency building and good citizenry.

Community relations is not "insurance" that can be bought overnight. It is tied to the bottom line and must be treated accordingly, with the resources and expertise to accomplish it effectively. It is a bond of trust that, if violated, will haunt the business. If steadily built, the trust can be exponentially parlayed into successful long-term business relationships.

Successful people are products of mentorship. So are our communities. I've remembered and recorded most of the worthwhile advice that I've been given. We make and honor our commitments, nurtured by our responsibility to mentor others. If we're going to be called role models, we show it without fanfare and inspire others to lead.

From *The $50,000 Business Makeover*

Here are 15 sure-fire steps to begin putting this information to immediate use in your business.

1. Business cannot exist in a vacuum. You must put everything that you produce into a Big Picture context.
2. Recognize that there is a Big Picture, and be skeptical about niche consultants and vendors who purport that their approach is the only one.
3. Choose your advisors very carefully. Insist that they benchmark everything they do for you toward a Big Picture of your business.
4. You must have both a Sales Plan and a Marketing Plan as sub-sets of your Strategic Plan.
5. Advertising is a process, part of marketing and a cousin of sales. Running an ad here and there does not constitute advertising.
6. Have concurrent programs in your plan, including direct marketing, sales promotions, advertising, internet presence, specialty advertising, public relations and other marketplace presence.

7.   Running a small business is tough. You cannot be a Lone Ranger. Develop a support system of friends and colleagues. Surrounding yourself with employees and consultants is not enough.

8.   Always think about new products to create.

9.   Never stop changing. Change is 90% positive. Every person and company changes 71% per year anyway. You might as well benefit from it, rather than become a victim of it.

10.   Use my Business Tree as a way of always looking at the whole of any situation, then at the parts and back to the whole again.

11.   You never stop paying dues. Opportunities create more successes.

12.   Take ownership of planning programs, rather than abdicate them to human resources or accounting people.

13.   Predict the biggest crises that can beset your company. 85% of the time, you'll prevent them from occurring.

14.   Challenge yourself to succeed by taking a Big Picture look, while others are still thinking and acting small-time. Your biggest resource is a wide scope … and the daring to visualize success and then all of its components.

From *The Future Has Moved … and Left No Forwarding Address*

In moving forward, one must review those junctures where leaders and their companies recognize when a business is in trouble. These are the high costs of neglect, non-actions and wrong actions, per categories on The Business Tree™:

1.   Product, Core Business. The product's former innovation and dominance has somehow missed the mark in today's business climate. The company does not have the marketplace demand that it once had. Others have streamlined their concepts, with greater success. Something newer has edged your company right out of first place.

2.   Processes, Running the Company. Operations have become static, predictable and inefficient. Too much band-aid surgery has been applied, but the bleeding has still not been stopped. Other symptoms of trouble have continued to appear … often and without warning.

3. Financial Position. Dips in the cash flow have produced knee-jerk reactions to making changes. Cost cutting and downsizing were seemingly ready answers, though they took tolls on the rest of the company. The overt focus on profit and bean counter mentality has crippled the organizational effectiveness.

4. Employee Morale and Output. Those who produce the product-service and assure its quality, consistency and deliverability have not been given sufficient training, empowerment and recognition. They have not really been in the decision making and leadership processes, as they should have been. Team members still have to fight the system and each other to get their voices heard, rather than function as a team.

5. Customer Service. Customers come and go … at great costs that are not tallied, noticed or heeded. After the percentages drop dramatically, management asks "What happened?" Each link in the chain hasn't yet committed toward the building of long-term customer relationships. Thus, marketplace standing wavers.

6. Company Management. There was no definable style in place, backed by Vision, strategies, corporate sensitivities, goals and beliefs. Whims, egos and momentary needs most often guided company direction. Young and mid-executives never were adequately groomed for lasting leadership.

7. Corporate Standing. Things have happened for inexplicable reasons. Company vision never existed or ceased to spread. The organization is on a downslide, standing still and doing things as they always were done constitutes moving backward.

These situations are day-to-day realities for troubled companies. Yes, they brought many of the troubles upon themselves. Yes, they compounded problems by failing to take swift actions. And, yes, they further magnify the costs of "band aid surgery" by failing to address the root causes of problems.